A Fascist Decade

MW01115192

From the invasion of Ethiopia in 1935 through to the waning months of World War II in 1945, Fascist Italy was at war. This Fascist decade of war comprised an uninterrupted stretch of military and political engagements in which Italian military forces were involved in Abyssinia, Spain, Albania, France, Greece, the Soviet Union, North Africa and the Middle East. As a junior partner to Nazi Germany, only entering the war in June 1940, Italy is often seen as a relatively minor player in World War II. However, this book challenges much of the existing scholarship by arguing that Fascist Italy played a significant and distinct role in shaping international relations between 1935 and 1945, creating a Fascist decade of war.

Marco Maria Aterrano is Post-doctoral Research Fellow in Contemporary History at the University of Padua, Italy. After receiving a PhD in History from the University of Naples Federico II, he has been a Research Fellow at the Einaudi Foundation in Turin and a Visiting Researcher at Georgetown University. He has published widely on the Anglo-American presence in Italy during World War II and is now focusing on the topic of civilian disarmament and gun control in 20th-century Europe.

Karine Varley is Lecturer in French and European History at the University of Strathclyde, Glasgow. She has published widely on French relations with Italy during World War II, and her forthcoming book is entitled *Vichy's Double Bind: French Axis Entanglements and Relations with Fascist Italy, 1940–1943.* She has also worked on Franco-British relations in World War II in collaboration with the British Embassy in Paris and the French Embassy in London.

Routledge Studies in Fascism and the Far Right

Series editors:
Nigel Copsey, Teesside University, UK and Graham Macklin, Center for Research on Extremism (C-REX), University of Oslo, Norway

This new book series focuses upon fascist, far right and right-wing politics primarily within a historical context but also drawing on insights from other disciplinary perspectives. Its scope also includes radical-right populism, cultural manifestations of the far right and points of convergence and exchange with the mainstream and traditional right.

Titles include:

CasaPound Italia
Contemporary Extreme-Right politics
Caterina Froio, Pietro Castelli Gattinara, Giorgia Bulli and Matteo Albanese

The International Alt-Right
Fascism for the 21st Century?
Patrik Hermansson, David Lawrence, Joe Mulhall and Simon Murdoch

Failed Führers
A History of Britain's Extreme Right
Graham Macklin

The Rise of the Dutch New Right
An Intellectual History of the Rightward Shift in Dutch Politics
Merijn Oudenampsen

A Fascist Decade of War
1935–1945 in International Perspective
Edited by Marco Maria Aterrano and Karine Varley

No Platform
A History of Anti-Fascism, Universities and the Limits of Free Speech
Evan Smith

For more information about this series, please visit: www.routledge.com/Routledge-Studies-in-Fascism-and-the-Far-Right/book-series/FFR

A Fascist Decade of War

1935–1945 in International Perspective

Edited by Marco Maria Aterrano and Karine Varley

Routledge
Taylor & Francis Group

LONDON AND NEW YORK

First published 2020
by Routledge
2 Park Square, Milton Park, Abingdon, Oxon, OX14 4RN

and by Routledge
605 Third Avenue, New York, NY 10017

First issued in paperback 2021

Routledge is an imprint of the Taylor & Francis Group, an informa business

Publisher's Note
The publisher has gone to great lengths to ensure the quality of this reprint but points out that some imperfections in the original copies may be apparent.

British Library Cataloguing-in-Publication Data
A catalogue record for this book is available from the British Library

Library of Congress Cataloging-in-Publication Data
Names: Aterrano, Marco Maria, 1986- editor. | Varley, Karine, editor.
Title: A fascist decade of war : 1935-1945 in international perspective / Marco Maria Aterrano and Karine Varley. Other titles: 1935-1945 in international perspective
Description: Abingdon, Oxon ; New York : Routledge, [2020] | Series: Routledge studies in fascism and the far right | Includes bibliographical references and index.
Identifiers: LCCN 2019058402 (print) | LCCN 2019058403 (ebook) | ISBN 9781138574151 ; (hardback) | ISBN 9780203701232 ; (ebook)
Subjects: LCSH: Italy–History–1922-1945. | World War, 1939-1945–Italy. | Italy–History, Military–20th century. | Fascism–Italy–History–20th century.
Classification: LCC DG571 .F296 2020 (print) | LCC DG571 (ebook) | DDC 940.53/45–dc23
LC record available at https://lccn.loc.gov/2019058402
LC ebook record available at https://lccn.loc.gov/2019058403

ISBN 13: 978-1-03-223622-3 (pbk)
ISBN 13: 978-1-138-57415-1 (hbk)

DOI: 10.4324/9780203701232

Typeset in Times New Roman
by Integra Software Services Pvt. Ltd.

Contents

Contributors

Marco Maria Aterrano, University of Padua (marco.aterrano@gmail.com)

Marco Maria Aterrano is Post-doctoral Research Fellow in Contemporary History at the University of Padua. After receiving a PhD in History from the University of Naples Federico II, he has been a Research Fellow at the Einaudi Foundation in Turin and a Visiting Researcher at Georgetown University. He has published widely on the Anglo-American presence in Italy during World War II and is now focusing on the topic of civilian disarmament and gun control in 20th-century Europe.

Andrew N. Buchanan, University of Vermont (andrew.buchanan@uvm.edu)

Andrew N. Buchanan teaches Global and military history at the University of Vermont. His *American Grand Strategy in the Mediterranean in World War II* was published by Cambridge University Press in 2014, and his new book, *World War II in Global Perspective 1931–1953: A Short History* was published in 2019 by Wiley. Buchanan is the author of several journal articles and book chapters on military-political and cultural aspects of World War II, and he is currently writing on the ideological work done by Henry Luce's 1940 'American Century' article.

Fabio De Ninno, University of Siena (fdn87@yahoo.it)

Fabio De Ninno is Adjunct Professor and Research fellow at the University of Siena. An expert of Naval and military history and historiography is author of two books on the Italian Navy, *I sommergibili del fascismo* (2014) and *Fascisti sul Mare. La Marina e gli ammiragli di Mussolini* (2017), and has published chapters and articles in international journals like *War in History* and the *Journal of Military History*.

Luca Fenoglio, University of Leicester (lf184@leicester.ac.uk)

Luca Fenoglio is Leverhulme Early Career Fellow and member of the Stanley Burton Centre for Holocaust and Genocide Studies at the University of Leicester. He is author of 'Between Protection and Complicity: Guido Lospinoso, Fascist Italy and the Holocaust in Occupied Southeastern France' (*Holocaust &*

Genocide Studies, 33:1, 2019) and 'Fascist policy towards Jews in south-eastern France, 1942–1943: Some remarks on the events and methodology', in G. Orsina and A. Ungari (eds), *The 'Jewish Question' in the Territories Occupied by Italians* (Rome: Viella, 2019).

MacGregor Knox, London School of Economics (m.knox@lse.ac.uk)

MacGregor Knox, Stevenson Professor of International History emeritus, London School of Economics and Political Science, was educated at Harvard College, the U.S. Army Infantry School and Yale University. His works include *Mussolini Unleashed, 1939–1941*; *The Making of Strategy: Rulers, States, and War* (ed., with Williamson Murray and Alvin Bernstein); *Common Destiny: Dictatorship, Foreign Policy, and War in Fascist Italy and Nazi Germany*; *Hitler's Italian Allies: Royal Armed Forces, Fascist Regime, and the War of 1940–1943*; and *To the Threshold of Power 1922/33: Origins and Dynamics of the Fascist and National Socialist Dictatorships*.

Nicola Labanca, University of Siena (labanca@unisi.it)

Nicola Labanca is Professor of Contemporary History at the University of Siena. He has published extensively on the history of Italian colonialism and military history in contemporary Italy. Among his many relevant publications, *Oltremare. Storia dell'espansione coloniale italiana* (2002); *La guerra d'Etiopia. 1935–1941* (2015); and *Caporetto. Storia e memoria di una disfatta* (2017). Labanca is also President at the Centro Interuniversitario di Studi e Ricerche Storico-Militari, and Director of *Italia Contemporanea*, journal of the Istituto nazionale di storia del movimento di liberazione in Italia.

Arturo Marzano, University of Pisa (arturo.marzano@unipi.it)

Arturo Marzano is Associate Professor at the Department of Civilization and Forms of Knowledge, University of Pisa. His research mainly deals with history of Judaism, Zionism, the Israeli-Palestinian conflict and the relationship between Italy and the Middle East in the 20th century. Among his main publications, there is the volume *Onde fasciste. La propaganda araba di Radio Bari (1934–1943)* (Rome, 2015).

Steven Morewood, University of Birmingham (s.morewood@bham.ac.uk)

Steven Morewood is Senior Lecturer in International History at the University of Birmingham. He is the author of *The British Defence of Egypt, 1935–1940* (Routledge, 2014) and chapters and articles about Britain's geostrategic position in the Eastern Mediterranean. Currently he is researching two books about the Italian invasion of Egypt and the British response and another on the British intervention in Greece in 1940–1941.

Ioannis Nioutsikos, University of Piraeus (giannis.nioutsikos@yahoo.gr)

Ioannis Nioutsikos is an Associate Lecturer in International Relations in the Department of International and European Studies at the University of Piraeus. He earned his PhD from the Department of War Studies, King's College London, and he is head of the Military History Research Programme in the Institute of International Relations of Panteion University. His research interests include the history of international relations and strategy, modern Greek history and guerrilla warfare.

Javier Rodrigo, Universitat Autònoma de Barcelona (javier.rodrigo@uab.cat)

Javier Rodrigo is ICREA-Acadèmia Research Fellow and Associate Professor at the Universitat Autònoma de Barcelona, Spain. He received his PhD at the European University Institute, his publications include nine books as author, including *La guerra fascista. Italia en la Guerra Civil Española, 1936–1939* (2016, English edition 2020) and *Comunidades rotas. Una historia global de las guerras civiles, 1917–2017* (2019). He is currently the Principal Investigator of a Project within the framework of the Horizon2020 Programme.

Andrew Stewart, Australian National University (andrew.stewart@kcl.ac.uk)

A graduate of King's College, London, Professor Andrew Stewart joined the Strategic and Defence Studies Centre at Australian National University in January 2020 as Professor of War Studies and Principal of the Military and Defence Studies Program at the Australian War College. The author of more than thirty books, book chapters, articles and other published work, his next book examines the volatile relationship between Winston Churchill and General Archibald Wavell during 1940 and 1941 and their clash in the Middle East. A founding Director of the King's Second World War Research Group, he is also a Trustee for the Liddell Hart Centre for Military Archives.

Andrea Ungari, Università Marconi (a.ungari@unimarconi.it)

Andrea Ungari is Full Professor in Contemporary History at Guglielmo Marconi University and Adjunct Professor in History of Political Parties at Luiss Guido Carli University in Rome. His main research interests are the political history of Italy from the monarchical period to the Republic and its military history, focusing on World War I. His most recent publications are *La guerra del Re. Monarchia, Sistema politico e Forze armate nella Grande guerra* (Luni, 2018) and the *Atlante Geopolitico del Mediterraneo 2019* (Bordeaux, 2019).

Karine Varley, University of Strathclyde, Glasgow (karine.varley@strath.ac.uk)

Karine Varley is Lecturer in French and European History at the University of Strathclyde, Glasgow. She has published widely on French relations with Italy during World War II, and her forthcoming book is entitled *Vichy's Double Bind: French Axis Entanglements and Relations with Fascist Italy, 1940–1943*. She has also worked on Franco-British relations in World War II in collaboration with the British Embassy in Paris and the French Embassy in London.

Valentina Villa, Università Cattolica Milano (valentina.villa@unicatt.it)

Valentina Villa is Research Fellow in History of the Political Institutions at the Catholic University of Milan. She completed her PhD in 2013 writing a dissertation about the British monarchy and carrying out most of her research at the National Archives during a visiting period at University College London. Her publications include *The Crown is a Living Bond: L'attività pubblica all'estero della monarchia Britannica, 1952–1972* (Aracne, 2018) and her interests lie in contemporary Italian history, particularly during the Fascist period, and in the evolution of the Italian and British monarchies.

Nicolas G. Virtue, University of Western Ontario (nvirtue2@uwo.ca)

Nicolas G. Virtue holds a PhD in History and teaches at King's University College at Western University in London, Ontario, Canada. His dissertation, 'Royal Army, Fascist Empire', examined the relationship between the Royal Italian Army and Fascist empire-building in Africa and Europe. He has also contributed chapters to *Italy and the Second World War: Alternative Perspectives* (2018), *The Concept of Resistance in Italy* (2017), and *Collision of Empires: Italy's Invasion of Abyssinia and its International Impact* (2013).

Introduction

A Fascist decade of war? The impact of the Italian wars on the international stage, 1935–1945

Marco Maria Aterrano and Karine Varley

From the invasion of Ethiopia in 1935 through to the waning months of World War II in 1945, Fascist Italy was at war. This decade of war comprised an uninterrupted stretch of military and political engagements in which Italian military forces were involved in Abyssinia, Spain, Albania, France, Greece, the Soviet Union, North Africa and the Middle East. It concluded with Italy itself being transformed into a military theatre, with the dramatic fall of the Fascist regime and the political transition under the aegis of foreign occupations.[1] Between 6–7 September 2016, forty-seven scholars from fifteen countries convened at the University of Strathclyde in Glasgow to discuss the latest developments in military, political and diplomatic studies on Fascist Italy between 1935 and 1945. This volume brings together contributions from fourteen of the speakers.

The main contention of this volume is that the significance of Fascist Italy in World War II and the years leading up to it was distinct and unique. Because Italy only entered World War II in June 1940, and was then subjected to a series of stark defeats, it has often been perceived as being on the periphery of the conflict. The role and impact of Italy as the junior partner to Germany in shaping the character of the war has consequently often been underestimated by historians.[2] While there has been extensive historical examination of the role of Nazi Germany in exacerbating the international tensions that led to war and on the nature of Nazi warfare and occupations during World War II, much of the existing scholarship confines the role played by Italy to the margins. The distinct role of Fascist Italy has been mostly the subject of a largely separate historical debate, often scarcely integrated within the broader international context and seldom available to an English-speaking readership.[3]

Building upon the work of scholars who have rejected Germanocentric perspectives in the analysis of the lead-up to World War II, the contributors to this volume argue in favour of the centrality of the Mediterranean in the period between 1935 and 1945.[4] The disintegration of the international community and the weakening of the League of Nations' powers of intervention were first put in motion in response to the actions of Fascist Italy; only then did they spread outwards across the continent and beyond.[5]

One of the elements of innovation in this book is its periodization. The contributions in this volume operate within a chronological framework that considers the

1935–1945 decade as a functional historical unit, in which long-established Fascist policy and ideology finally came to full fruition, albeit unsuccessfully. This volume challenges the periodization and the military focus proposed by previous historians by adopting a broader thematic approach across a ten-year period that also includes the period after the Italian surrender of September 1943. Expanding upon Giorgio Rochat's attempts to frame his examination of Italy's war experience between 1935 and 1943, this volume explores the political, ideological and military reasons for the prolonged period of conflict.[6] Whereas Rochat's analysis concludes in 1943, this volume suggests the need to incorporate the developments of 1944 and 1945, which saw much of Italy under occupation and still at war.[7] Indeed, as the creation of the Italian Social Republic (RSI) showed, Fascism did not suddenly evaporate with the fall of Mussolini in July 1943 or with the Italian surrender in the following September. Among the other chronological interpretations that have been constructed on the Italian war experience, we offer a different perspective to that suggested by Simon Ball, who sees Libyan independence in 1951 as marking the real end of a Fascist policy of challenging British hegemony in the Mediterranean that began in 1935.[8] At the same time, the starting-point of our periodization is more aligned with the interpretation put forward by Robert Mallett, who suggests that May 1935 marked a significant shift in aligning Italian policy with Nazi Germany, leading directly to World War II.[9]

These two elements – a longer chronology and a broader thematic scope of investigation – allow the contributors to further consider additional aspects in the analysis of Italy's role in the development of the European crisis before and during World War II. This volume suggests that Italy was one of the principal causes of the new climate of instability that, developing from the mid-1930s, gave rise to the European conflict in 1939. Furthermore, Italy played a decisive role in expanding the scope of the war by bringing the European conflict into the Mediterranean theatre, which in turn became critically important for the development of the strategies of Britain, France and the United States, as well as to the overall outcome of World War II and the global post-war order.

Consequently, one of the distinguishing features of the analytical framework being proposed in this volume is the suggestion that 1935 marked a critical turning-point and shaping factor in the lead-up to World War II. Drawing from an expanding body of work on the topic, contributors suggest that Italy played a primary role in the creation of a weak and precarious European balance.[10] While many histories of this period see the Spanish Civil War as the decisive turning-point in the breakdown of international relations that eventually led to the outbreak of war in 1939, we argue that the Abyssinian Crisis of 1935 gave rise to a new international landscape. The key elements that were to characterize the Fascist decade of war were already in place during the Abyssinian Crisis, while the diplomatic fallout caused Rome to move more decisively towards rapprochement with Berlin, accelerating the militarization of Italian society.

The decision to intervene in Abyssinia therefore triggered a chain reaction that made the conflict in Spain part of an existing continental trend, while aggravating the deterioration of relations between the non-allied powers in

Europe. Domestically and internationally, in the aftermath of the Abyssinian Crisis, the Fascist regime turned to develop a more ideologically cohesive programme, attempting to lay the foundations of a totalitarian society. As the ideology of the Fascist regime became clearer and more manifest, so it brought graver consequences for Italy, Europe and the wider world. Refocusing upon the role and impact of Italy provides us with a more nuanced understanding of World War II and of the factors that shaped its character.

The Fascist wars are considered here from the military to the cultural dimensions, from the diplomatic to the political, adopting a dual perspective. The Italian angle considers the ways in which Fascist policy, strategy and ideology made this decade of war a by-product of the consolidation of the regime. The international angle, on the other hand, seeks to evaluate how Fascist regional challenges affected the policies, strategies and ideologies of other countries. The contributors to this edited collection revisit and challenge traditional military histories of this period by exploring violence, propaganda, perceptions, ideology, empire, race and occupation, engaging with new methodological approaches. By interacting critically with the book's main arguments, the authors highlight the wide international connections that shaped Italian conduct between 1935 and 1945, while exploring Italian – as well as international – scholarship and providing a necessary update on the state of the field for an English-speaking readership.

Outline

This volume's contributions are framed within a contention that Fascist Italy's role and its impact upon the late inter-war period and World War II can be better understood through the analysis of five key elements that led to the development of a decade of war between 1935 and 1945. These elements, which define the sections into which the volume is structured, comprise the weakening of the system of international relations; the formulation and implementation of a strong imperialistic ideology; the development of an innovative Fascist warfare; the adoption of a signature use of violence; and the use of propaganda. The chapters explore some of the major themes that have emerged in the recent scholarship on Italy at war: from the colonial inspiration to the relevance of a Fascist ideology, from the outward projection of images of power to the occupation policies, the authors update the state of the research, connecting their field with the most recent international historiography.

In line with the overall objectives of this volume, the first section focuses on the international dimensions of the decade of war, exploring not just the foreign policy of the Italian Fascist government, but how some of the key international players engaged with the regime. By focusing their attention outwards upon the international ramifications of Fascist policies and engagements and by looking at other international players' responses to Italian actions, the first four authors suggest that the Fascist decade of war represented a complex, sometimes inconsistent, shaping influence upon the conflicts being played out across the European, Mediterranean and global stages. In this sense, the volume adopts a different approach to that taken by Emanuele Sica and Richard Carrier in their edited volume on Italy and World War II, which seeks to explore the conflict 'through the lens of Italian soldiers and civilians, and of populations occupied by the Italian army', incorporating a range of perspectives from high politics to history 'from below'.[11]

In his chapter on the international significance of the Italian invasion of Abyssinia in 1935, Steven Morewood suggests that the episode represented a missed opportunity for the British to thwart Fascist aggression. Dismissing the episode as a minor colonial war, the British government failed to capitalize on its military advantage, and in so doing, bolstered Mussolini's ambitions. The crisis over Abyssinia has tended to be downplayed in favour of an emphasis upon the remilitarization of the Rhineland in 1936 and the Munich crisis of 1938. Yet, as Morewood observes, it fundamentally altered the strategic balance in the Mediterranean.

Andrew Buchanan also sees the 1935 Abyssinian Crisis as a critical turning-point, transforming the American approach towards Italy. Washington began to see Italy in terms of an aggressor, shifting its perceptions of Mussolini's government as it moved towards closer alignment with Germany. At the same time, American popular opinion of Fascist Italy began to change as well. From the end of World War I, Buchanan argues, American elites had sought to incorporate Italy into a Wilsonian liberal capitalist international order and to use it as a bulwark against the threat posed by Communism. That policy scarcely changed with the Italian entry into the war in 1940, nor did the long-term American aim of hegemony in the Mediterranean region.

Analysing the relations between Italy and Spain during Fascism's republican epilogue between 1943 and 1945, Andrea Ungari argues that Franco's policy continued to be shaped in part by an ongoing gratitude for Italian Fascist intervention in the Spanish Civil War. Focusing upon the attempts by the RSI to form a coherent and independent foreign policy, Ungari highlights how the loyalty of many Italian diplomats in Spain lay with the Royal government rather than the RSI. Mussolini's tribulations were further aggravated by the Spanish government's unwillingness to commit itself to either of the sides in play. Ultimately, Ungari concludes, Mussolini failed to make the RSI an autonomous international player and never managed to restore in full Italian Fascist relations with Spain.

Marco Maria Aterrano examines British policy towards Italy following the armistice of September 1943. On one level, Aterrano observes, the British government returned to a position similar to that of the pre-1935 period, no longer regarding Italy as a threat in the Mediterranean. On another, however, London engaged in what has sometimes been regarded as a 'vindictive' approach that stood in contrast with Washington's more benevolent policy. Harold Macmillan, Resident Minister in the Mediterranean, led the development of more progressive British policy that helped engineer a change in British and Allied policy so that Italy would be treated as a friendly cobelligerent.

Moving from the international stage to the field of battle, the second section asks whether and to what extent it might be argued that there was a distinctive Fascist way of waging war. The four chapters examine the specificities of the

Italian conflicts, looking at the centrality of ideas of war within Italian Fascist ideology. In contrast with Alan Kramer, who suggests that Fascist warfare eliminated the distinction between combatants and non-combatants, the chapters in this section focus more on the ideological intentions of the Fascist regime, rather than on its actual achievements.[12] With the militarization of society being a core aim of the Fascist regime, the Italian involvement in World War II was the logical and, in some respects, inevitable result of its ideological trajectory.[13]

How far this can be characterized as Fascist might, however, appear to be contested by continuities with the pre-Fascist era. Indeed, while the regime's vision of empire drew influences from classical Rome, there were continuities with the liberal colonialism of the late-nineteenth century as well. The violent repression of Libya in 1922, moreover, predated Fascism, and drew upon notions of Italian 'racial superiority'.[14] The Fascist regime also reasserted liberal Italy's irredentist territorial claims. As Roberta Pergher has highlighted, at the heart of Fascist ideology on empire were tensions with Fascist visions of the Italian nation. Mussolini found himself having to balance his ambition for a racially and culturally cohesive nation with his desire to gain new territories populated by diverse peoples.[15]

The second section of this volume also looks at the Fascist regime's use of violence. The chapters explore the escalation of violence that characterized Fascist military campaigns, zooming in on the Spanish Civil War, the Italian occupation of Albania, the defence of the Eastern African Empire and Italian participation in the resistance movement in Greece.

Within the framework of the Fascist decade of war, Javier Rodrigo explores Italian intervention in the Spanish Civil War as a turning-point for Italian Fascist ambitions in Europe and the Mediterranean, sealing the connection between the regime's visions of war and violence. Rodrigo argues that while concern that a lack of intervention would leave Spain under German influence and the desire to limit support for the Popular Front were core considerations, Mussolini was also driven by the desire to control maritime traffic in the western Mediterranean to lay the foundations for Fascist supremacy. Developments in Spain, concludes Rodrigo, showcase the 'inseparable relation between Fascism and war, between expansion, penetration and violence, obedience, combat and belief'.

Turning to the relatively neglected subject of the Italian invasion of Albania, Valentina Villa suggests that while the military incursion of April 1939 marked the real beginning of World War II for Italy, the Italian action was long in preparation, beginning with the Fascist regime's efforts to increase its economic, political and cultural influence in the region in the 1920s. By the time the invasion took place, Villa argues that Albania was a *de facto* Italian colony. Ciano was a pivotal figure in persuading Mussolini to annex Albania, but the wider European situation played a part as well. Hitler's decision to invade Czechoslovakia without consulting Mussolini led the Italian leader to believe that Italy must act to counterbalance German expansion. Fascist Italy's seizure of Albania was to be its final military victory, but it was to prove a hollow one.

In his chapter on British perceptions of the Italian army at war, Andrew Stewart notes a lack of balance in historical assessments of military performance, especially in the campaign between Italy and Britain in Italian East Africa. The same was true in the 1930s, Stewart observes, as British representations of Italy and the Italian army were shaped by racial prejudices and by the press in particular. Colonial stereotypes also informed the way that British officers evaluated the Italians' conduct in war, leading to an unjustly harsh assessment of their collective performance in East Africa. Drawing from a variety of sources that include magazines, pictures and military records, Stewart concludes that the Italian war in the region was hampered by poor strategic planning and incompetence, rather than the lack of bravery depicted in British representations of the African campaign.

Detailing the Italian participation in the Greek resistance after the September 1943 armistice, Ioannis Nioutsikos draws our attention to the role individual political and ethical choices played in transnational fighting during World War II. Nioutsikos highlights how this case study can be situated within a wider European civil war, with Italians in Greece confronting the same moral dilemmas as Italians in Italy. Indeed, combatants were engaged in three connected conflicts: a liberation struggle, a civil conflict and a revolutionary struggle. What bound them together was a common opposition to Fascism. They were thus engaged in a transnational war of liberation against the German occupying forces, a revolutionary struggle against royalist forces and rival resistance groups and a civil war against Italian Fascists.

Focusing on the ideological dimension of the Italian military campaigns, the third section seeks to explore the relevance of Fascism's expansionist beliefs in bringing about the 1935–1945 decade of war. The four authors in this section analyse the racial dimensions of Italian policies in this period. Dealing with anti-Semitism and drawing comparisons between Fascist policies in relation to France, the Balkans and Africa, they tackle issues related to propaganda policies both in the Italian Navy and through the air waves across the Eastern Mediterranean.

Historians have long debated the significance of ideology in Mussolini's foreign policy. One of the leading historians of Fascist Italy and a contributor to this volume, MacGregor Knox, has been at the forefront of the argument that ideology drove Mussolini's imperialist ambitions and his alliance with Nazi Germany. For Knox, war against the western powers was to be the prelude to a deeper internal Fascist revolution within Italy itself.[16] On the other side of the argument, Renzo De Felice has suggested that Mussolini was driven by little more than pragmatism, not taking a definitive position on Fascist Italy's international alignments until the spring of 1940.[17] Taking the middle ground, H. James Burgwyn and Christian Goeschel have suggested that it was not so much ideology driving the *Duce*'s actions as ambition, arguing that while Mussolini and Hitler had much in common in their quest for a new order, contempt for liberal democracy and use of political violence, ideological affinities did not make their alliance inevitable.[18]

Our contention is not merely that the Italian involvement in the war fundamentally shaped its character, but that Italian Fascism showed a distinct ideological influence as well. The Abyssinian war was a Fascist enterprise, driven by ideological notions of empire and race.[19] It marked, arguably, the apogee of consensus about the regime.[20] In this respect, some chapters engage with notions of an ideological 'civil war' in Europe advanced by some scholars. Historians such as Enzo Traverso, Eric Hobsbawm, Ernst Nolte and François Furet have suggested that the years 1914–1945 should be conceived in terms of a struggle between Fascism and Communism, Fascism against the resistance, and anti-Fascism and revolution against counterrevolution.[21] Within the wider continental conflict were local civil wars, Traverso suggests, including not just the Spanish Civil War but World War II itself.[22] Fascist Italy, led by a strong ideological drive, was a major player in this context.

In his chapter on navalism and empire, Fabio De Ninno shifts our attention towards the role played by the Italian navy in shaping the Fascist decade of war. He suggests that the Regia Marina acted as a 'think tank', influencing Fascist ideological notions of the need for vital space and the militarization of society. Indeed, De Ninno argues, the Italian navy's geopolitical vision served as source of inspiration for Mussolini's conception of the Mediterranean as a 'trap', thwarting Italian expansionist ambitions and pushing the regime towards war.

Dealing with the colonial heritage in Italian military practices in the Balkans, Nicolas Virtue examines the debate over whether there were symmetries between the actions of the Italian army in Africa and Europe, drawing upon the theoretical frameworks of transfer history. Comparing the policies and attitudes that fuelled mass violence, he highlights the differing contexts of Africa and Europe and their places in the Fascist vision of a racial hierarchy. Virtue suggests that there was a complex process in which military and political elites transferred knowledge between the Ethiopian and Yugoslavian experiences, but that their actions were shaped by structural factors and circumstances. He finds little evidence of a distinct colonial mentality that transferred across to Yugoslavia, arguing that Italian military culture helps explain the linkages in Fascist violence.

Turning to the Fascist role in the persecution of the Jews, Luca Fenoglio looks at the Italian zone of occupation in France. Drawing upon comparative genocide scholarship, he explores the question of whether anti-Semitic theories led inexorably to the extermination of the Jews. The Italian occupation in France brought into sharp relief the divergences between German and Italian policies on the Jews. The Fascist regime did not see dealing with the 'Jewish question' as being critical to the success of its ideological vision. Rather, Fenoglio highlights the pragmatic nature of Italian policy that was adjusted to fit political and military needs.

Focusing upon the significance that Fascist ideology ascribed to propaganda, Arturo Marzano's chapter looks at how the Fascist regime sought to project its values outwards through Radio Bari's broadcasts to Arab populations. Marzano observes that Italian broadcasts were characterized by levels of anti-Semitism comparable with Radio Berlin and an exaggerated triumphalism that presented the war as if an Axis victory was inevitable. In response, between 1940 and 1943, Marzano finds that Arab audiences switched over either to the BBC or to Radio Berlin. A reduction in the levels of cultural output, the perceived objectivity of the BBC or the greater zeal of Berlin left listener figures to Radio Bari languishing.

In the final section of the volume, two of the leading historians of Fascist Italy and World War II, MacGregor Knox and Nicola Labanca, offer some broader reflections on the Fascist experience between 1935 and 1945, on its public and private memory and on the evolution of its historiographical narrative.

Placing the Fascist decade of war in a longer-term perspective, Knox reminds us that war was far from being a new experience for united Italy. While he notes that the wars which began in 1935 were qualitatively different to those which had come before, Knox also identifies elements of continuity. At the heart of the imperatives driving Italy to engage in war was the realization that territorial unification had brought neither great power status nor succeeded in uniting the country. The Fascist regime sought to harness war as a means of pursuing its totalitarian ambitions of a fascistized Italian 'race' that had been toughened by the experiences of war. It was only with the events of 1943 to 1945 that Italy was able to break free from the myths which had lain at the heart of unification and which the Fascist regime had radicalized through violence.

In his wide-ranging overview of the historiography on Italy's role in World War II and the state of the field more broadly, Nicola Labanca re-evaluates the relevance Fascist Italy had in the shaping of World War II. Despite many global studies barely mentioning the role played by Fascist Italy, Labanca observes that the war would not have been possible without its sequence of destabilizing actions before 1939. Italy played a key role in the breakdown of the international system in the 1930s and Hitler would not have been able to carry out his policies as ambitiously and swiftly as he did without the support of other Fascist governments. However, Labanca suggests that the relative neglect of Italy's role may change as new generations of scholars trained in transnational and international methodologies begin to shape the field. It is with this in mind that this volume proposes a new approach towards the role of Italy in shaping a Fascist decade of war between 1935 and 1945.

Notes

1 Studies on the end of the war, the fall of Fascism and the liberation of Italy have included: D.W. Ellwood, *Italy 1943–1945* (Leicester: Leicester University Press, 1985); P. Morgan, *The Fall of Mussolini: Italy, Italians and the Second World War* (Oxford: Oxford University Press, 2007); R. Atkinson, *The Day of Battle: The War in Sicily and Italy, 1943–1944* (New York: Henry Holt and Company, 2008).

2 Some of the major publications on the Second World War in Europe have included: M. Mazower, *Dark Continent: Europe's Twentieth Century* (New York: Verso Books, 1998); R. Vinen, *A History in Fragments: Europe in the Twentieth Century* (London: Little Brown, 2000); M. Mazower, *Hitler's Empire: Nazi Rule in Occupied Europe* (London: Allen Lane, 2008); I. Kershaw, *To Hell and Back: Europe 1914–1949* (London: Allen Lane, 2015). The international tensions of the 1930s continue to be debated by scholars, with new studies including: R. Boyce and J. Maiolo, *The*

Origins of World War Two: The Debate Continues (Basingstoke: Palgrave Macmillan, 2003). Edited collections on this subject have included: P. Liddle, J. Bourne and I. Whitehead (eds.), *The Great World War 1914–1945* (London: HarperCollins, 2000); and R. Gerwarth (ed.), *Twisted Paths, Europe 1914–1945* (Oxford: Oxford University Press, 2007). The complexity of international rivalries, ideological clashes and domestic upheaval in this period is such that it continues to generate fresh interpretations and debates, such as that advanced in E. Traverso, *Fire and Blood: The European Civil War, 1914–1945* (London: Verso, 2016).

3 For a detailed historiographical reflection on Italy in the Second World War, see Nicola Labanca's chapter at the end of this volume.

4 As part of a broader historiographical shift away from a Germanocentric and European focus towards a more global understanding of this period, several studies have explored the significance of the conflict over the Mediterranean region. These have included R.M. Salerno, *Vital Crossroads: Mediterranean Origins of the Second World War, 1935–1940* (Ithaca, NY: Cornell University Press, 2002); D. Porch, *The Path to Victory: The Mediterranean Theater in World War II* (New York: Farrar, Strauss and Giroux, 2004); A. Buchanan, *American Grand Strategy in the Mediterranean During World War II* (Cambridge: Cambridge University Press, 2014); C. D'Este, *World War II in the Mediterranean, 1942–1945* (Chapel Hill, NC: Algonquin, 1990). However, none of these studies have focused specifically upon the important impact of Italian actions before and during the Second World War.

5 Fascist Italy's role in international affairs during the 1930s is the subject of numerous publications. These have included: H.J. Burgwyn, *Italian Foreign Policy in the Interwar Period 1918–1940* (Westport, CT: Praeger, 1997); G. Bruce Strang, *On the Fiery March. Mussolini Prepares for War* (Westport, CT: Praeger, 2003); J. Gooch, *Mussolini and his Generals: The Armed Forces and Fascist Foreign Policy, 1922–1940* (Cambridge: Cambridge University Press, 2007); M. Knox, *Mussolini Unleashed, 1939–1941: Politics and Strategy in Fascist Italy's Last War* (London: Cambridge University Press, 1982); R. Mallett, *Mussolini and the Origins of the Second World War, 1933–1940* (Basingstoke: Palgrave Macmillan, 2003). Focusing upon the ideological dimensions of Fascist Italy's policies is: A. Kallis, *Fascist Ideology: Territory and Expansionism in Italy and Germany, 1922–1945* (London: Routledge, 2000).

6 G. Rochat, *Le guerre italiane 1935–1943. Dall'impero d'Etiopia alla disfatta* (Turin: Einaudi, 2005).

7 See, for instance: Ellwood, *Italy 1943–1945*; J. Holland, *Italy's Sorrow: A Year of War, 1944–1945* (London: Harper Press, 2008); and R. Bailey, *Target: Italy: The Secret War against Mussolini, 1940–1943* (London: Faber & Faber, 2014).

8 S. Ball, *The Bitter Sea: The Struggle for Mastery in the Mediterranean, 1935–1949* (London: Harper Press, 2009), pp. 322–3.

9 R. Mallett, *Mussolini in Ethiopia, 1919–1935: The Origins of Fascist Italy's African War* (Cambridge: Cambridge University Press, 2015), p. 158.

10 In a recent article, Bastian Matteo Scianna aptly defines the Italian intervention in Abyssinia as a 'prelude to total war', B.M. Scianna, 'A Prelude to Total War? The Abyssinian War (1935–36) in the eyes of Foreign Military Observers', *International Journal of Military History and Historiography*, 38 (2018), pp. 5–33.

11 E. Sica and R. Carrier (eds), *Italy and the Second World War: Alternative Perspectives* (Leiden: Brill, 2018), p. 1. Recent studies on the Italian occupations in Europe, such as D. Rodogno, *Fascism's European Empire: Italian Occupation During the Second World War* (Cambridge: Cambridge University Press, 2006); E. Sica, *Mussolini's Army in the Riviera: Italy's Occupation of France* (Urbana: University of Illinois Press, 2016); A. Osti Guerrazzi, *The Italian Army in Slovenia: Strategies of Antipartisan Repression, 1941–1943*, trans. E. Burke and A. Majanlahti (New York: Palgrave, 2013) have explored the significance of violence and race in Fascist occupation policies.

12 A. Kramer, *Dynamic of Destruction: Culture and Mass Killing in the First World War* (Oxford: Oxford University Press, 2007), p. 329.

13 For a recent historiographical reflection on Fascist Italy and the World War, see G. Fiocco, 'Guerra fascista e guerra italiana (1940–1943)', *Studi Storici*, 55:1 (2014), pp. 271–85, where an insufficient dialogue between histories of Fascism and histories of war is denounced. On this point, also see Rochat, *Le guerre italiane*, p. xiv.

14 J. Gooch, 'Re-conquest and Suppression: Fascist Italy's Pacification of Libya and Ethiopia, 1922–1939', *Journal of Strategic Studies*, 28:6 (2005), pp. 1005–32.

15 R. Pergher, *Mussolini's Nation-Empire: Sovereignty and Settlement in Italy's Borderlands, 1922–1943* (Cambridge: Cambridge University Press, 2017), pp. 244–50.

16 M. Knox, 'The Fascist Regime, its Foreign Policy and its Wars: An Anti-Anti-Fascist Orthodoxy?', *Contemporary European History*, 4:3 (1995), pp. 346–65. See also M. Knox, *Hitler's Italian Allies: Royal Armed Forces, Fascist Regime, and the War of 1940–1943* (Cambridge: Cambridge University Press, 2000).

17 See Renzo De Felice's eight-volume biography of the Duce, specifically *Mussolini il duce. Vol. I: Gli anni del consenso, 1929–1936* (Turin: Einaudi, 1974); *Mussolini il duce. Vol. II: Lo stato totalitario 1936–1940* (Turin: Einaudi, 1981); and *Mussolini l'alleato. Vol. I. L'Italia in guerra, 1940–1943. Tomo I: Dalla guerra 'breve' alla guerra lunga* (Turin: Einaudi, 1990).

18 H.J. Burgwyn, *Mussolini Warlord. Failed Dreams of Empire, 1940–1943* (New York: Enigma Books, 2012); C. Goeschel, *Mussolini and Hitler: The Forging of a Fascist Alliance* (New Haven, CT and London: Yale University Press, 2018).

19 The Italian invasion of Abyssinia and the Fascist regime's approach to colonial rule in Africa have been the subject of several recent books. These have included: M. Fiore, *Anglo-Italian Relations in the Middle East, 1922–1940* (Farnham: Ashgate, 2010); G. Bruce Strang (ed.), *Collision of Empires: Italy's Invasion of Ethiopia and its International Impact* (London: Routledge, 2016).

20 For an overview on popular opinion in Fascist Italy, see, among others, P. Corner (ed.), *Popular Opinion in Totalitarian Regimes: Fascism, Nazism, Communism* (Oxford: Oxford University Press, 2009); and C. Duggan, *Fascist Voices: An Intimate History of Mussolini's Italy* (Oxford: Oxford University Press, 2012).

21 See, for a starting point on the debate, E.J. Hobsbawm, *The Age of Extremes: 1914–1991* (New York: Vintage Books, 1994); and F. Furet and E. Nolte, *Fascism and Communism* (Lincoln: University of Nebraska Press, 2004).

22 Traverso, *Fire and Blood*, pp. 1–44.

Part I

The international dimension

Policy-making and diplomacy

1   An opportunity missed

Britain and the Abyssinian Crisis

Steven Morewood

Introduction

When Saddam Hussein invaded Kuwait with overwhelming Iraqi forces in August 1990, American political commentators spoke of 'the Abyssinia moment'. Amid comparisons between the situation facing the American-led international community and the 1930s, Republican President George H.W. Bush rose to the challenge, which became his most lauded achievement in office. The credibility of the United Nations, successor to the League of Nations, was on the line. In the event it imposed the most crippling and far-reaching sanctions in its history. When they failed to succeed in removing the aggressor, decisive military intervention followed.

All this was in stark contrast to the international reaction following Benito Mussolini's invasion of Abyssinia in October 1935. Despite quickly declaring Fascist Italy an aggressor in breach of the League Covenant, it took several weeks for the League Council to agree and implement soft sanctions, which lacked any persuasive power. Closure of the Suez Canal, thereby severing Italy's sea communications with East Africa, and an oil sanction, were conspicuous by their absence. Not surprisingly, this 'test case' – the one and only occasion when Article XVI, the supposedly coercive fulcrum of the League edifice, was tried out – ended in abysmal failure. The League of Nations became an irrelevance in the international crises that followed, leading to World War II.

Causes and consequences

In ascribing blame for the disastrous train of events, much culpability can be laid at the door of the French.[1] But much more responsibility resides with the British who, like the Americans in 1990, had the opportunity to take the lead, indeed created expectations that they would act decisively, but instead fell back on excuses for inaction. During May 1936, Italian troops having recently marched into Addis Ababa, the Abyssinian capital, the House of Commons convened for a post-mortem. Anthony Eden, once seen as the League's 'golden boy', who had succeeded the disgraced Sam Hoare as Foreign Secretary following the abortive Hoare-Laval Pact – often seen as the first act of 'craven appeasement' – faced hostility during his speech, including shouts of 'resign', 'shame' and 'sabotage'. Unconvincingly, he claimed there was no support for military action, whose burden would fall predominantly on Britain as the most proximate military power. Arthur Greenwood, for Labour, replied that 'no more deplorable speech has ever fallen from the lips of a British Minister'.[2]

Within a short period, Leo Amery, formerly Secretary of State for the Colonies (1924–1929), a leading Conservative backbencher and staunch opponent of war in 1935–1936, changed his opinion. 'Everyone knows now that our Abyssinian policy was crazy. [...] We might have done better to have shut the Suez Canal on Mussolini in the summer of 1935 and run the risk, or more than the risk of war'.[3] In April 1937, Sir Eric Phipps, the departing British Ambassador to Berlin, appraised his four-year tenure thus:

> British influence and prestige reached its height towards the end of 1935 (when, for a brief space, it was thought that England, at the head of the League, might succeed in stopping Mussolini's Abyssinian adventure). I reported at the time that in existing circumstances the policy of Anglo-German understanding would be abandoned with the greatest reluctance. [...] The victory of Italy opened up a new chapter. It is inevitable that in a country where Might is worshipped English prestige should then fall. The German began to ask himself whether it was necessary to conciliate a power, without whose favours Italy appeared to be doing very well.[4]

For British decision-makers, the Abyssinian Crisis presented a golden opportunity to thwart an aggressor that was not taken. As the pre-eminent power in the League of Nations whom the majority of members, and especially the smaller nations, were looking towards to take a lead and as the dominant naval power in the Eastern Mediterranean, Britain could have pushed through and implemented crippling military sanctions. 'By putting his great army on the other side of the Suez Canal', Neville Chamberlain wrote to his sister, Ida, 'Mussolini has tied a noose round his own neck and left the end dangling for anyone with a noose to pull'.[5] Instead of playing hangman, however, the Baldwin government championed soft sanctions and while it persuaded the League Council to lift the arms embargo on Abyssinia crucially the funding which Emperor Haile Selassie so desperately needed to buy modern weapons to defend his country was not forthcoming. Only in successfully proposing the lifting of sanctions, in July 1936, did the Baldwin government finally and ignominiously take the lead.

Britain averted war with Italy in 1935–1936 for selfish reasons, thereby dealing a fatal blow to the League-centred international system that had arisen since 1919. Mussolini's defiance of the world order was of momentous significance in setting off a chain of events leading to another world war. What was not recognized by British decision-makers at the time was the fact that the Duce was deadly serious in his oft-stated ambition to recreate the Roman Empire in the Eastern Mediterranean. As the men on the spot, diplomats and senior military figures recognized, this was bound in the end to produce a clash of arms.

It did lead, in the interim, to a propaganda war which Italy won because it seemed to the Arab world and beyond that Britain was afraid of the new Italy and its substantial air force and submarine fleet which had the potential to wreak havoc with the British Mediterranean Fleet, guardian of the citadels of imperial influence such as Malta, Alexandria, Suez and Aden. The actuality was rather different in 1940, but by then the damage had been done as the situation got out of control and the League became an irrelevant bystander to the aggressive moves of the fascist powers from July 1936, when they became embroiled in Spain's civil war, moving onto the absorption of a succession of weak states whose last victim, Poland, finally produced a military response from the Western Powers. Only belatedly did Neville Chamberlain recognize the turning point represented by December 1935 when Britain opted for appeasement over the imposition of an oil sanction. 'It is from that moment', he conceded in parliament two years later, 'that the difficulties of this country have increased and the world situation has deteriorated'.[6]

The Italians led the way for the Germans to follow. They became brothers in arms, cementing their relationship politically through the Rome–Berlin Axis and military through the Pact of Steel. In the interim, Mussolini dropped his resistance to *Anschluss* in return for a free hand in the Mediterranean. Chamberlain deluded himself that the Duce could once more become a partner for peace, as in the later 1920s, when in reality the resulting agreements (the Gentleman's Agreement and the Anglo-Italian Agreement) merely bought time for Rome and were quickly contravened through retaining 'volunteers' in Spain and reinforcing the Libya garrison to frighten the Egyptians and undermine British influence in Cairo. The fact was that the imperial impulse in Italian foreign policy went unheeded in Whitehall. This represented another illusion which underpinned Britain's foreign policy, the other being that the fascist powers would not naturally gravitate towards one another and conspire to bring down the international order.

Why Mussolini was allowed to snatch victory from the jaws of defeat over Abyssinia has exercised political commentators and historians ever since.[7] The furore surrounding the Hoare-Laval Pact, which exposed the hypocrisy of the Baldwin government's professed adherence to the League of Nations as the cornerstone of its foreign policy, moved the Prime Minister to tell an angry parliament that his lips were sealed while claiming that if he disclosed the underlying reasons he would be able to carry every member of the House of Commons with him. Cartoonists had a field day.[8]

The underlying reason for British passivity was the neglect of defence spending occasioned by mistaken presumptions, the priority accorded to social spending after 1918, and the ravages of the Great Depression. Rearmament only began in 1934–1935 and was then directed against Germany and Japan. Since November 1933, Italy, alongside France and the United States, had been placed on a list of friendly powers against which no defence preparations were deemed necessary. This led to the neglect of Malta and a failure to upgrade the anti-aircraft defence system of the capital ships in the Mediterranean Fleet.

Mussolini, by contrast, while paying lip service to the international system through signing up to Locarno, concluding friendship treaties with various small states (including Abyssinia) and joining in with agreements to ban the use of gas in war and renounce conflict as an instrument of foreign policy, went in the opposite direction. His speeches were often laced with imperialist rhetoric. In May 1927, he proclaimed:

> The precise, fundamental and paramount duty of Fascist Italy is that of putting in a state of readiness all her armed forces on land, sea and in the air. We must be in a position to arm them. Our navy must be reinforced, and our air force – in which I have growing faith – must be so numerous and so powerful that the roar of its engines will drown any other noise in the peninsula. [...] We shall be in a position then – tomorrow – when, between 1935 and 1940, we shall find ourselves at a crucial point in European history – we shall be in a position to make our voice felt, and at least to see our rights recognised.[9]

The Regia Aeronautica accordingly received funding for expansion and began to establish new air bases in the Eastern Mediterranean. In April 1935, a new air force programme was announced with emphasis on a new tri-engine heavy bomber, the Savoia Marchetti 81. It could reportedly attain 180 mph, had a range of 248 miles and carry a 2,000-pound bomb load. Potentially, this advanced design could wreak havoc with the Mediterranean Fleet and target Egyptian cities and British bases. British intelligence on Italy was poor, but one guestimate suggested that 400 had been ordered.[10] When the critical Cabinet meeting was held to consider whether to back an oil embargo or a peace overture, critically reference was made to the expectation that 150 Savoia Marchetti 81s would be available by January 1936.[11]

Besides the tangible Italian air threat, other considerations came into play. The Baldwin government was caught on the horns of a dilemma. Italy was an ally within the anti-German Stresa front.[12] The League of Nations Union's Peace Ballot result, in June 1935, indicated overwhelming public support for the League and applying sanctions against an aggressor. It was felt that the sanctions machinery of Article XVI of the League Covenant must be applied should Italy invade Abyssinia, as it did on 3 October 1935.[13] The situation was also viewed in imperial terms. Should Italy be decisively defeated by Abyssinia, repeating 1896, then this might stimulate revolts against British dominance in the empire. Last, but not least, rearmament had barely begun, leading the Chiefs of Staff to advise the government on 28 May 1935 'of the utmost importance that this country should not become involved in war within the next few years'.[14]

The League of Nations Union stridently advocated the closure of the Suez Canal to Italian troop and supply ships as the most lethal way of bringing Italy's imperialist adventure to a juddering halt.[15] This was never seriously entertained despite the counsel of the Foreign Office's Legal Adviser that by its aggression Italy had placed itself outside international law, which meant that the

1888 Suez Canal Convention could be overridden. During the Great War, British warships constantly flouted its edict to keep the waterway open to all nations, denying access to Central Powers' ships.[16] But Mussolini had decreed that closure meant war, an eventuality the Baldwin government was determined to avoid. In the 1935 election campaign, Neville Chamberlain denounced Lloyd George's advocacy of closure to induce negotiations:

> What does this mean? It means sending British warships to stop Italian transports and supply ships which may be convoyed by Italian warships, from passing through the Suez Canal. But that means war. Signor Mussolini has said so himself. So the peace policy of Mr. Lloyd George is to begin by going to war.[17]

On 13 November 1935, Chamberlain went further and publicly stated that military sanctions 'would [...] reduce the League to a farce'.[18] The day before the Foreign Secretary, Sir Samuel Hoare, issued an official statement, condemning Lloyd George and Clement Attlee, the Labour leader, as 'warmongers' for proposing military sanctions. Following their policy would destroy collective security. 'We will', Hoare insisted, 'take our full share boldly and locally in collective action, but we refuse to take isolated action'.[19]

The Baldwin government reinforced the Eastern Mediterranean from far and wide with aircraft, tanks, troops and warships not as a prelude to military intervention but as insurance lest Mussolini turned into a mad dog in response to sanctions. This was always an unlikely eventuality in the absence of biting sanctions. The effect of the extraordinary reinforcements, which remained in theatre for eleven months, was to create an expectation in Britain and beyond of decisive action. When it failed to materialize, Britain suffered an immense loss of prestige, especially in the Middle East where the impression was that the British were running scared of the Italians.[20]

It is apparent that the perception of Britain's military capabilities and the likely losses she would sustain in bringing Italy to heel influenced, indeed impelled, Hoare to embrace a sell-out of Abyssinia rather than back the imposition of a potentially crippling oil embargo. The military advice remitted to the Foreign Office was tinged with pessimism and reflected the Chiefs of Staff's disinclination to risk war with Italy. As a consequence, they accentuated the deficiencies of the British forces massed in the Eastern Mediterranean while failing to emphasize the perilous strategic position of the Italian forces. After reviewing the Chiefs of Staff's doom-laden memoranda Rosaria Quartararo concluded:

> They appeared to be unable to devise any effective means of defence. [...] Imperial defence policy remained chaotic and confused. [...] The Chiefs of Staff must, in retrospect, have been profoundly relieved that Mussolini never dared to put their dispositions to the test. [...] In 1935–1936 Britain could not defend Egypt or the Suez Canal, let alone fight in defence of the Covenant.[21]

The implication of this analysis is that Italian military capability peaked at this time and a wider conflict would have produced a different outcome to 1940–1941 when Italian forces performed lamentably in Egypt and Greece.

An alternative perspective

Quartararo conspicuously failed to examine the views of the senior military commanders in the Eastern Mediterranean. The men on the spot relished rather than feared the prospect of war with Italy. 'To us in the Mediterranean Fleet', reflected Rear Admiral Andrew Cunningham, 'it seemed a very simple task to stop [Mussolini]. The mere closing of the Suez Canal to his transports [...] would effectively have cut off his armies concentrating in Eritrea and elsewhere'.[22] Admiral Sir Roger Backhouse, Commander-in-Chief Home Fleet, made frequent visits to Admiralty House in Whitehall during the crisis. He discerned that 'the Mediterranean atmosphere [was] quite definitely very different from what it was at home. Their *one* thought is operations'.[23]

What operations were being planned? Admiral Sir William Fisher, Commander-in-Chief of the Mediterranean Fleet, contemplated bombarding the vulnerable Italian ports and coastal rail communications to puncture Mussolini's bombastic anti-British propaganda and bring home the superiority of British naval power.[24] Fisher was in the Nelson mould but was also keenly aware of the latent threat posed by the Italian air force. On 25 February 1936, he reported to Admiral Chatfield, the First Sea Lord, that 'the carriers are ready for war now. War of every kind against ships or shore, day or night'.[25] Had war come then, the two aircraft carriers would have played a vital role, Fisher recognizing that the Fleet Air Arm was essential to catch the faster Italian warships. The genesis of the famous raid on the Italian fleet base at Taranto can be traced to this period. Particularly intensive fleet exercises were undertaken between January and March 1936, including a night exercise when a sabotage force attacked a fleet in harbour. Fisher also contemplated dawn raids by the Fleet Air Arm on Italian warships at Augusta and Catania.[26] Significantly, the Italian naval high command feared an 'English battle fleet, escorted by a powerful mass of destroyers [...] able to ramble about the Mediterranean inflicting whatever damage it wants to our scarcely defended coast'.[27]

Where the pessimism of the Chiefs of Staff clashed with the optimism of the men on the spot, the former's view prevailed. At the start of the crisis, Fisher audaciously proposed to combine the Home and Mediterranean fleets at Malta, but his superiors deemed this provocative and risky, presenting the Regia Aeronautica, only thirty minutes flying time away in Sicily, with too tempting a target. Again, Fisher's proposal of 11 August 1935 to send substantial naval units to Port Said, which would have given Mussolini pause for thought, was overridden. The Admiralty ruled that the Suez Canal Convention, which only permitted one battleship and another ship to be stationed at the canal's Mediterranean entrance, must be observed.[28] Fisher was livid when he received the Chiefs of Staff's pessimistic appraisal which deemed that his fleet could not act without the certain support of the French. Indeed, Fisher confessed his astonishment to his historian brother at the reinforcements being sent out since he felt able to 'blow the Italians out of the water with the ordinary Mediterranean Fleet'.[29] In January 1936, General Sir George Weir, General Officer Commanding in Egypt, wanted to adopt an aggressive forward posture on the border with Libya only to find himself overruled by the Chiefs of Staff despite intelligence that there were no major Italian forces immediately across the frontier.[30]

None of the optimism emanating from the forces gathered in the Eastern Mediterranean was channelled to ministers. Incredibly, no minister visited the theatre for a first-hand assessment which meant that the Chiefs of Staff, their aides and abettors – the service ministers, Sir Maurice Hankey (secretary to the Cabinet and Committee of Imperial Defence) and Sir Robert Vansittart (permanent under-secretary at the Foreign Office) – controlled and manipulated appreciations to suit their war-avoidance agenda. They painted a bleak picture. While there was no question that Italy could be defeated if it came to war, the potential losses, especially in warships, could jeopardise Britain's standing as a world power, encouraging the Japanese to commit aggression in the Far East.[31] The unrelenting pessimism had the desired effect. Hoare complained that the Chiefs of Staff were 'the worst pacifists and defeatists' in the country.[32]

The issue of anti-aircraft ammunition stocks came to the fore in the debate over whether to back an oil sanction which the Canadians had inconveniently tabled at Geneva. There was undoubtedly a severe shortage at the start of the crisis. By November, however, when League sanctions came into effect, there had been a considerable improvement. At a critical Defence Policy Requirements Committee meeting on 26 November 1935, the situation was examined. Alfred Duff Cooper, the new Secretary of State for War, broke ranks with his fellow service ministers, departing from their unrelenting pessimism. Ammunition production had doubled to 8,000 rounds per week and if it came to war an extra 5,000 rounds a week was available. He postulated that there were now enough stocks at Eastern Mediterranean ports to defend them against 300 air raids. The War Office representative countered that ammunition expenditure depended on the weight of attack, the only precedent being a Great War raid on London when each anti-aircraft gun fired an average of 5,000 rounds. For the navy, Sir Bolton Eyres-Monsell, First Lord of the Admiralty, emphasized that there was only enough fleet ammunition for 22 minutes of continuous firing at long range and 13 minutes at short range.[33] This statement was misleading since air raids would take seconds, leaving ample ammunition to counter many attacks. Hoare, who had inclined towards supporting an oil sanction, was suitably panic-stricken. As Major-General Pownall recorded in his diary, the Foreign Secretary implored the service departments to 'do this, that and the other, including the production of more anti-aircraft ammunition than it is physically possible to produce'.[34]

Issues came to a head at a three-hour Cabinet on 2 December. Pownall summarized the outcome from the Chiefs of Staff's perspective:

> Mercifully reasonable councils prevailed. [...] Hoare's urgency was overborne by the service ministers (less Duff Cooper who was, I gather, most

ineffective) and the PM. They decided not to go for an immediate oil sanction on 12 December at Geneva but rather to use the intervening week for
negotiations to get Mussolini to heel. [...] Great emphasis was laid on the
unreadiness of our services to take the brunt of a League war, and the
losses we should incur.[35]

Five days later, Hoare met Laval in Paris, under firm instructions from Baldwin
to 'keep us out of war'.[36] The French proved very willing bed partners and the
infamous pact was agreed. Ironically, the Abyssinians launched a successful
counter-offensive at the same time which led retired General 'Boney' Fuller, who
was in Abyssinia, to describe the Italian position as 'hopeless, helpless, paralytic'.[37]
Soon, however, the illegal use of mustard gas, delivered in massive quantities
through the Suez Canal, would turn the tide decisively in Mussolini's favour.

The failure to save Abyssinia and uphold the authority of the League of
Nations represents one of the most shameful episodes in British foreign policy.
It was the one occasion in the 1930s when Britain held a credible military card
in its hands. By contrast, the later guarantee to Poland lacked all credibility,
with no British or French armed forces deployed to indicate that a German
invasion really meant war. Why it was not played in 1935–1936 had much to
do with the military advice remitted to civilian ministers, which failed to reflect
the supreme confidence of the men on the spot that a firmer hand could have
been dealt with little risk of incurring the losses so feared by the Chiefs of
Staff. They and their supporters clearly regarded this crisis with Italy as
a transient episode, an inconsequential colonial war, steadfastly refusing to be
deflected from defence preparations against Germany and Japan by risking war
with Italy.[38] These were, they insisted, the greater menaces to national security.
But this was all the more reason to deal decisively with the lesser Italian threat
at this stage. Within the Foreign Office, the Egyptian Department and the Colonial Office were lone voices emphasizing that the Italian challenge would grow
unless it was confronted.[39]

On 25 June 1936, Geoffrey Dawson, *The Times'* editor, found Admiral Fisher
'very insistent that the Italians would have had short shrift in the
Mediterranean'.[40] The Italians did not have the tactics and weaponry to inflict
serious damage to the Royal Navy. They lacked any armour piercing bombs,
modern capital ships, aircraft carriers, midget submarines, dive bombers or torpedo bombers. Their submarines were slow to dive and easily detected in the
clear waters of the Mediterranean. To quote Admiral Sir Guy Grantham, then
Staff Officer (Operations) to Admiral Sir Dudley Pound:

I do not think the Italians would have succeeded in seriously damaging the
fleet and stopping it cutting communications to Libya and Ethiopia. Admit-
tedly, as war later proved, our anti-aircraft equipment was inadequate, but
constant anti-aircraft practices were carried out, as the fleet was frequently
at sea. [...] We often practised a system which involved all ships firing
their heavy anti-aircraft guns to produce an umbrella of bursting shells over

the fleet, or towards an attacking formation. In World War Two ships managed to drive off Italian high-level bombers with guns that were standard equipment in 1936. [...] I personally felt a great opportunity was missed, although of course it was a political matter.[41]

For the Regia Aeronautica to have dominated the Eastern Mediterranean in 1935–1936, the new Savoia Marchetti 81 long-distance, high-level bomber would need to have been a wonder plane with wonder pilots. This was far from the reality. Its bomb mechanism did not facilitate accurate bombing, drag reduced speed and aside from self-sealing tanks it was unarmoured. During the Spanish Civil War, the Savoia Marchetti 81 operated well only with fighter cover. Moreover, the best Italian fighter plane, the Fiat CR 42, could only provide escorts as far as Mersa Matruh so that over Alexandria the Savoia Marchetti 81 would have been vulnerable to fighter interception by the RAF and Fleet Air Arm.[42] In a telling incident, Hawker Fury fighters forced a Savoia Marchetti 81 on a reconnaissance mission over Egypt to land, its pilot having been briefed that no British aircraft could attain its height. In his post-crisis evaluation, Air Chief Marshal Sir Robert Brooke-Popham, Air Officer Commanding in Chief Middle East, conceded that the Savoia Marchetti 81

> was certainly faster than our fighters. On the other hand, if the pilot put the Savoia Marchetti 81 into a dive the top surface of the plane blew off. Therefore, the obvious solution was to get above the Savoia Marchetti 81 and make them dive.

In this knowledge, Brooke–Popham dissuaded Fisher from moving his fleet to Haifa to place it at a greater distance from Savoia Marchetti 81s operating from Libya. The RAF also planned to target Savoia Marchetti 81s on the ground, a tactic that was later successfully employed in the Desert War. After continual drills in harbour and at sea Fisher wrote to Chatfield on 25 February 1936 that a 'big formation of Savoia Marchetti 81s, approaching to bomb the fleet, and keeping together, is now a pleasant dream, certainly not a nightmare'.[43] Moreover, Savoia Marchetti 81s were not being mass produced. It is doubtful whether Italy possessed even a hundred by early 1936. Furthermore, British intelligence reported in May that the Italians were finding difficulty in servicing this aircraft. By December 1936, RAF Intelligence detected that Caproni 133 bombers had replaced Savoia Marchetti 81s in Abyssinia after 70% of them became unserviceable through forced landings and technical failures. In 1937, the Savoia Marchetti 79 superseded the Savoia Marchetti 81 which in World War II was relegated to a transport role.[44]

Nor, in 1935–1936, was there any prospect of an Italian invasion of Egypt to seize Alexandria and the Suez Canal. Most ground forces were tied up in East Africa and any invasion force would have faced the Mobile Force supported by the RAF and Royal Navy along the coast. On 26 February 1936, Major-General

Sir John Dill, Director of Military Operations and Intelligence at the War Office, briefed the Chiefs of Staff after visiting Egypt:

> The risk of a serious invasion of inhabited Egypt by Italian land forces does not exist. [...] To project and maintain a land force of sufficient strength to be effective over the 300 miles [...] of stony and practically waterless wastes of the Western Desert would be an undertaking far beyond the powers of the Italians. [...] Victory for them is unattainable and they know it. It is doubtful if they would be capable of any serious effort beyond seventy miles of the Cyrenaican frontier. [...] We are running no risks in the Western Desert. Our position there is fully insured.[45]

Dill's confidence was not misplaced. In September 1940, the Italian Tenth Army advanced no further than Sidi Barrani, sixty miles inside the Egyptian border. But this report was of no consequence to the Chiefs of Staff who failed to consider it until 31 March 1936. At their meeting on that date, they pronounced that neither Dill's prognosis nor the optimistic combined offensive appreciation remitted by the commanders in Egypt changed the situation.[46] The Chiefs' profound irritation with developments was reflected in their unsolicited report on the military ramifications of the German remilitarization of the Rhineland when they warned their government that

> if there is the smallest danger of being drawn into commitments which might lead to war with Germany, we ought at once to disengage ourselves from our present responsibilities in the Mediterranean, which have exhausted practically the whole of our meagre forces.[47]

Chatfield was chairman of the Chiefs of Staff. Although part of him inclined towards teaching the impudent Italians a lesson, throughout the crisis he failed to utilize the optimism of Admiral Fisher, with whom he corresponded, to press for military sanctions. In March 1936, Chatfield gave evidence to the Committee of Imperial Defence's committee on the Vulnerability of Capital Ships to Air Attack. Chatfield was incensed by press articles and parliamentary comments which suggested that the Royal Navy had been rendered impotent by the air threat. One opposition MP impudently suggested that the Mediterranean Fleet was transfixed 'at Alexandria, Haifa and Aden [...] completely at the mercy of the Italian Air Force [...] like sitting rabbits against hawks'.[48] Chatfield told the committee:

> I wish we could prove it [fleet defence] because we might have less of these remarks. Of course, I do not want to prove it, because, in proving it, we should lose some ships inevitably and so weaken our imperial defence position, until our navy has been rebuilt.

Chatfield was looking beyond the present emergency. He maintained that once heavy anti-aircraft guns were installed in capital ships, the effects would be 'so tremendous that no chief of a foreign air staff will hurl his valuable aircraft against this terrific fire'. Once modernized, he insisted, the *Queen Elizabeth*, Fisher's flagship, bristling with anti-aircraft guns, could destroy half of attacking aircraft, which proved to be a fanciful claim when war came.[49]

Conclusion

The Baldwin government's line of least resistance was not without consequences. Churchill commented at the time: 'our communications cannot be left at the mercy of so unreliable a thing as Italian friendship'.[50] The failure to make a stand in 1935–1936 effectively ended the Naval Plans Division's cherished Main Fleet to Singapore strategy which planned to send a reinforced Mediterranean Fleet through the Suez Canal and Red Sea, the shortest route to the Far East.[51] Chatfield conceded in his memoirs that he had failed to anticipate Mussolini's vindictive nature.[52] Far from being grateful to Britain for its magnanimity, Mussolini deluded himself into believing that ultimately he could wrest Egypt and the Sudan from British dominance and create a swathe of neo-Roman territories running from Libya to Italian East Africa, directing the Italian High Command to begin planning in the wake of his Abyssinian triumph.[53] Germany was also brought out of isolation. Having considered Mussolini foolhardy for venturing into Abyssinia against British wishes, Hitler now hailed the Duce as a genius. Anglo-French disarray provided the opportunity for Germany to march into the Rhineland. Soon Mussolini and Hitler intervened in Spain, further destabilizing the Mediterranean. By this time, the Chiefs of Staff were anxious to avoid further commitments in the region, refusing to back Eden's proposed guarantees to Greece and Turkey against outside aggression. That policy would be revisited in 1939 after Italy invaded Albania by which time, ironically, Britain was in a far weaker position in the Eastern Mediterranean than in 1935–1936 and its guarantees accordingly lacked credibility.

Lord Salisbury's dictum that one of the cardinal errors in foreign policy is to stick with the carcasses of dead policies is very apt in this case. Britain had never been to war with Italy since its creation and with France and the United States it remained on the list of friendly powers until the late 1930s. The illusion of a benign Italy persisted. Winston Churchill's verdict still rings true: 'if ever there was an opportunity of striking a decisive blow in a generous cause with the minimum of risk, it was here and now'.[54] In the event, in 1935–1936, the Baldwin government allowed itself to be out-bluffed by the poseur Mussolini, further inflating his imperious ego until the gallant Greeks punctured it in autumn 1940, followed swiftly by the British who had ejected the Italian invaders from Egypt by the end of the year.

The Italo-Abyssinian crisis, once a centrepiece of the historiography on the origins of World War II, has latterly been relegated to a sideshow, with the Rhineland and Munich crises becoming the key turning points towards another global conflict. In fact, the feeble British response to Mussolini's challenge played heavily on the mind of Adolf Hitler in moulding his perception that the

Western Powers would not implement their guarantee to Poland and actually go to war with Germany. To quote Geoffrey Waddington:

> Hitler's view of the value of British friendship was profoundly influenced by the latter's policy during the Abyssinian crisis. Far from witnessing a display of the formidable power with which he associated the British Empire and which he wished to share, the Führer looked on in amazement as Britain tried desperately to avert an Anglo-Italian breach with offers of compensation and compromise solutions. Such was the impression which Italy's military achievements appear to have made upon the Chancellor that Sir Eric Phipps found him in May 1936 expatiating on the 'greatness and genius of Signor Mussolini'.[55]

Already, in March 1936, Hitler decided to take advantage of Anglo-French disarray and bring forward his plans to remilitarize the Rhineland. By August 1939, Hitler was deluding himself that if he attacked Poland, the war could be localized. Foreign Minister, Joachim von Ribbentrop, led the Fuhrer to believe that Britain would stay out because of the Italian and Japanese threats to the empire. He anticipated a repeat of the Abyssinian episode from the Western Powers: futile gestures, like ineffectual sanctions, but not declarations of war in honour of the Polish guarantee. Mussolini, he told his doubting generals, 'has demonstrated his strength in [the] Abyssinian conflict'.[56] Again harking back to 1935–1936, Hitler assured a sceptical Count Ciano, the Italian Foreign Minister: 'France and England will certainly make extremely theatrical anti-German gestures but will not go to war'.[57] When they did, he was dumbfounded, turning on Ribbentrop to ask: 'what now?'[58]

Mussolini, too, drew the wrong conclusions from his Abyssinian adventure. Rather than viewing the outcome as fortuitous, his deluded dream of recreating the Roman Empire in the Eastern Mediterranean gained further sustenance. He encouraged his generals to contemplate the seizure of Egypt and the Sudan, which if successful would provide the last piece of the jigsaw linking East and North Africa.[59] The final showdown came in December 1940, when the Italian invaders were ignominiously expelled from Egypt by British and Commonwealth forces which, despite manifold difficulties, were, as in 1935–1936, supremely confident of besting the Italians. 'Never in the field of human conflict', Eden, restored as Foreign Secretary, wrote to Prime Minister Winston Churchill, paraphrasing his famous Battle of Britain speech, 'has so much been surrendered by so many to so few'.[60] Mussolini's bluster had finally been exposed for what it was. But, unlike in 1935–1936, a far more formidable opponent was waiting in the wings, as Rommel's Afrika Korps emerged to stretch out the Desert War. Closer Italo-German ties were another consequence of the reverberations of Rome's victory over the League. So too was the 'triple threat' – the prospect of war in three theatres against Germany, Italy and Japan – which the British Chiefs of Staff warned was unwinnable. It is difficult to disagree with David Omissi: 'the Abyssinian war completely altered the strategic picture in the Mediterranean[and] struck a blow at the delicate equilibrium of British global strategy from which it never fully recovered'.[61]

Notes

1 See, for example, F.D. Laurens, *France and the Italo-Ethiopian Crisis 1935–1936* (Paris: Mouton, 1967); G. Warner, *Pierre Laval and the Eclipse of France* (London: Eyre and Spottiswoode, 1968); R. Davis, 'Mesentente Cordiale: The Failure of the Anglo-French Alliance. Anglo-French Relations during the Ethiopian and Rhineland Crises, 1934–6', *European History Quarterly*, 23:4 (1993), pp. 513–27.

2 *Hansard Parliamentary Debates*, Commons, vol. 313, 18 June 1936, cc. 1197–211. Just over three years later, Greenwood again led the attack on the government by castigating Neville Chamberlain for not immediately declaring war on Nazi Germany following the invasion of Poland.

3 Amery diary, entry 31 December 1937, in J. Barnes and D. Nicolson, (eds.), *The Empire at Bay: The Leo Amery Diaries 1929–1945* (London: Hutchinson, 1988).

4 Sir Eric Phipps (Berlin) to Eden, 13 April 1937, *Documents on British Foreign Policy 1919–39: European Affairs, January–June 1937*, I, (London: HMSO, 1980), vol. XVIII, 2nd series, no. 399.

5 Neville to Ida Chamberlain, 8 December 1935, University of Birmingham Special Collections (UBSC), NC 18/1/941.

6 *Hansard*, 5th Series, House of Commons, CCCXXX, 21 December 1937, c. 1816.

7 See, for example, A.J. Marder, 'The Royal Navy and the Ethiopian Crisis of 1935–36', *American Historical Review*, 75 (1970); F. Hardie, *The Abyssinian Crisis* (London: Harper Collins, 1974); T.M. Vench, *The European Powers and the Italo-Ethiopian War, 1935–1936: A Diplomatic Study* (Salisbury, NC: Documentary Publications, 1980); A.J.P. Galardi, *Sir Eric Drummond, Britain's Ambassador to Italy, and British Foreign Policy during the Italo-Abyssinian Crisis of 1935–26* (British Columbia: Simon Fraser University, 1998); M. May, *Fuelling Fascism: British and Italian Economic Relations in the 1930s and the Abyssinian Crisis* (London: University of London, 2000); G. Bruce Strang (ed.), *Collision of Empires: Italy's Invasion of Ethiopia and its International Impact* (Farnham: Ashgate, 2013).

8 M. Potter, 'What Sealed Baldwin's Lips?', *The Historian*, XXVII:1 (1964), pp. 21–36.

9 Cited in E. Monroe, *The Mediterranean in Politics* (Oxford: Oxford University Press, 1937), pp. 141–2.

10 S. Morewood, *The British Defence of Egypt 1935–1940: Conflict and Crisis in the Eastern Mediterranean* (London: Routledge, 2014), pp. 36–7.

11 Cabinet meeting, 2 December 1935, The National Archives, Cabinet Papers (CAB) 23/82.

12 See A.L. Goldman, 'Sir Robert Vansittart's Search for Italian Cooperation against Hitler, 1935–1936', *Journal of Contemporary History*, IX:3 (1972), pp. 93–130.

13 See D.S. Birn, *The League of Nations Union* (Oxford: Clarendon Press, 1981).

14 Chiefs of Staff, Imperial Defence: Revision of Defence Requirements, 28 May 1935, TNA, AIR 8/200.

15 On two occasions the League of Nations Union sent delegations to Downing Street calling for a tougher line only to be rebuffed.

16 Walter Beckett, 'The Legalities of Closing the Suez Canal', 11 June 1936, TNA, FO 371/19117.

17 *The Times*, 4 November 1935, p. 1.

18 *The Times*, 14 November 1935, p. 1.

19 *The Times*, 11 November 1935, p. 1.

20 See M.A. Williams, *Mussolini's Propaganda Abroad: Subversion in the Mediterranean and Middle East 1935–1940* (London: Taylor & Francis, 2006).

21 R. Quartararo, 'Imperial Defence in the Mediterranean on the eve of the Ethiopian Crisis (July–October 1935)', *The Historical Journal*, 20:1 (1977), p. 198.

22 Viscount Cunningham, *A Sailor's Odyssey* (London: Hutchinson & Co., 1951), pp. 173–4.

23 Backhouse to Chatfield, 3 February 1936, NMM, CHT 4/4/1.
24 Fisher to Admiralty, 20 August, 6 September 1935, TNA, ADM 116/3038.
25 Fisher to Chatfield, 25 February 1936.
26 Admiral Fisher memorandum, March 1936, ADM 116/4324.
27 Quoted in G. Baer, *The Coming of the Italo-Ethiopian War* (Cambridge, MA: Harvard University Press, 1967), p. 360.
28 Admiralty to Fisher, 16 August 1935, ADM 116/3476.
29 Fisher comment quoted in Philip Noel-Baker to Hugh Dalton, 16 December 1935, CAC Noel-Baker Papers.
30 Chiefs of Staff to Admiral Fisher, 13 January 1936, CAB 53/5. As the most senior commander, all telegrams went through him.
31 Morewood, *The British Defence of Egypt 1935–1940*, chapter 3.
32 Hoare to Eden, 17 September 1935, UCL, Templewood Papers, VIII, 3.
33 Defence Policy Requirements Committee, 14th meeting, 26 November 1935, CAB 16/139.
34 Pownall diary, 26 November 1935, LHCMA.
35 Pownall diary, 2 December 1935, LHCMA.
36 Eden, The Hoare-Laval Pact, February 1953, UBSC AP 19/4/12.
37 Notes on discussion at Duff Cooper's Dinner – Buck's Club, 14 February 1936, LHCMA LH II/1936/40.
38 See S. Morewood, '"This Silly African Business": The Military Dimension of Britain's Response to the Abyssinian Crisis', in Strang (ed.), *Collision of Empires*, pp. 73–107.
39 Morewood, *The British Defence of Egypt*, pp. 84–5.
40 Dawson diary, 25 June 1936, Bodleian Library (BL) Oxford: Dawson Papers.
41 Admiral Grantham undated letter to author.
42 Air Marshal Sir Robert Brooke-Popham, 'Recent Events in the Near East', lecture to RAF Staff College, 10 December 1936, LHCMA, Brooke-Popham Papers, BP II/9/10.
43 Fisher to Chatfield, 11 January 1936, NMM, Chatfield Papers, CHT/4/5.
44 'Italian Aircraft Industry', 3 December 1935, CAB 2/6.
45 Dill, 'Defence of Egypt: The Situation in the Western Desert', 26 February 1936, CAB 53/26.
46 Chiefs of Staff, 170th meeting, 31 March 1936, CAB 53/5.
47 Joint Planning Committee report, *Documents on British Foreign Policy 1919–39: The Rhineland Crisis and the Ending of Sanctions, March–July 1936*, London, HMSO, 1978, vol. XVI, no. 3.
48 Dingle Foot remarks, *Hansard Parliamentary Debates*, 5th Series, House of Commons, CCCVIIII, 19 February 1936, c. 1762.
49 Vulnerability of Capital Ships Committee, 1st meeting, 31 March 1936, CAB 16/147.
50 Dawson diary, 25 June 1936, BL, Dawson Papers.
51 See Morewood, *The British Defence of Egypt*, chapter 10.
52 Lord Chatfield, *It Might Happen Again, Volume 2: The Navy and Defence* (London: Heinemann, 1947), p. 90.
53 J. Gooch, *Mussolini and His Generals: The Armed Forces and Fascist Foreign Policy, 1922–1940* (Cambridge: Cambridge University Press, 2007), pp. 356–8.
54 W.S. Churchill, *The Second World War, Volume I: The Gathering Storm* (London: Cassell, 1947), p. 154.
55 G. Waddington, 'Hassgegner: German Views of Great Britain in the Later 1930s', *History*, 81:261 (1996), pp. 27–8.
56 Conference held by Führer (Obersalzberg), 22 August 1939, in C. Burdick and H.-A. Jacobsen (eds.), *The Halder War Diary 1939–1942* (Novota, CA: Presidio, 1989).
57 Cited in J. Holland, *The War in the West, Volume I: Germany Ascendant 1939–1941* (London: Bantam Press, 2015), p. 31.

58 Ribbentrop responded, correctly, that, following the British declaration of war at 11 a.m. on 3 September 1939 a French one would follow, which it did at 5 p.m.

59 Gooch, *Mussolini and his Generals*, pp. 356–7.

60 Eden to Churchill, January 1941, TNA, WO 106/712.

61 D. Omissi, 'The Mediterranean and the Middle East in British Global Strategy, 1935–39', in M. Cohen and M. Kolinsky (eds.), *Britain and the Middle East in the 1930s: Security Problems, 1935–39* (New York: St Martin's Press, 1992), p. 6.

2 American policy towards Italy during its 'decade of war'

Andrew N. Buchanan

Introduction: American policy after World War I

At the very end of his 1980 book *The United States and Fascist Italy* – now available in English translation for the first time – Gian Giacomo Migone poses a suggestive and challenging question. Did 'fear of Soviet-led subversion', he asks, provide an 'element of continuity' in American policy towards Italy that 'ran right through to the period following the Second World War?'[1] What is startling is not the suggestion that Washington's pre- and post-war policy was guided in part by opposition to communism, whether Soviet-led or not: Mussolini's popularity among pre-war American elites has long been viewed in the light of his offering a bulwark against the left, and the political warfare waged in Italy in the immediate post-war is widely understood as an opening move in the construction of Cold War containment.[2] What *is* striking is the assertion that Washington's *wartime* policy was shaped by similar considerations – in other words, that, rather than being discrete and conjunctural, America's pre-war, wartime and post-war policies towards Italy were in fact shaped by powerful elements of continuity. This suggestion becomes even more salient when we remember that Washington's anti-communism advanced in the framework of a broader effort to promote a new global economic order under American leadership, and that this, too, displays significant continuities through pre-war, wartime and post-war periods.

Washington's course was fundamentally rooted in the emergence of the United States as the predominant global economic power during and immediately after World War I. As Adam Tooze has recently argued, the United States, emerging unscathed and economically powerful from the war, set out to remake the world order around the liberal principles of free trade, the Open Door and, within carefully delineated limits, national self-determination.[3] Moreover, despite the wreck of President Woodrow Wilson's hopes for a new world political order, the United States did not retreat into isolationism during the 1920s. On the contrary, both in the Pacific – through the 1921 Washington Naval Conference – and, even more decisively, in Europe – through the 1924 Dawes Plan and the 1925–1926 Locarno Treaties that were its 'natural result' – the United States played a decisive role in structuring the new world order.[4] Moreover, American predominance forced leading politicians across Europe – including

Gustav Stresemann in Germany, Aristide Briand in France and Austen Chamberlain and Ramsay MacDonald in the United Kingdom – to orient their countries towards the United States and to accept, with more or less good grace, the subordinate status that implied.[5]

What was true for the strongest European countries was doubly so for the weakest of the 'great' powers, and in Italy 'L'Americano' Francesco Nitti, Trade and Industry Minister in 1911–1914, Finance Minister in 1917 and Prime Minister in 1919–1920, charted a similar course towards the United States. Moreover, while radical nationalist Benito Mussolini would ultimately side with Germany to mount a powerful challenge to American predominance in Europe, during the first decade of Fascist rule he was careful to position himself within the ambit of American hegemony. Mussolini famously sought approval for his 1922 March on Rome from American ambassador Richard Washburn Child, and his key ally Dino Grandi – the Minister of Foreign Affairs in 1929–1932 – pursued a consistently pro-American course.[6] Ambassador Child's admiration for Mussolini was hardly unique, and he was joined in his adulation by his ambassadorial successors Henry Fletcher and William Breckinridge Long.[7] What is often overlooked is that American enthusiasm for Mussolini was not simply the product of ruling class prejudice, but was deliberately cultivated by an Italian regime that understood that it had to operate within an American-dominated world system.[8] It also, of course, underscored the degree to which hostility to the Soviet Union and to radical working class movements within individual countries had become a key driver of American policy.

This relationship was a two-way street. While Italian leaders recognized the importance of securing inflows of American capital, American bankers and businessmen understood that the dictatorial character of the regime gave it a capacity for decisive economic and financial decision-making that compared favourably to the political divisions that seemed to compromise firm action in the parliamentary democracies. Likewise, they viewed the effective liquidation of organized labour through its incorporation into the corporate state and the resulting decline in wages in an extremely positive light.[9] The intimacy between Italian Fascism and American capital had direct and measurable consequences. In 1930, Italy received the fourth largest inflow of dollars in both direct (voting) and portfolio investments, trailing only Germany, Britain and France, and if only non-voting portfolio investment is considered, it came in second place after Germany.[10] Not surprisingly, given the strident nationalism of the Fascist regime, political and business leaders were less enthusiastic about the construction of American-owned plant in Italy; their goal at this point was neither autarky nor economic dependency, but the development of Italian manufacturing within a global environment dominated by American capital. In this, the years from the establishment of Fascism to the onset of the Great Depression proved beneficial to both parties.

Change and continuity in American policy as the 'decade of war' unfolds

The onset of the Great Depression, and the response of the American and Italian governments to it, did much to wreck this carefully constructed relationship. This was a two-sided process, driven both by President Franklin Roosevelt's emphasis on domestic recovery and by the turn to autarky – and the concomitant orientation towards Nazi Germany – in Rome. It would, however, be a mistake to exaggerate the depth of this divergence, at least in the early 1930s. Roosevelt did not entirely abandon his Wilsonian vision of a global capitalist economy under American leadership even as he responded to domestic economic and political pressures by turnings inwards, and architects of the New Deal saw much that they found appealing in Fascist Italy. Until the middle of the decade, Mussolini continued to enjoy high standing in the eyes of the American elite and to receive a great deal of positive press coverage. The Italian invasion of Ethiopia in 1935 prompted a shift in American attitudes towards the Fascist regime, setting it among the 'aggressors' that, by 1937, Roosevelt wanted to place in 'quarantine'.[11] In parallel with this shift, which at root reflected hostility to German-Italian domination of Europe, Mussolini began a rapid slide from modernizing superman to buffoon in the American popular imagination.[12]

Even after the Ethiopian crisis, however, the picture was by no means one-sided. As Migone points out, a coalition of commercial and banking interests backed by senior State Department figures ensured that Washington's 'moral' sanctions against Italy actually allowed for an expansion of critical oil exports.[13] From Rome, ambassador Long urged Washington to recognize Italy's conquest of Ethiopia, while his successor William Phillips hoped that such a policy, combined with increased economic aid, might dissuade Mussolini from 'dancing' to Berlin's 'tune'.[14] Even as Germany's gravitational pull on the Italian regime became overwhelming, Washington continued to harbour hopes that recognition of Rome's conquests in Africa, combined with a favourable trade deal, might be enough to keep Mussolini out of the war. Carrying this message to Rome in the spring of 1940, Undersecretary of State Sumner Welles reported to Roosevelt that the Italian dictator struck him as being a 'man of genius'.[15] The fact that these hopes were dashed barely weeks later by the Italian invasion of southern France in June 1940 should not obscure the conciliationist impulse that prompted them.

From the end of World War I through to the opening of World War II in Europe, American elites had sought to find ways of integrating Italy into the Wilsonian vision of a liberal capitalist order under United States' hegemony. Carried forward by administration policy prior to the rejection of the League of Nations, and then sustained primarily by the actions of bankers and businessmen supported by key State Department figures, this course was not fundamentally modified by the political nature of the Fascist regime; indeed, Mussolini's appearance as a bulwark against foreign and domestic communism enhanced his appeal to America's rulers. Rome's decision to enter the war alongside

Germany ended any lingering hopes of drawing Mussolini into an American-sponsored order, forcing a drastic re-evaluation of the previous course. It is important to note, however, that while the war in Europe forced the adoption of new *means*, the fundamental *goals* of American policy remained largely unchanged.

The emphasis on American military *means* that was demanded by the outbreak of war had been intellectually prepared during the 1930s by 'realist' notions generated by practitioners in the influential new field of security studies. Organized in prestigious institutions, such as the Princeton-based Institute of Advanced Study (IAS) and the Yale Institute for International Studies, and funded by the foundations of key American businesses, these interdisciplinary forums were designed to integrate academic study and state-level policy-making. Their goal, as David Ekbladh points out, was the development of a 'fully-fledged grand strategy that would [...] coordinate the diplomatic, military, and executive branches' of American state power.[16] These perspectives meshed closely with Roosevelt's own grand strategic concerns, rooted as they were in muscular Mahanian navalism and in his own wartime experience as Assistant Secretary of the Navy (1913–1920).[17] Italy did not loom large in the work of the security studies institutes except insofar as it formed part of a broader 'totalitarian' threat, but the Mediterranean more generally was conceived by geopolitical analyst Nicholas Spykman as a key component of the maritime 'rimland' from which power could be projected into an Asiatic 'heartland'.[18]

American strategic planning for war with Italy

These two sources of American wartime grand strategy – the long-standing effort to integrate Italy into an American-led world system, and the more recent development of an assertive and 'realist' policy capable of giving Wilsonian liberalism a sharp militarized edge – coalesced in the strategic planning of the early 1940s. Shifting gears in the light of the new geopolitical situation created by the fall of France, American planning was framed by Chief of Naval Operations Admiral Stark's insistence on prioritizing the defence of Britain and of its imperial outposts in the Mediterranean, some of which might provide a launching pad for an 'ultimate offensive' against Germany.[19] As Mark Stoler points out, this emphasis on Europe over Asia reflected earlier strategic priorities reflected in the *Red-Orange* plan for war against an Anglo-Japanese alliance in the 1920s, and in Army War College studies of war against the Axis powers drafted in the 1930s.[20] Stark's Germany-first orientation was quickly approved by the president and incorporated into joint Anglo-American planning at the ABC-1 talks in March 1941. Here planners sketched out a series of offensive actions, including commando raids, a naval blockade, an escalating bombing campaign and an effort to secure the 'early elimination' of Italy from the war, all of which would precede a decisive final offensive against Germany.[21] This Anglo-American agreement was then incorporated into America's own strategic planning with the adoption of the *Rainbow 5* plan in November 1941. Like ABC-1, *Rainbow 5* emphasized the importance of defeating Germany before concentrating on Japan, but it also called for a campaign to force Italy out of the war.[22] The hope of separating Italy from Germany that had been central to American diplomacy in the late 1930s was thus reprised in militarized form.

Given the subsequent tortured development of American strategic planning, which saw the newly formed Joint Chiefs of Staff fighting a long-running battle with President Roosevelt to force the abandonment of the Mediterranean aspects of these early plans, the Italian components of ABC-1 and *Rainbow 5* are easily overlooked. But they were not an aberration. On the contrary, the permissive algebra of these early plans gave U.S. grand strategy a flexibility denied to it by the simplistic concentration of mass and effort that was central to Joint Chief's cross-Channel design and, as I have argued at length elsewhere, it continued to guide Roosevelt's thinking throughout the first phases of America's intervention in the European theatre.[23] The result, beginning with the dispatch of air assets, brand-new Sherman tanks and other war material to the Western Desert in the summer of 1942, moving through the *Torch* invasions of French North Africa in November 1942, and culminating in the operations designed precisely to secure the 'early elimination' of Italy in the summer and fall of 1943, was inspired by the ABC-1 playbook.

If these steps registered the military aspects of Washington's unfolding grand strategic orientation towards the Mediterranean and towards Italy in particular, the political aspects did not lag far behind. Formed in February 1942 and chaired by Undersecretary of State Sumner Welles, the State Department's Advisory Committee on Postwar Foreign Policy prepared a set of guidelines for the political organization of post-fascist Italy. This interdepartmental committee included senior State Department personnel along with influential figures from outside of government, including *The New York Times* editorial board member Anne O'Hare McCormick, president of the Council on Foreign Relations Norman Davis and geographer Isaiah Bowman. Reviewing detailed studies prepared by several sub-committees, Advisory Committee members concluded that an American victory over Italy would lead to the establishment of a new political order that, while shorn of overt Fascist trappings, would nevertheless retain significant elements of the existing regime. Former chairman of U.S. Steel, Myron Taylor, argued that only the monarchy could provide solid anchor when 'everything else [was in] confusion', while Anne O'Hare McCormick added that the maintenance of the monarchy was the key to heading off a 'popular uprising'.[24] In this vein, a summary of the meeting concluded that a royal government based on the 'upper bourgeoisie', military leaders and the Catholic Church would offer the best chance of political stability following an Allied victory and the ouster of Mussolini.[25] Needless to say, committee members also assumed that such a regime would also be compliant with American interests.

American planners also turned their attention to the emergence of a potentially dangerous interregnum between the military defeat of Italy and the establishment of a pro-Allied regime in Rome. They assumed that some form of Allied military government would be necessary to bridge this gap and to prevent radical forces establishing local organs of political power. During this period, the Advisory

Committee concluded, the existing Italian state apparatus at provincial and local level could be incorporated into the structures of military rule. Judging it unlikely that the overthrow of Mussolini would result in the entire Fascist state being 'swept into the discard', they suggested that the 'agencies of local government' could be purged of the most 'culpable and intransigent Fascists' and thereby rendered 'amenable to a new political orientation'.[26] Committee members conceptualized Fascism as a 'stucco surface' plastered over the edifice of government, and they argued that if this outer covering was removed, the underlying building could be rehabilitated.

Invasion, military occupation and the advance of American influence

To a remarkable degree, the main outlines of this approach began to be realized in practice following the Allied invasion of Sicily, the ouster of Mussolini and the establishment of a new Italian government sponsored by King Vittorio Emanuele III and headed by Marshal Pietro Badoglio in July 1943. Beginning in Sicily and then carried into mainland Italy, existing elites at local and regional level were regrouped around officials of the Allied Military Government of Occupied Territories (AMGOT) in very much the manner suggested by the Advisory Committee; as *The New York Times* later editorialized, Allied authorities had no choice but to 'utilize' local officials 'not too strongly tainted by the Fascist brush'.[27] Needless to say, the question of how much 'taint' was too much was not closely examined, and many former fascists continued to play leading roles in local administrations.[28]

These developments were paralleled on the national level by the signing of an armistice between the Allied governments and the new government of Italy on 3 September 1943. Under the terms of the armistice, the Allies recognized Italy as a 'co-belligerent', and a military mission – later the Allied Control Commission (ACC) – was dispatched to Brindisi to oversee the work of the Badoglio government. In a matter of months, the ACC grew into a sprawling bureaucracy that effectively sustained the Italian state, even if it made little progress in modernizing it.[29] Front line zones and the key port of Naples remained under direct AMGOT control, but rear areas were turned over for administration by the Italian government working under the guidance of the ACC; thus, in theory, the whole country would be returned to Italian rule as the fighting advanced northwards. These initial steps conformed closely to the Advisory Committee's plan to regroup business, military and religious elites around the monarchy. Soon, however, these assumptions began to come unstuck as large sections of the Italian people asserted their right to have a say in the disposition of their country. The popular uprising against the Germans in Naples in September 1943 heralded the re-emergence of public politics, and soon six anti-fascist parties – the Communists, Socialists, Christian Democrats, Labour Democrats, Liberals and the Party of Action – formed the Committee of National Liberation (CLN). To various degrees, all were hostile to the monarchy, which was widely viewed as an adjunct of Fascism.

American leaders on the ground in the region, including Dwight D. Eisenhower, the Allied Commander in Chief in the Mediterranean and Robert Murphy, President Roosevelt's personal representative, quickly grasped that the revival of popular politics meant that the Advisory Committee's project of reorganizing the Italian ruling classes around the monarchy would have to be abandoned. Continued reliance on a deeply unpopular monarchy, they argued, now carried the risk of having to array Allied troops against the Italian people in a contest whose outcome would surely be politically disastrous. By November, President Roosevelt had endorsed this change of course, and he instructed Eisenhower to pursue a 'democratic government [in Italy] whether the House of Savoy remains as a figurehead or not'.[30] Prompted by Washington, Allied authorities revoked their ban on public political activity, agreeing that the 'Italian people may be permitted to participate in such political activities as do not lead to rioting and disorder'.[31] Acting with American encouragement, the CLN brushed aside British opposition and organized a broad anti-fascist congress in Bari at the end of January 1944.

Far from overturning the Advisory Committee's vision of an Italy reorganized under American leadership, however, these policy shifts – and the more liberal-democratic government that they were intended to produce – were in fact tactical adjustments designed to realize the committee's hegemonic goal. Moreover, while this change of course led to a series of sharp political clashes with the British, who argued forcefully against 'breaking up the present King/Badoglio show', it opened the road to collaboration with the Soviet Union.[32] Taking advantage of the division of Europe into spheres of influence sketched out at the Tehran conference in November 1943, American officials in Italy quickly came to see Moscow and the Italian Communist Party (PCI) as associates in the battle to liberalize the Italian government. Moreover, they recognized Soviet-style communism as a key ally in containing the threat of unpredictable and destabilizing popular uprisings within Italy. In March 1944, Moscow extended diplomatic recognition to the Badoglio government, a surprise move that facilitated the even more surprising decision of the PCI to drop its campaign against the monarchy and join the government. This abrupt change of course unfolded following the return to Italy from exile in Moscow of PCI leader Palmiro Togliatti. Shaped by Moscow's insistence on avoiding revolutionary developments in Western Europe in order to secure its predominance in Eastern Europe, Togliatti's line neatly dovetailed with the desire of many PCI leaders to champion a broad cross-class process of national renewal.[33]

American officials had already developed a close working relationship with Russian representatives posted to Allied Forces HQ in Algiers, where the new advisory Allied Council on Italy was based. They quickly recognized the significance of Moscow's new policy; as American ambassador to Moscow Averell Harriman noted in May 1944, Russian backing for a liberalization of the Italian government 'solved our difficulty', making possible the outcome that 'we wanted from the beginning'.[34] Togliatti, Robert Murphy reported to Washington, was acting as an 'intelligent national patriot' rather than as a Communist.[35]

This Washington–Moscow axis now established the political framework for the final act in the liberalization of the Italian government, the ouster of Badoglio and the establishment of a cabinet of anti-fascist parties led by Ivanoe Bonomi. The opportunity for this bloodless coup, carried out in the face of vigorous opposition from London, was provided by the seizure of Rome by General Mark Clark's Fifth Army on 4 June 1944. As I have argued in detail elsewhere, there is strong circumstantial evidence that Clark's drive on Rome, carried out in direct violation of orders from his British superior, was prepared in a secret meeting with President Roosevelt in White Sulfur Springs in late April or early May 1944.[36] While this assertion remains unproven, American military control of Rome clearly facilitated the exclusion of senior British officials, thus depriving London of an opportunity to block the change of government until it was presented with an irreversible *fait accompli*.

June 1944: Italy enters the 'post-war period'

With the liberal coalition government in place, Italy could now begin, as head of the State Department's Office of European Affairs James Dunn observed, to 'enter […] the post-war period'.[37] It was a bold assertion, and it showcased Washington's confidence that the basic structures of its post-war hegemony were now emerging. In particular, American officials sought to engage American business interests, along with governmental and non-governmental agencies, in their effort to make Italy into a 'stable, peaceful, and constructive element among the nations of Europe' that was integrated into 'multilateral and non-discriminatory foreign trade'.[38] This approach, centred on the rehabilitation of Italy and pushing towards the normalization of relations between Rome and the Allies, was registered in the 'New Deal for Italy' adopted by Roosevelt and Churchill at their Hyde Park, New York meeting in September 1944. The British, who sought a more punitive policy towards Italy, were markedly less enthusiastic about this turn than the Americans, but with American aid flowing into the country in significant quantities, their room for manoeuvre was increasingly limited. In February 1945, Churchill issued what amounted to a 'public withdrawal' of Britain's more punitive policy when he signalled London's acceptance of American efforts to rehabilitate Italy.[39]

The American government put significant political resources into its Italian policy. Senior administration figures visited Italy, including Secretary of War Henry Stimson (July 1944), Secretary of State Edward Stettinius and Roosevelt's special envoy Harry Hopkins (both in January 1945). A 19-person delegation from the House Military Affairs Committee that included future ambassador to Italy Clare Booth Luce also visited in December 1944. This top-level political interest was reinforced by a number of fact-finding missions, including those by Supreme Court Justice Frank Murphy, who undertook a survey for the President in July 1944, and attorney and trade expert William Culbertson, who visited with a high-level trade delegation in November 1944. In their various ways, these visits pressed Washington's case. Hopkins, for example, who had not informed

British authorities of his visit, argued forcefully that the United States had to play a leading role in Italy, including by mobilizing its merchant shipping to overcome ongoing food shortages.[40] Similarly, Culbertson's team produced a 55-page report on the economic situation in Italy that concluded, not surprisingly, that the time had come to loosen Allied controls over the Italian economy in order to allow the development of free trade through normal commercial channels.[41]

The work of these official visitors and delegations was supported by the efforts of non-governmental agencies, with the newly formed United Nations Relief and Recovery Administration (UNRRA) foremost among them. UNRRA was set up by 44 Allied governments in November 1943 to coordinate the distribution of relief supplies to 'liberated peoples'.[42] From its inception, Washington – which provided 73% of the agency's funding along with its leader, former New York governor Herbert Lehman – saw UNRRA as playing a crucial role in heading off social unrest flowing from wartime hardship, and in the summer of 1944 American officials proposed that it begin supplying aid to Italy.[43] As a former Axis power, Italy was not initially considered as a 'liberated' nation eligible to receive UNRRA supplies, and Washington's proposal to extend aid to a former enemy aroused fierce British opposition. Not surprisingly, Washington won its point in the UNRRA council. After long discussions with the Italian government, which insisted on being treated as an equal member of the United Nations, $50 million of aid for displaced persons, children and expectant mothers began to arrive in Italy in February 1945.[44]

UNRRA was widely – and not inaccurately – seen as an American-led organization delivering American-supplied aid, and its operations bolstered Washington's carefully burnished image. These efforts were reinforced by the operation in Italy of various American charities headed by the new American Relief for Italy. Led by Myron Taylor, American Ambassador to the Papal See, and sponsored by President Roosevelt, American Relief for Italy raised, shipped and distributed over $37m in aid.[45] In addition, Taylor persuaded the Pope to chip in an additional 5 million lira, a move that won widespread publicity in Italy. Britain's representative to the Vatican Sir D'Arcy Osborne complained that Taylor's 'charitable instincts' were designed to win President Roosevelt Italian American votes back home, but there was no denying that American Relief for Italy's operations put America in a very good light in Italy as well.[46]

Italian political leaders were acutely aware of this great inrush of American soft power and positioned themselves as reliable local allies of the emerging hegemon. Meeting with Allied Council for Italy leader and soon-to-be American ambassador Alexander Kirk to discuss the 'New Deal for Italy', Prime Minister Bonomi noted that while Italy had to 'work out its own salvation', it would lean on ongoing American aid and guidance as it did so.[47] Italian politicians became adept at telling the Americans what they wanted to hear, with Bonomi impressing Clare Booth Luce with his enthusiastic support for women's suffrage.[48] This was not, of course, an entirely one-way street: even as they worked to position themselves within the new framework of America's consensual hegemony, Italian leaders sought to reassert Italian sovereignty, often by exploiting divergences between Washington and London or tensions between different layers of American officialdom.[49]

These divisions, framed both by sharpening international tensions between the United States and the Soviet Union and by intensifying social and political conflict within Italy, shaped an extremely tense and complex post-war period. Between 1945 and 1948, Washington built on the political capital accrued since 1943, and the main thrust of American policy increasingly hinged on forging an alliance with Alcide De Gasperi's Christian Democrats (DC). Given DC's 'amoebic' blend of 'Catholic populism and bourgeois moderation' and De Gasperi's desire to rebuild and reassert Italian sovereignty, this was not always an easy relationship.[50] As Italy came to be seen as a critical battleground in the rapidly deepening Cold War, large amounts of both overt and covert aid flowed to the DC, its partners and its associated labour and cultural organizations. American policy-makers also made particularly good use of pliant American trade union officials, encouraging them to champion the cause of 'free labour' in Italy. Channelled through the embassy and the CIA, this exercise in political warfare is widely credited with securing the climactic electoral defeat of the PCI and its allies in the 1948 general election. It also, almost in passing, registered Britain's relegation to the sidelines of Italian politics.[51]

Consolidating the post-war order

De Gasperi's American-assisted victory in 1948 overlapped with the launching of the European Recovery Program (ERP), better known as Marshall Plan. DC leaders recognized that the ERP would help advance economic reconstruction, strengthen Italian integration in the American-dominated West and limit the appeal of the PCI, and they participated enthusiastically in the talks that prepared the aid programme.[52] In the ERP's first year of operation, Italy received the third largest allocation of funds (following the United Kingdom and France), and overall it came fourth, trailing Germany. In turn, the DC's electoral victory paved the way for Italy's inclusion in the NATO alliance, formally established in March 1949. Addressing Washington's Cold War concerns, De Gasperi argued that the exclusion of Italy from the pact would enhance the prospect of a PCI takeover.[53] With Italy's place within the post-war 'security' architecture secure, Washington proceeded to fund and to organize the country's rapid rearmament. These integrationist measures were reflected at the level of economic relations by an expansion in trade between the two countries, with American exports to Italy rising from an average of $141 million in the years 1926–1930 (the last half-decade before the onset of depression and war) to $456 million in 1951.[54]

In the light of these outcomes, Washington's first great outing into post-war 'political warfare' seemed to have been entirely successful, and 'Italy 1948' came to be seen as a repeatable blueprint that was applicable to sites of so-called communist subversion from Iran to Guatemala.[55] It is important to remember, however, that these successful steps in the advance and consolidation of American hegemony rested not only on the exercise of economic, diplomatic and political influence, but also on the assertion of military force. By the end of World War II, the Mediterranean – as geopolitical commentator Joseph Roucek put it in 1953 – had effectively become an 'American lake'.[56] American naval forces dominated the waters of the Mediterranean, and its land and air forces projected power outwards from much of the littoral. The American government negotiated a series of 'status of force' agreements with Rome that permitted the stationing of substantial American forces on Italian soil and established Naples as the base of the U.S. Navy's Sixth Fleet and the southern headquarters of NATO.[57]

This position of military predominance was the direct product of the execution, at President Roosevelt's direct and persistent urging, of military strategies designed to secure the 'early elimination' of Italy from the war. Given Italy's geopolitical position, as William Reitzel explained to an American audience in 1948, predominance within the peninsula was necessarily connected to the exercise of broader regional power within the Mediterranean.[58] On the face of it, of course, none of this should be surprising. As Mark Stoler points out in a recent study of the continuity of George Marshall's 'Europe-first' strategy from war to post-war, 'diplomacy and war are always linked'.[59] Yet this simple and seemingly self-evident relationship is easily and often overlooked, so that America's post-war 'empire by invitation' arrives more or less unsullied by the projection of armed force and military occupation across an entire continent.

Commenting on this process in 1951, Edward Mead Earle, one of the leading lights in the development of security studies in the 1930s, suggested that the critical distinction between President Wilson's policy after World War I and that of Roosevelt and Truman after World War II lay in the new willingness of American leaders to accept the necessity of large-scale and ongoing engagement with Europe.[60] Earle was not suggesting that the broad goals of American policy had changed, arguing that since the United States 'can be prosperous only in a stable and prosperous world', its 'economic stake' in Europe was necessarily both 'economic *and* political'. Moreover, American concern with the containment of the Soviet Union, although now viewed as even more pressing, had been a driver of American policy since 1917.[61] What had changed was not so much the goal of American policy as the means of achieving it. Here, of course, Earle endorsed the realist policy of global engagement that he and other security studies advocates had championed since the thirties. It is striking, however, that this advocacy pointed not to the antithesis of Wilsonian liberal internationalism, but rather to a heavily armed rendition of it; in Italy, as elsewhere, American free trade liberalism arrived gun in hand.[62]

What stands out here is not, as David Ellwood suggests, that the United States had 'the means but no organized strategy' in Italy, but rather that Washington had *both* a long-term hegemonic goal – however hazily defined – and an increasing willingness to apply the military *means* necessary to achieve, consolidate and defend it.[63] As Migone suggested in his provocative conclusion, it is indeed the continuities that are primary. Their pursuit was necessarily advanced not primarily through predetermined plans, but through the zigzag course of progressive approximation; this is in the nature of grand strategy, and it required, as Williamson Murray points out, a capacity to act 'beyond the demands of the present' and to respond to complex and contingent events as they unfolded while holding fast to a vision of the desired post-war outcome.[64] It was in this, and in particular in the combination of military, economic and political power, that Roosevelt and Truman were able to succeed where Wilson had failed; in success, however, they realized Wilson's vision rather than negating it.

Notes

1 G.G. Migone, *The United States and Fascist Italy: The Rise of American Finance in Europe* (New York, NY: Cambridge University Press, 2015), p. 396.
2 For an extended account of Mussolini's popularity in the United States, see J.P. Diggins, *Mussolini and Fascism: The View from America* (Princeton, NJ: Princeton University Press, 1972); for the United States–Italy relations in the immediate post-war period, see K. Mistry, *The United States, Italy and the Origins of the Cold War: Waging Political Warfare, 1945–1950* (New York, NY: Cambridge University Press, 2015).
3 See A. Tooze, *The Deluge: The Great War, America and the Remaking of the Global Order, 1916–1931* (New York, NY: Viking, 2014), esp. 'Introduction'.
4 Migone, *The United States and Fascist Italy*, p. 25.
5 Tooze, *The Deluge*, p. 23.
6 Migone, *The United States and Fascist Italy*, p. 301.
7 D. Mayers, *FDR's Ambassadors and the Diplomacy of Crisis: From the Rise of Hitler to the End of World War II* (New York, NY: Cambridge University Press, 2013), p. 74.
8 Migone, *The United States and Fascist Italy*, pp. 82–4.
9 Migone, *The United States and Fascist Italy*, pp. 189–91.
10 Migone, *The United States and Fascist Italy*, pp. 166–7.
11 See S. Casey, *Cautious Crusade: Franklin D. Roosevelt, American Public Opinion, and the War against Nazi Germany* (New York, NY: Oxford University Press, 2001), p. 36.
12 A. Buchanan, '"Good Morning, Pupil": American Representations of Italianness and the Occupation of Italy, 1943–1945', *Journal of Contemporary History*, 43:2 (2008), p. 222.
13 Migone, *The United States and Fascist Italy*, pp. 395–6; R. Dallek, *Franklin D. Roosevelt and American Foreign Policy, 1932–1945* (New York, NY: Oxford University Press, 1979), pp. 110–21.
14 Mayers, *FDR's Ambassadors and the Diplomacy of Crisis*, pp. 76–81.
15 Welles to Roosevelt, 19 March 1940, Welles Report, PSF, Franklin D. Roosevelt Library.
16 See D. Ekbladh, 'Present at the Creation: Edward Earle Meade and the Depression-Era Origins of Security Studies', *International Security*, 36:3 (2011/12), p. 117.
17 On this understudied chapter in Roosevelt's life and intellectual formation, see J. Tertius de Kay, *Roosevelt's Navy: The Educations of a Warrior President, 1882–1920* (New York: Pegasus Books, 2012).
18 F.P. Sempa, 'The Geopolitical Realism of Nicholas Spykman', in N.J. Spykman (ed.), (1942) *America's Strategy in World Politics* (New Brunswick, NJ: Transaction, 2008), p. xxiii.
19 *Plan Dog*, 12 November 1940, in S.T. Ross (ed.), *U.S. War Plans: 1938–1945* (Boulder, CO: Lynne Rienner Publishers, 2002), p. 56.

20 M.A. Stoler, 'George C. Marshall and the "Europe-First" Strategy, 1939–1951: A Study in Diplomatic as well as Military History, *Journal of Military History*, 79:2 (2015), p. 296.

21 ABC-1, 27 March 1941, Ross, *U.S. War Plans: 1938–1945*, p. 70.

22 Rainbow 5, 19 November 1941, Ross, *U.S. War Plans: 1938–1945*, pp. 138–9.

23 See A. Buchanan, *American Grand Strategy in the Mediterranean during World War II* (New York, NY: Cambridge University Press, 2014), esp. 'Introduction' and 'Conclusion'.

24 Advisory Committee on Postwar Foreign Policy, minutes of meeting P#39, 2 January 1943, Notter Files, microfilm.

25 Advisory Committee document P170, 7 January 1943, Notter Files, microfilm.

26 Advisory Committee document T195, Dec. 17, 1942, Notter Files, microfilm.

27 Editorial, *The New York Times*, 19 July 1945.

28 For a recent regional study, see A. Muschamp, 'Living under Allied Military Government in Southern Italy during the Second World War: A Case Study of the Region of Molise', *Journal of Military History*, 79:2 (2015), pp. 379–80.

29 D. Ellwood, *Italy, 1943–1945* (New York, NY: Holmes & Meier), p. 237.

30 Roosevelt to Eisenhower, 9 November 1943, Map Room, Box 34, Franklin Delano Roosevelt Presidential Library, Poughkeepsie, NY.

31 CCS to AFHQ, 1 January 1944, R363, FO 371/43836, The National Archives, London.

32 Churchill to Roosevelt, Nov. 6 1943, *Complete Correspondence*, 2: 587.

33 On the 'national communist' framework of sections of the PCI leadership, see A. Brogi, *Confronting America: The Cold War between the United States and Communists in France and Spain* (Chapel Hill, NC: University of North Carolina Press, 2011), esp. Chapter 1.

34 Harriman, press conference, 4 May 1944, Harriman papers, box 172, Library of Congress.

35 Murphy to Hull, 22 April 1944, U.S. Department of State, *Foreign Relations of the United States Diplomatic Papers (FRUS), 1944*, vol. 3 (Washington, DC: U.S. Government Printing Office, 1944), p. 1103.

36 Buchanan, *American Grand Strategy in the Mediterranean*, pp. 151–7.

37 Dunn to Hilldring, 6 July 1944, in H.L. Coles and A.K. Weinberg, *Civil Affairs: Soldiers Become Governors* (Washington, DC: Office of the Chief of Military History U.S. Army, 1964), p. 497.

38 State Dept. Interdivisional Country and Area Committee, CAC#248, *The Treatment of Italy*, 31 August 1944, microfilm T1221, National Archives and Record Administration (NARA), College Park, MD.

39 M. Gat, *Britain and Italy 1943–1949: The Decline of British Influence* (Brighton: Sussex Academic Press, 1996), p. 104.

40 Gat, *Britain and Italy 1943–1949*, p. 101.

41 Buchanan, *American Grand Strategy in the Mediterranean*, pp. 234–5; For a more comprehensive account of Culbertson's mission to the Mediterranean, see J.A. DeNovo, 'The Culbertson Economic Mission and Anglo-American Tensions in the Middle East, 1944–1945', *The Journal of American History*, 63:4 (1977).

42 G. Woodbridge, *UNRRA: The History of the United Nations Relief and Recovery Administration* (New York, NY: Columbia University Press, 1950), vol. 1, p. 3.

43 W.I. Hitchcock, *The Bitter Road to Freedom: A New History of the Liberation of Europe* (New York, NY: Free Press, 2008), p. 220.

44 See Woodbridge, *UNRRA*, vol. 2, pp. 262–3.

45 J.E. Miller, *The United States and Italy, 1940–1950* (Chapel Hill, NC: University of North Carolina Press, 1986), p. 105 ff.

46 Osborne to Eden, 6 October 1944, R15955/95/22, FO 371/43865, NA.

47 Kirk to State Department, 30 September 1944, *FRUS 1944*, vol. 3, p. 1155.

48 Kirk to State Department, 20 December 1944, 033.1165/12-2044, RG 59, NARA.

49 See, for example, the discussion of Italian postwar diplomatic maneuvering with Britain and Spain in P. del Hierro, *Spanish-Italian Relations and the Influence of the Major Powers, 1943–1957* (London: Palgrave Macmillan, 2015), pp. 16–68; for a framework for analyzing the divisions between American policymakers, see Mistry, *The United States, Italy and the Origins of the Cold War*, pp. 22–6.

50 Mistry, *The United States, Italy and the Origins of the Cold War*, pp. 31–2.

51 Gat, *Britain and Italy 1943–1949*, p. 128.

52 Mistry, *The United States, Italy and the Origins of the Cold War*, pp. 84–5.

53 Mistry, *The United States, Italy and the Origins of the Cold War*, pp. 172–4.

54 *Statistical Yearbook* (Washington, DC: U.S. Department of Commerce, 1939, 1948, 1952).

55 On the 1948 election, see Mistry, *The United States, Italy and the Origins of the Cold War*, pp. 204–5.

56 J.S. Roucek, 'The Geopolitics of the Mediterranean', *American Journal of Economics and Sociology*, 13:1 (1953), p. 82.

57 'France and Italy', in J.B. Hattendorf (ed.), *Naval Policy and Strategy in the Mediterranean: Past, Present and Future* (New York, NY: Routledge, 2000), pp. 201–2.

58 W. Reitzel, *The Mediterranean: Its Role in American Foreign Policy* (New York, NY: Harcourt, Brace and Co., 1948), p. 19.

59 Stoler, *George C. Marshall and the "Europe-First" Strategy*, p. 316.

60 E.M. Earle, 'The American Stake in Europe: Retrospect and Prospect', *International Affairs*, 27:4 (1951), pp. 423–33.

61 Ibid., p. 432.

62 On the 'convergence' of liberalism and realism, see A. Anievas, *Capital, the State and War: Class Conflict and Geopolitics in the Thirty Years' Crisis, 1914–1945* (Ann Arbor, MI: University of Michigan Press, 2014), pp. 112–18.

63 Ellwood, *Italy, 1943–1945*, p. 240.

64 W. Murray, 'Thoughts on Grand Strategy', in W. Murray, R. Hart Sinnreich, J. Lacey (eds.), *The Shaping of Grand Strategy: Policy, Diplomacy, and War* (Cambridge: Cambridge University Press, 2011), p. 2.

3 Repubblica Sociale Italiana and Spain

An ideological relationship in the decade of war

Andrea Ungari

Introduction

Italo-Spanish relations between 1943 and 1945 are fully immersed in the 1935–1945 decade, during which Italy was in turn victim and perpetrator. An increasing detachment from Fascist foreign policy of the preceding years characterized the period. Inheriting the great power status gained by achieving victory in World War I, Fascist international policy during the 1920s remained close to Italian long-standing traditions, maintaining collaborations with old allies, even in the presence of some revisionist instances. In the 1930s, once Dino Grandi had been removed from the Ministry of Foreign Affairs in 1932, Fascist policy became more aggressive and grew progressively closer to the authoritarian regimes that emerged on the European continent. The rise of National Socialism and its willingness to redraw the political map that emerged from Versailles led Mussolini towards a more active foreign policy in Ethiopia and then Spain. With these two events, which saw Italy as a protagonist, began the decade of war that ended with the definitive defeat of Fascism in April 1945.

Italian support for Francisco Franco during the Spanish Civil War is to be placed within this framework. If this support was consistent with Mussolini's intentions of emphasizing and reiterating Italy's international role, it also served to attest clearly the new direction taken by Fascist foreign policy. It is not by chance that the Rome–Berlin Axis was created in the aftermath of the common Italo-German participation in the Spanish Civil War. This event, by further accentuating the Axis's anti-communist dimension, highlighted an increasing ideological proximity both between Italy and Germany and between Italy and Francoist Spain. A commonality that, as demonstrated in the following pages, led the Spanish government to allow in later years the activity of Italian Social Republic (RSI) agents on its national territory, despite being against both the Italian Royal Government and the Allies. Franco's gratitude for Fascist support in the shared anti-communist battle which led him to secure power in Spain remained. This debt of gratitude acknowledged by Spain can be interpreted as a clear manifestation of the continuity between the Fascist regime and the RSI.

The difficult situation of autumn 1943

This is not the place to discuss the foundation of the RSI and its relations with the German occupier. However, as suggested by historians,[1] at the time of Mussolini's liberation from Campo Imperatore, there were main currents within the German leadership: one willing to simply occupy Italy militarily and the other, personally favoured by Hitler, to reconstruct a Fascist government led by the Duce. The former took precedence and on 14 September 1943 the creation of the RSI was proclaimed.[2]

Such a proclamation did not entail the immediate constitution of an entire cabinet, so much so that only around the end of September the various RSI government officers were appointed. Establishing a pro-German government was made difficult by the opposition of several Nazi leaders and further complicated by the sequence of events that occurred after the armistice, when most of the Italian ruling and administrative class joined the Badoglio government. The difficulties in rebuilding a Ministry of Foreign Affairs[3] were a case in point. Several phone calls, made by future RSI ambassador to Germany Filippo Anfuso[4] when the foundations of the new government were being laid, led the Duce to acknowledge that, in most cases, the diplomatic corps abroad were loyal to the King and therefore unavailable to serve in the Republican government. Such stances, in addition to causing a measure of resentment among German diplomats, elicited great dissatisfaction in Mussolini.

Among the many disappointments, the refusal of the ambassador in Madrid – Giacomo Paulucci de' Calboli, whose diplomatic career had been favoured by the Duce – was particularly significant. Paulucci's decision to remain loyal to the Badoglio government had already matured by the afternoon of September 8. His rejection and the passage of most of the Italian diplomatic agents in Spain at the service of the Royal Government was a tough blow to Mussolini's prestige, leaving, throughout 1943, freedom of diplomatic activity to the 'Kingdom of the South'. This also made the RSI unable to reaffirm the old friendly ties with Franco's government and to defend the interests of Italians residing in Spain who did not recognize the Royal Government. Indeed, the activities of the royal embassy in Madrid were twofold: on the one hand, they meant to strengthen control over the Italian community, while on the other, to put pressure on Spain to surrender the Italian merchant and warships that had fled to Spanish ports after the armistice.[5] In this regard, in a telegram to Franco, Badoglio highlighted how Italy perceived the shipping issue as of primary importance, also in consideration of future relations with Spain:

> There are still in Spanish waters thirteen Italian merchant ship totalling over sixty thousand gross tons. They are essential for this country's supplies. On the threshold of winter eighteen million Italians are threatened by impending famine. [...] I cannot believe that during this dark hour General Franco would contribute in any way to aggravate our situation. I therefore personally turn to him with confidence. Should our ships be immediately

set free, they would help us to solve part of our problems which are mostly due to lack of transport. General Franco knows well that, whatever may be the political vicissitudes, there cannot be between Spain and Italy reasons of discord or motives of quarrelling. He knows well that it is our firm intention to maintain old and traditional friendship with Spain. His personal intervention would immediately solve all difficulties. And this is exactly what I hope for and look forward to.[6]

On this issue, the Royal Embassy repeatedly sought the Anglo-American ambassadors' support. In a conversation with Spanish Minister of Foreign Affairs, Count Jordana on 22 October 1943, in addition to the US legal recognition of Badoglio,[7] US Ambassador Haynes confirmed backing the Royal Government:

The Italian Ambassador is extremely interested in the issue of Italian warships and merchants held in Spanish ports. He said that he [...] understood perfectly the right of any belligerent ship to, once supplied with fuel, leave the neutral port within twenty-four or forty-eight hours that the international precepts determine; and that, therefore, his Government considered that the Spanish authorities should have allowed such vessels to leave port.[8]

These international pressures confirmed how weak the RSI position was, in the absence of an official representative. In that first period, in fact, the German embassy was the only one trying to protect the RSI government by favouring local Fascist groups. Despite this lack of directives, some consular agents, stationed in Pamplona, Logroño, Gijo and Vigo, and some soldiers, assisted by the consul of Malaga Eugenio Morreale, had joined the RSI and had decided to reorganize themselves to protect the interests of the Italians residing in Spain. The group had then proceeded to re-establish contacts with the Spanish military hierarchies and organize fascists in civic groups. The need for an official representative, however, was reaffirmed with the urgent appointment of 'a representative of the Republican Fascist Government indispensable to carry out all activities, a more profitable work in protecting the interests of the Republican Fascist Government in Spain where there are still strong sympathy currents for Mussolini'.[9]

Faced with the demands of both loyal fascists and German authorities, the RSI government had thought in early October to entrust the regency of the Italian embassy to Edgardo Nostini, general consul in Madrid.[10] Nostini's position in favour of the Badoglio government, however, persuaded Mussolini to choose Count Rogeri di Villanova, who was supposed to travel to Spain as the official Italian representative.[11] His appointment fell through as well. Behind the failure to appoint Rogeri were the Germans, probably harbouring a measure of mistrusts for the diplomat's loyalty to the Duce[12] and the real difficulty in accrediting an RSI-Minister Plenipotentiary in Franco's government. Although the Spanish *chargé d'affaires* in Italy, Josè Comin, had seemingly favourably received

Rogeri's scheduled appointment, it was known to Mussolini that Franco had decided, after being pressured by the Allies, to maintain diplomatic relations with the Badoglio government and to avoid officially recognizing Mussolini's government.[13] In a meeting between German ambassador Dieckhoff and Franco, the position of the Spanish dictator towards the two Italian governments clearly emerged:

> Caudillo noted that it was clear to him that the King of Italy could not have any 'weight' either morally or politically – that the government was in fact a government of traitors and masons. Even politically, it would not be a major factor because the part it governed is occupied by Anglo-American troops and the government has little to say. Caudillo, in spite of this, could not immediately make a decision regarding the official recognition of the Fascist government, but reserved to make a decision about it. [...] He let it be understood that he did not foresee in any way to send an Ambassador to the King (Ambassador to the Quirinal Fernandez Cuesta will have to return to Madrid and stay there). With the Duce's Government, Caudillo made him understand, he would have established factual relations, but always taking into account Spanish interests.[14]

Franco's position was then communicated by Morreale to Serafino Mazzolini in his October 12 report. Morreale underlined how the Spanish government was reluctant to assume clear stances, such as an open acknowledgement of the Fascist republican government. On the contrary, it was willing to tolerate any situation that would allow him to eventually manoeuvre any contrary pressure applied by the Anglo-Americans. For this reason it was necessary, in Morreale's opinion, that the appointed RSI representative would initially have to 'assume an unofficial position tasked with using his personal reputation to endorse [...] and coordinate the work of the specialists, able and motivated by the tenacious determination to prevail against the Spanish time-taking attitude, hand-picked by the various Italian ministries'.[15] Morreale's personal reputation, that had previously led him to occupy special positions on behalf of the Fascist government,[16] as well as his actions in Spain after September 8, led him on 23 November 1943 to be appointed as Agent for the Protection of Italian interests in Spain.

Eugenio Morreale and the agency for the protection of Italian interests in Spain

The appointment of Morreale was certainly the best choice the government could make, both for his personal qualities and his knowledge of the Spanish political framework. Morreale was well aware of the real relations between the RSI and the Spanish government and how the international scene would influence them:

> To put the Spanish government in a position of responding more readily to Paulucci and foreseeable Anglo-American opposition to the recognition – even if de facto – of a representative of the Republican Fascist Government

in Spain, I would propose to accredit me for the moment as 'General Commissioner' (or any other name) for the assistance of Italians in Spain. The Spanish government should not be able to avoid the existence of Italians in Spain (the majority) whose ties lie with Mussolini's Italy or the even more serious circumstance that these Italians risk – were they to express their feelings – being denied a passport from the Royal Consolates and become stateless, a situation which the Spanish government itself should find unwelcome.[17]

Halted in Berlin by Spanish bureaucratic resistance, after obtaining a regular diplomatic visa, Morreale arrived in Madrid on 17 December 1943.[18] Upon his arrival in Spain, he had to face a serious diplomatic crisis. In early January 1944, a rumour was circulating about the Spanish government's acknowledgement of the RSI. The news, obviously false, had offered the Spanish Foreign Ministry reasons 'to delay conversations about the provisional statute for the protection of our interests and our communities'.[19] Iberian diplomacy was truly affected by the strong Anglo-American pressures and adopted a dilatory technique, but it needed to respond to such a clumsy attempt by the Fascist government. On 3 January 1944, the US ambassador Haynes met Count Jordana, asking for explanations about the news spread by radio in Rome and Berlin. Jordana clearly explained the Spanish 'tactical' position:

> The Minister specifically states that the Spanish Government has not recognized the Mussolini, not even de 'facto', but that the circumstance that most of Italy [...] is not controlled by neither the King of Italy or the Government of General Badoglio, which is the Government which Spain recognizes and which has its Ambassador in Madrid, is therefore not strange.[20]

Allied pressures on the Spanish government, however, were not limited to whether or not to recognize the Fascist Republican government, but also about Italian ships in Spanish ports. Again, Jordana assumed a tactical and prudent attitude, reflecting the international situation. Spain, in fact, was not yet convinced that the Allies would achieve final victory, and therefore feared that exposing itself diplomatically would bind them to the Anglo-American powers. Spanish ties with Germany were kept alive by the fear of possible reprisals of German troops deployed along the Pyrenean border and their shared anti-communist ideological struggle. This struggle was felt so strongly by the Iberian government that Franco's government deployed the Azul Division, a chosen division of his Army, on the Russian front. In such a context, it was obvious that Spanish diplomacy was essentially trying to stall for time between Allied pressures and German demands.

As far as the protection of the Italians that remained loyal to the Duce was concerned, the Iberian government was substantially condescending to republican representation, trying to withstand the increasingly insistent pressures coming from the Allies and the Italian Royal government. This Spanish stance was certainly due to the fact that the Italian economic and industrial structures were still under Republican control, but it was also motivated by a sense of gratitude for Fascist support in the civil war and an ideological communion which was particularly felt by large sectors of the 'Falange'. Fostering such a bond with the RSI there was the behaviour of the royal consular representatives in Spain, who had delivered all secret correspondence to the Allies providing them with powerful blackmail against the regime – a reason that could explain the hostile attitude of the Spanish Government to Badoglio's demands.[21] However, Franco's benevolence did not change the obvious weakness of the RSI's representation in Spain. It was a weakness of which Morreale was fully aware, so much so that on 17 January, he highlighted the need to 'act on the remnants of Spanish representation in Italy and Spanish interests in our country to flank my work'.

Caught between having to defend himself from combined pressures to expel him and the need to strengthen his position in the face the Spanish government stalling tactics, Morreale began to organize 'his' representation. At the end of January, the RSI agent informed Secretary of the Ministry of Foreign Affairs, Serafino Mazzolini, of the composition of the Agency of the Republic (Agenzia della Repubblica), requesting confirmation of the various appointments. Once the approval was obtained and the Representation conclusively established, Morreale's action was directed towards obtaining the best possible legal and consular *status* while, at the same time, defending the Republican interests in Spain and protecting the rights of Italians who had remained loyal to Mussolini.

The agency's recognition

As for the potential recognition of its Spanish mission, Morreale did not obtain any formal success. On 5 February, Anfuso informed the Ministry of Foreign Affairs that on 27 January

> Jordana told the Ambassador of France, Pietri, that the Spanish government had decided against granting the representative of the De Gaulle National Liberation Committee (Minister Plenipotentiary Truelle) and the Republican Fascist Government any 'political' recognition. These representatives would be allowed to deal exclusively on commercial and administrative matters. Instructions complying with this line of conduct would be given to Spanish representatives in republican Italy.[22]

On 16 February, Morreale communicated to the Ministry of Foreign Affairs that contacts within the Spanish Government allowed him, in principle, to carry out an activity that was beginning to give results, especially as far as assistance to nationals was concerned. Legal recognition, however, was not discussed. Despite this caution, Morreale was granted diplomatic immunity for the Republic, right to cipher and courier, as well as other provisions normally accorded to diplomatic agents, probably fearing possible retaliations with restrictions imposed on the Spanish Embassy in Italy. It was a *de facto* recognition that would allow the RSI agent to play a more profitable role in defending republican interests.

In this sense, all possible ways to prevent the departure of Italian ships from Spanish ports were tested by Morreale and his naval representative. As it has been pointed out, Royal and Anglo-American pressures to this effect had been very strong since the beginning of the issue. Anglo-American demands clashed again with the Spanish government's dilatory action. In truth, behind the controversy for the not-so important issue regarding Italian ships, a real issue was hidden, namely Spain's future position in the international context that was taking shape. Morreale emphasized in one of his communications how

> Spain tends to take time especially because behind the Anglo-American requests hide the problem of what orientation should be given to Spanish neutrality. Nor do Anglo-Americans seem alien to give time to the leaders of the Madrilean politics, but in the meantime (they) act indirectly.[23]

Commercial relations

Beyond the protection of fellow countrymen residing in Spain, Morreale also sought to restore the more general trade relations between Spain and Italy. Just a day after 8 September, the German embassy in Madrid suggested that branches of major Italian industries and companies were in danger of escaping Mussolini's government control. The German warning substantially fell on deaf ears, also in view of the abovementioned difficulties in constituting the RSI representation. This situation favoured Badoglio's government by helping the main Italian companies' Spanish branches to remain loyal to the Royal government, a very successful attempt.

To confront this situation, Morreale had been trying since January 1944 to put forward the problem of reactivating commercial relations between the two countries, but had to face some trade-related difficulties. Indeed, in addition to the non-recognition of RSI as the holder of the right to exercise the war debt Spain incurred with Italy during the civil war, the commercial situation of the two countries was further complicated by other factors, highlighted by Morreale in an *ad hoc* report addressed to Filippo Anfuso:

> The trade clearing between Italy and Spain is passive, to the detriment of Italy for 360 million lire. A resumption of trade may, given the current impossibility of filling the passive asset, be taken into account only on the basis of commodity compensation. Meanwhile, however, it is necessary to know which goods can be exported from Italy to Spain and vice versa, if the German authorities are willing to withdraw the order of seizure of Spanish goods destined for Italy that transit in France, issued immediately after the armistice. On the other hand, my attempt to make the purely financial part independent from the commercial, trying to establish a financial clearing between Spain and Italy, would immediately stumble in the question

of how to value the Lira, issue that in the present stagnating situation of all commercial traffic would be at our disadvantage.[24]

After an intense effort to try to smooth the mutual resistance to the establishment of trade relations between the two countries and the Republican Finance Ministry's substantial support, in mid-April the foundations for the re-establishment of Italo-Spanish trade relations were laid, with a reciprocal exchange of goods for the sum of twelve million pesetas.[25] The contacts between the Representation and the General Manager of the Spanish Ministry of Industry and Commerce continued during June, although it was evident that Germany had to authorize any resumption of trade from and to Spain. The Republican Ministry of Commerce's business management at the Ministry of Foreign Affairs replied in mid-May 1944, sending a precise statement to the German embassy asking what decisions the German authorities would take about that resumption of trade.

By the end of June, the foundations of the Italian–Spanish trade agreement had been put in place and were only waiting for German approval. This consent was never given by the German government, delaying the anticipated authorization for the sale of Italian products.[26] Thus, Antonio Cantoni Marca, general manager of business affairs at the Ministry of Foreign Affairs, exemplified the real situation of RSI's subjection to Germany:

'Inter nos' we are a de facto occupied country, while abroad we figure as independent. In private conversations with the German Embassy official, who has been responsible for years of the commercial deals and whom I have known for a long time, I have clearly stated that the Germanic attitude towards us is a source of public opinion irritation and furthermore it compromises their opinion of the Duce. [...] Moreover, our trade negotiations with other states [...] so far have remained a dead letter.[27]

This private reflection by Cantoni Marca confirms the judgement about the RSI's lack of autonomy from the German occupants and, therefore, Mussolini's failure to make RSI an autonomous power. This was the most obvious discontinuity from the Fascist regime, when Italy played a major role on the international chessboard. Italo-Spanish trade relations were never truly resumed and were limited to the arrival of a few trains that were already in transit but were stopped at the French border. The events of June–July 1944 and the progressive Allied conquest of France prevented the transalpine communication route from being exploited, effectively preventing any commercial exchange.

The May agreements and the altered international context

The relations between Spanish authorities and the Representation began to strain with the signing of the May agreements between Spain and the Anglo-Saxon powers. Between February and April, there was a tug of war between Franco's regime and the Anglo-Americans after the blockade of crude oil supply. This situation became progressively unsustainable for Spain, as the lack of oil supply threatened to determine the collapse of the not-flourishing Iberian economy. So, in early May, the negotiations carried out in those months resulted in an epistolary exchange between Jordana and the Allied ambassadors that led to the formal stipulation of the agreement. This established the reduction of wolfram exports to Germany to 600 tons per year and prohibited its contraband;

> it prescribed the complete withdrawal of volunteers from the Soviet front, the closure of the German consulate in Tangier, the dismissal of the Japanese attaché and the expulsion of the Reich's secret agents from Spanish territory; the dispute over Italian warships would be subject to arbitration and Madrid would return all merchants except two; they would proceed to restore oil supplies to Spain.[28]

This agreement meant, far beyond the clauses envisaged, the shift of Spain towards a more marked alignment with the Anglo-Americans. The proclaimed Spanish neutrality had shown itself to be increasingly oriented towards the Allies. Morreale, analysing this situation, clarified this new course of Iberian diplomacy in a report to his Foreign Minister:

> The speech in which Generalissimo Franco in Alicante (on the 11th of the current month) broke the silence [...] contains the following elements: an obvious act of tribute to the *Falange* – from which, after the recent agreement with the Anglo-Americans, dissatisfaction stemmed more intensely; a justification for the current Spanish policy accompanying a statement of friendship towards those countries that are currently in war alongside Russia; a manifestation of disbelief for a domesticated communism accompanied by a return to the tone of open hostility towards Russia. The supposition that the Spanish-Anglo-American agreements to which that discourse followed have also touched on the issue of the positive attitude of Spanish politics is not out of place. [...] If, as it is to be believed, this concern [...] has been shared by England, with the discretion imposed on it by the Russian alliance, the prospect of an agreement between England and Spain emerges. Agreement in which Franco would replace England, in the forms that the contingencies will advise, in that Mediterranean anti-communism which during the civil war led Italy to help the Spanish national forces.[29]

It was clear that such a move would further damage the positions reached by the republican representation. In that sense, Morreale made clear that the first repercussions would concern the issue of the Italian ships in Spanish ports.

> As it was to be expected [...] the greater collapse would be along the line of lesser resistance: that of Italian ships. It is that the Anglo-Americans, while saving the Spaniards face and for not being perceived as anxious that could be interpreted as weakness, have accepted the arbitration for war units, registering a given success: the transfer of six merchant units. [...] As for the war unit's

arbitration, it is to be assumed that it will have to decide on whether, under the current conditions, these ships are to be considered 'interned', given the continuation of war, or undoubtedly the object of the September 3 armistice between the United Nations and the Badoglio government.[30]

Further aggravating the situation was the capture of Rome by Allied troops and the subsequent landings in Normandy. During the summer of 1944, it was evident that although some Spanish military sectors still trusted German military capabilities, the conflict was about to take a clear direction. Spain, which had assumed a dilatory position waiting for events to unravel, could only suffer the progressive pressure of Allied diplomacy, beginning to see the possibility of economic and political coexistence with the Anglo-Saxon world, especially in the attempt to re-obtain a hegemonic role in the Mediterranean, perhaps replacing Italy.

Although in July Morreale penned a long memorandum in which the relations between Spain and the RSI were described as rosy,[31] it was clear to him that the situation was evolving unfavourably for the republican government.[32] Morreale's punctual analysis immediately found validation. During the summer, Spain expedited the disembarkation of Italian sailors who had opted for the RSI, interning them or making them voluntarily return to Italy, arranging the subsequent departure of these boats towards Allied ports in February 1945 as well. The pressures of both the Royal and the Allied embassies became more and more insistent in particular on the need to stop the action of the republican representation in Spain.

On 30 June, following a previous verbal note of 13 January, the embassy of the Italian Royal Government cited the 'harmful' activity carried out by the Agency, requesting its suppression.[33] The Italian initiative was not isolated, as the US embassy[34] sent a series of memorandums to Jordana starting in July and, after he died of heart attack in early August, to his successor Lequérica in order to obtain the suspension of Morreale and his agency. In September, the grip on the republican representation became more intense, with direct pressure from the British embassy as well.[35] In this delicate situation, Morreale's action was forcibly destined to manoeuvre between the Allied pressures and the Spanish attitude, increasingly yielding to the Anglo-American demands.

On 30 November 1944, the Ministry of Foreign Affairs summoned Morreale for an interview with the Director-General for Political Affairs, Minister Doussinague. Despite the firm intention of the Spanish to show their benevolence towards the representatives of Mussolini's government, the minister pointed out that

> the Spanish position would have been facilitated if I myself were to lighten the Representation staff by indicating the names of a couple of people – particularly belonging to the Representation Military Offices – to be written up in a measure of deportation from Spain, so appeasing the Anglo-Americans.

After a lengthy conversation with the minister to point out that the Representation had acted correctly, the interview ended with a suspensive statement that, however, for Morreale had a clear meaning: 'I cannot, however, exclude, given the current climate within the Spanish Ministry of Foreign Affairs, that the removal from Spain of some members of this Representation could be imposed before I have any other contact with Doussinague'.[36]

The contacts and meetings between the members of the Representation and the Spanish authorities continued in December, always addressing the need to lighten the Agency and, in particular, its military offices. The turning point in these meetings happened on 10 January 1945, when the head of the European affairs section of the Spanish Ministry of Foreign Affairs delivered a list of ten Italians whose expulsion the Anglo-Americans demanded to Captain Antonio Boserman. Faced with Morreale's subsequent protests to Minister Doussinague, he left full liberty to the Representation's members who had to be repatriated. Morreale, analysing the situation, underlined that such attitude from the Spanish, in addition to Allied pressures, was due to two main reasons:

> a reorganization of the Embassy in Spain with the Lieutenant Government and the recent exchange of ambassadors between the Spanish Government and the Lieutenant Government, a diplomatic activity which currently does not have any reason to find a counterpart in the de facto relations between himself and the RSI Government; and 'the re-emergence of the problem of representations of exiled governments (French, Romanian, Hungarian), a problem that advises the Spanish Government to be more cautious towards us'.[37]

For Morreale, these demands were not to be underestimated by the ministries, especially the military ones. In his report to the Ministry of Foreign Affairs, the republican agent did not fail to point out some possible solutions: either keep resisting the Spanish pressures until reached by an official expulsion order, or – the solution recommended by Morreale – 'take the initiative of streamlining the various branches of the service to be carried out promptly and in such a way that would not affect the continuity of the services themselves'.[38]

The line proposed by Morreale was immediately considered by the Ministry of Foreign Affairs and adopted, under the pressure of the Minister of Finance Giampietro Pellegrini, by Mussolini himself, so that on 1 February 1945 a telegram was sent to all the interested clerks emphasizing the need to reduce personnel.[39] As it also interested Colonel Collu, head of the Republican National Guard in Spain, Mazzolini clarified the Republican government's new needs: according to the Spanish Ministry of Foreign Affairs,

> it would be appropriate for the Italian Government to take the initiative to reduce its Technical Representations (Military Offices and Press) to that Agency which appear numerically disproportionate considering the non-official situation of the Representation itself. Evidently – and although the

Spaniards do not want to admit it – this strong demand is not alien from the Anglo-American pressures to definitively close the RSI Agency in Spain.

The Duce, Mazzolini continued, 'has, without fail, approved and has given the task to this ministry of informing the other qualified ministries in other that staff reduction, and therefore the costs, will be realized as soon as possible'.[40]

Financing reasons, therefore, seemed to prevail over the unchanged Spanish pressures. Different reactions followed such request from the Ministry of Foreign Affairs. If the Ministry of Popular Culture (Minculpop) accepted the directive, the Armed Forces, and particularly General Rodolfo Graziani, opposed this reduction.[41] Only after the pressures of Alberto Mellini Ponce de Leon – successor to Mazzolini who died on 23 February – Graziani was forced to agree to the reduction of the military body in the Representation. That the main reasons for these reductions were of an economic nature was highlighted by the fact that Morreale, while reporting to the Ministry of Foreign Affairs that it was possible to consider Spanish authorities' pressure suspended, clarified on 28 March the economic and non-political factors that had determined this choice: 'It was superiorly decided not for Spanish pressures the Military Offices reduction [...]. The measure has been determined by various reasons, among which it is mainly necessary to reduce expenditure drastically'.[42]

At that time, in truth, the fate of the conflict was already decided.

Conclusions

The analysis of the relations between the RSI and Spain highlights the persistence of the link between the Iberian country and Mussolini's regime; a bond that was characterized by dilatory attitudes and ambiguous behaviours, political sympathy for their shared past, and the awareness of the harsh reality of a new world order. This was a sign that support in the civil war and ideological affinity had not reduced Caudillo's debt to the Duce.

If this is a clear testimony of the continuity of Fascist foreign policy towards the Iberian country, it is beyond doubt that the lost war and the events of 25 July had greatly weakened Mussolini's authority. The subordination of the RSI to German occupation is the most important element of discontinuity from the previous Fascist regime; even though Mussolini sought in all ways to carve out a role of autonomy for himself to not appear like any other Quisling, the events briefly described in these pages show how the RSI's margins of autonomy with Germany were always very limited and the interferences, especially in important areas such as foreign policy, were significant.

The June 1940 'bluff' that should have led Italy, in Mussolini's vision, to quickly gain a place at the peace table, after liquidating France and its presence in the Mediterranean, turned into a failure. Unlike during World War I, there had not been a battle like the Marne to induce greater caution in government spheres and, furthermore, to remember the priority bond with Britain that Liberal Italy had always preserved. This wrong assessment led to a stark defeat, the fall of the regime, and the loss of that great power status that Liberal Italy had succeeded in obtaining after the victory in the Great War, despite the millions of military and civilian deaths. This really marked the most remarkable element of discontinuity between monarchical and republican Italy: between a country with an autonomous foreign policy and a country subject to the wishes of other powers. All this stemmed from the failure of Italian liberalism between 1919 and 1922, the Crown's uncertainties and weaknesses, and a dictatorial regime that lost its totalitarian bet in the tough test of the war.

Notes

1 F.W. Deakin, *Storia della Repubblica di Salò* (Turin: Einaudi, 1963); R. De Felice, *Mussolini l'alleato 1940–1945*, tomo II, *1943–1945* (Turin: Einaudi, 1997).
2 About the Republican Fascist party see R. D'Angeli, *Storia del partito fascista repubblicano* (Rome: Castelvecchi, 2016).
3 On the reconstruction and functioning of the RSI Foreign Affairs Ministry see M. Viganò, *Il Ministero degli Affari Esteri e le relazioni internazionali della Repubblica Sociale Italiana 1943–1945* (Milan: Edizioni Universitarie Jaca, 1991).
4 F. Anfuso, *Da Palazzo Venezia al Lago di Garda (1936–1945)* (Rome: Settimo Sigillo, 1996), pp. 318–24.
5 On 8 September 1943, seven Italian merchant ships were in Spanish continental ports, another seven in the Canary Islands; four warships were interned in the Balearics. On board, they hosted the *Rome* battleship castaways and the crew of two self-sunk destroyers. Two navy *Marinefährprahm* (Motozattere-MZ) had taken refuge in Barcelona.
6 Pietro Badoglio telegram 231/123 to Paulucci di Calboli 8 December 1943, in Ministero degli Affari Esteri, *I documenti diplomatici italiani*, 10th series: *1943–1948*, vol. I: *9 settembre 1943–11 dicembre 1944* (Rome: Istituto Poligrafico e Zecca dello Stato, 1992), p. 107.
7 'The Ambassador […] states that he once again wishes to underline, with the utmost emphasis, that the Government of the United States fully and with all rights, recognizes the General Government of General Badoglio, which it considers to be the only genuine representative of the Italian State, and that by no concept or at any time it intends to modify this criterion', in Archivo Central Ministero des Asuntos Exteriores (ACMAE), Leg. R.2300, *Conversaciones reservadas del Ministro de Asuntos Exteriores con representantes diplomaticos 1941–46*, conversation between the Minister of Foreign Affairs and the United States Ambassador, 22 October 1943.
8 Ibid.
9 Ibid.
10 Archivio Storico-diplomatico del Ministero degli Affari Esteri (ASMAE), *Archivi Rsi*, b. 38, f. *Rappresentanze diplomatico-consolari italiane – Rappresentanza italiana in Spagna. Missione Rogeri*, Ministry of Foreign Affairs note to the Duce, 8 October 1943.
11 Ivi, Ministry of Foreign Affairs note addressed to the Duce, 20 October 1943.
12 Anfuso, *Da Palazzo Venezia al Lago di Garda*, pp. 336–8.
13 Ramon Serrano Suñer in his meeting with the American Ambassador Haynes underlined how 'the Minister states that Spain is not facing any problem of recognition, but rather to continue its relations with the Government that constitutionally appointed the King of Italy. On the other hand, it must be confessed that the relations which the Spaniard maintains with the Government are not normal, and suffer from such defect by the circumstance that Spain is prevented from having its diplomatic representation near it, that the embassy that represents it is in Madrid. And that, as the Minister

continues, with regard to the recognition of another Italian Government, apart from General Badoglio, there is no such fact', see document in note 7.

14 ASMAE, *Archivi Rsi*, b. 38, f. *Rappresentanze diplomatico-consolari italiane – Rappresentanza italiana in Spagna. Missione Rogeri*, Rahn report translated in Italian. On the meeting see Deakin, *Storia della Repubblica di Salò*, pp. 568–9; M. Guderzo, *Madrid e l'arte della diplomazia. L'incognita spagnola nella seconda guerra mondiale* (Florence: Manent, 1995), p. 319.

15 ASMAE, *Archivi Rsi*, b, 38, f. *Spagna – Adesioni alla Repubblica Sociale Ital.*, Malaga consul Eugenio Morreale's report, 12 October 1943.

16 F. Niglia, 'Mussolini, Dollfuss e i nazionalisti austriaci. La politica estera italiana in Austria nei rapporti di Morreale', *Nuova Storia Contemporanea*, VII:1 (2003), pp. 63–82.

17 ASMAE, *Archivi Rsi*, b. 78, f. *Rappresentanze italiane in Spagna*, memorandum to Mazzolini about the mission in Spain, 20 November 1943.

18 About the relations between RSI and Spain also see A. Albonico, 'La Spagna tra Badoglio e Mussolini (1943–1945)', *Nuova Rivista Storica*, III–IV (1985), pp. 217–76.

19 ASMAE, *Archivi Rsi*, b. 78, f. *Rappresentanze italiane in Spagna*, Morreale telegram to the Ministry of Foreign Affairs, 10 January 1944.

20 ACMAE, Leg. R.2300, *Conversaciones reservadas del Ministro de Asuntos Exteriores con representantes diplomaticos 1941–46*, conversation between the Minister of Foreign Affairs and the Ambassador of the United States, 3 January 1944.

21 Spanish executives cannot forgive the government's diplomatic representatives, particularly Paulucci in Madrid and De Minerbi in Barcelona, for delivering secret archives to the British, which among other things documented the aid that Spain had secretly given Italy during the war, ASMAE, *Archivi Rsi*, b. 81, f. *Appunto per il Duce. Relazione dalla Spagna del sig. Luigi Gatti*, Luigi Gatti note to the Duce, s.d. [May 1944].

22 ASMAE, *Archivi Rsi*, b. 38, f. *Spagna. Affari politici – Riconoscimento del Gov. Naz. Rep.*, Filippo Anfuso telegram to Minister of Foreign Affairs, 5 February 1944.

23 Ibid.

24 ASMAE, *Archivi Rsi*, b. 220, f. *Scambi commerciali italo-spagnoli – Rapporti commerciali italo-spagnoli*, Morreale letter to Anfuso, 12 February 1944.

25 Ibid., memorandum, 18 April 1944.

26 Ibid., telegram to Ministry of Foreign Affairs, 21 July 1944.

27 Ibid., Antonio Cantoni Marca's confidential note, 30 June 1944.

28 Guderzo, *Madrid e l'arte della diplomazia*, p. 375.

29 ASMAE, *Archivi Rsi*, b. 77, Eugenio Morreale secret report addressed to the Foreign Affairs Ministry, 16 May 1944.

30 ASMAE, *Archivi Rsi*, b. 220, f. *Rapporti sulla Spagna e rassegna della stampa spagnola – Rassegna stampa spagnola*, Morreale's letter to Mazzolini, 3 May 1944.

31 Ibid., Antonio Bosermman's reserved note to Mazzolini, 26 July 1944.

32 Ibid.

33 ACMAE, Leg. R.2300, *Conversaciones reservadas del Ministro de Asuntos Exteriores con representantes diplomaticos 1941–46*, verbal note of Italian Royal embassy, 30 June 1944.

34 Ibid., American embassy note to Jordana, 28 July 1944, and to Lequérica, 21 August 1944.

35 Ibid., British embassy note to Lequérica, 9 September and 23 November 1944.

36 ASMAE, *Archivi Rsi*, b. 38, f. *Spagna – Rappresentanze diplomatiche e consolari del Governo regio. Attività in Spagna*, Morreale's report to Foreign Affairs Minister, 5 December 1944.

37 Ivi, Morreale's report to Mazzolini, 15 January 1945.

38 Ibid.

39 ASMAE, *Archivi Rsi*, b. 38, f. *1945-Spagna – Rappresentanza italiana in Spagna*, Mazzolini's confidential note to Graziani, 1 February 1945.
40 Ibid., Mazzolini's note to Colonel Collu, 5 February 1945.
41 Ibid., Graziani letter to Foreign Affairs Minister, 18 February 1945.
42 Ibid., Alberto Mellini Ponce de Leon's telegram to Morreale, 28 March 1945.

4 A new deal for Italy

Rethinking Britain's punitive attitude and the making of the Allied policy in occupied Italy, 1944

Marco Maria Aterrano

Anglo-Italian relations during the decade of war

Anglo-Italian rivalry was a defining factor of the period comprised between the invasion of Ethiopia and the end of World War II. The challenge the Fascist regime posed in the Mediterranean to British vital regional interests resulted in the inevitable degeneration of their relationship. This mutual hostility shaped policies, dictated strategies and engendered long-lasting animosities. As a result, the Italian defeat in 1943 changed the landscape without clearing the air.[1]

In the decade that followed the onset of the Abyssinian crisis, the Anglo-Italian relationship was one of the most relevant factors in creating the tensions that would lead up to World War II in Europe, the Italian surrender and subsequent co-belligerency. It was defined by a fluctuating series of ups and downs, dictated by the ever-shifting nature of regional and continental events, with the need to keep reciprocal ambitions in the Mediterranean in check on the one hand, and the mutual unpreparedness to fight a war on multiple fronts on the other.[2]

The evolution of an Anglo-American policy for Italy during World War II has been at the centre of several studies over the past decades, even though it has recently experienced a marked decline in the historians' interest.[3] The purpose of this chapter is to reappraise the spirit and the relevance of the British political stance in occupied Italy during the crucial year of 1944 within the framework of the Allied policy-making. The post-armistice period, due to its liberating effect on Anglo-Italian relations, can be considered the breaking point that allowed Britain to return to its pre-1935 policy towards Italy. The elimination of Britain's most active rival in the crucial crossroads of the Mediterranean and the creation of a new geopolitical order in the region eased the strategic situation. Lasting tensions, however, were not defused by the end of the military confrontation between the two countries. The pivotal role played by London in the administration of occupied Italy made it possible for the British to implement a vindictive policy within an institutional framework of strict subordination.

Traditionally, these key passages have been interpreted by commentators and historians alike mainly as a manifestation of British intention to adopt a punishing approach to Italian affairs, driven by a desire for revenge after the 'stab in the back' of June 1940. From the British point of view, victory over the

Italians meant 'the elimination of a local rival who had come dangerously close to making good his boasts', and rewarded a long-term British strategic interest.[4]

Historians Antonio Varsori and David Ellwood have written extensively on this 'punitive policy' adopted by London towards the defeated Italian government, and considered the Allied policy for Italy mainly a regional by-product of British imperialism: a thesis that restated the substance, if not the form, of Gaetano Salvemini's definition of Italy as a 'second Ireland'.[5] The position taken in favour of the preservation of the monarchy and Marshal Pietro Badoglio's government contrasted with what was believed to be a 'merely punitive political choice' and perhaps motivated, as pointed out by Ellwood, 'by the idea of elevating Vittorio Emanuele and Badoglio to the rank of long-term vassals in Italy'.[6] Even after the signing of the *long terms*, 'the prolongation and exacerbation of conflict increased hostility towards Italy. [...] In particular, the conviction that Italians did not pay enough for their aggression was affirmed'.[7]

The Americans, on the other hand, were credited with the positive turns the Allied policy in Italy had taken after the September 1943 double armistice. According to this perspective, military occupation had been 'a defeat administered more in sorrow that in anger' by the Americans.[8] The United States, while more severe with regards to administrative and political issues, were largely perceived as the element of the alliance able to ease the sufferings of the local population and allow a faster reconstruction of the Italian State. The U.S. approach, then, as highlighted by historian Andrew Buchanan, seemed to offer a more benevolent alternative to the British: 'America's paternalistic intervention in Italian politics had a fundamentally redemptive rather than punitive thrust'; where London threatened, Washington offered hope.[9]

This chapter contends that these arguments contain both positive and negative elements. The fact that the British government maintained an essentially hostile stance against the defeated enemy is beyond doubt. Between April and May of 1944, when the Allied capitals started discussing the Italian request for a full alliance, London was firmly opposed to approving any recognition of a co-belligerent status to the Italians, and averse to encouraging 'too rapidly a marked tendency on her part to forget altogether her position as a defeated enemy or to claim privileges of an ally at the expense of an armistice'.[10] After the turbulent arrival in power of Ivanoe Bonomi in June, Churchill was also wondering 'whether it was they who had unconditionally surrendered to us or whether we were about unconditionally to surrender to them', finding in the Italians' requests 'an unpleasant flavour of blackmail'.[11]

The analysis of some of the most relevant policy-related issues the occupying forces had to deal with in 1944 could however offer an additional perspective on this narrative. This chapter analyses a second trend, as important as the first, in order to take a fresh look at the evolution of the British policy in occupied Italy as it slowly but surely broke away from the retaliatory attitude it maintained during the post-armistice period.

The new deal for Italy and the relaxation of control, August–December 1944

In June 1944, after months of unrelenting political struggle, the Allies decided not to meddle in the reconstruction of the Italian institutional framework and let the Committee of National Liberation form a new representative cabinet under the leadership of Bonomi. It was the beginning, or rather the actualization, of the long-overdue process of political rehabilitation that was promised to Marshal Badoglio, the Italian Prime Minister who succeeded Mussolini, on the occasion of the signing of the *long terms* in Malta at the end of September 1943.[12] Following the liberation of Rome and the Italian government's growing involvement in Allied military efforts against the German forces active in the region,[13] the adoption of a *new deal* for Italy in the Fall of 1944 signified the implementation of a softer policy, paving the way towards reintegration of the country within the Western 'family of nations'. This new policy was implemented with the intention of turning the peninsula into a bulwark of the new American-led geopolitical network in the Mediterranean.

This adjustment was the Anglo-American response to the rapidly shifting international context. The considerable relevance the Italian situation now had on the European socio-political scene, and the growing hardships the Italian civil population was subjected to, prompted the Allies to intervene with humanitarian urgency through the modification of the institutional parameters that were to shape the impending rehabilitation of Italy. On 26 September 1944, in the context of the second Quebec conference, the Anglo-American leaders agreed on a policy statement that promised to launch a new phase in the relations between Italy and the Allies. The occupying powers established that an 'increasing measure of control will be gradually handed over to the Italian administration' through the re-establishment of full diplomatic relations and a progressive reduction of the functions and prerogatives that the Allied Control Commission had in occupied Italy.[14] It is on this occasion that the agency's denomination lost its first C, the one standing for control (AC).

The impression that the liberal element in the Allied policy for Italy was contributed by the American side of the alliance rather than the British one was widespread among contemporaries and later confirmed by the historiography, as mentioned previously. According to this established narrative, the shift operated by the Anglo-Americans was almost exclusively to be credited to the amicable attitude displayed by the Americans since January 1944, when the U.S.-sponsored policy of non-intervention – part of that liberal turn that the Allies adopted throughout the Mediterranean[15] – led to the removal of King Vittorio Emanuele from the Italian political landscape and to the formation of the first anti-fascist cabinet.[16]

This attitude also seemed to strongly clash with the strict, conservative policy adopted by the British government in handling the evolution of the political game in Italy. However, next to the faction headed by the Prime Minister and the Foreign Secretary Anthony Eden – fundamentally opposed to the recognition of any privileges to the defeated Italians, still fully regarded as enemies – a different trend in the British policy for Italy started to gain momentum.[17] A second faction, moderate and pragmatic, acknowledged the precarious British position in the region and the risk of losing control over the Italian situation in the absence of a concrete show of trust towards the local liberal forces. This led London – at least her agents on the field – to endorse the implementation of a less harsh form of control.

Starting in January 1944 at the latest, Harold Macmillan, Resident Minister in the Mediterranean and chief British diplomat in the region, began to denounce the dualistic nature of the policy implemented by Britain in Italy. This set of contradictions, he argued, made substantial progress difficult to achieve. Therefore, he urged London to play a constructive role in weaving a renewed relationship with the Italians, without having to support the Badoglio government while, at the same time, constantly showing a 'tendency to deal him fresh blows'.[18] Resorting to a religious analogy, the Resident Minister thought it wrong 'to refuse absolution altogether, however tactfully'. Furthermore, referring to the Foreign Office's refusal to include the Italians within the Atlantic Charter, he quipped that if Saul of Tarsus had adopted a similar attitude towards the Gentiles, 'Christianity would have remained a small Jewish sect'.[19]

In May, Macmillan continued to emphasize the anomaly intrinsic in the concept of co-belligerency, nothing more than a 'convenient word invented on the spur of the moment immediately after the armistice to gain the maximum military help', and devoid of any legal significance. It was the refusal to accept the consequences of the Italians' involvement in military and administrative duties that inevitably led to London's inability to identify and pursue a well-defined policy in Italy.[20]

An additional factor occupying the mind of Macmillan was the risk that delaying the implementation of a fairer treatment would lead the Italians 'to be drawn willy-nilly into the arms of Russia'.[21] Some concessions to the Italians were thus necessary in order to restore British prestige in Italy and cast off any fears of growing Anglo-Russian competition in the region.[22] According to future ambassador to Italy Noel Charles, within the process of codifying short- and long-term set of British interests in Italy, 'some move is indicated to keep the new cabinet sweet and avoid giving a second game in the rubber to Vyshinsky'.[23]

Macmillan was not alone in his mission to soften British policy in Italy. His recognition of the limits highlighted by the restrictiveness of British policy, and the risks it exposed London to, was shared by the British men in the field that worked closely with the Italian authorities. Harold Caccia, senior political advisor at the Allied Control Commission, and, at a more advanced stage of the Anglo-Italian relations, Charles both told the story, through long and detailed reports from Italy, of a country in desperate need of political guidance as much as material aid. In two startling reports from Rome, Charles described a further deterioration of the political situation so serious that unless urgent measures were taken, the Allies would be left powerless while witnessing Italy's transition 'from the present form of democratic interregnum to extremism'. He therefore suggested that London make use of an increased number of Italian troops in the fight against the Germans, released Italian prisoners of war from the labour camps and intervened against the rising inflation.[24]

In mid-1944, the Foreign Office too was forced to acknowledge the distortions of the policy it had hitherto implemented in Italy. The British government was determined to treat Italy as a defeated enemy, insisting, when convenient, on the strict compliance with armistice terms, but at the same time expecting from her the performance of an ally in the war against Germany. This line of reasoning led the Foreign Office to promote the construction of a 'more forward policy in Italy' with three objectives: to contain the spread of communism; to create a prosperous and friendly Italy that could have in London, rather than Moscow or Berlin, a future point of reference; and to facilitate the task of post-war reconstruction. The best results in the pursuit of these objectives would be guaranteed, according to Whitehall, by the improvement of conditions in Italy through the loosening of control, granting Italy a partial restoration of her sovereignty, and a full alliance.[25]

During the first half of 1944, these growing concerns had thus found expression in a subterranean debate within the upper echelons of London's Mediterranean policy-making, which challenged the foundations of what appeared to have been the British repressive policy implemented in Italy throughout the first months of the occupation. This policy, centred upon the verbatim observance of the *long terms*, was subjected to an in-depth process of review in the months between February, when Churchill had strengthened his support of the Badoglio government with his notorious 'coffeepot speech',[26] and August 1944, when the Prime Minister embarked for the first time on an official visit to Italy.

On 22 August 1944, Churchill met with the entire structure of the British policy-making with the notable exception of Eden at the British Embassy in Rome. In the presence of Churchill, Macmillan, Charles and two senior Foreign Office officials, Pierson Dixon and Roger Makins, the details of the Italian situation were discussed. Echoing the positions outlined in the previous months, Charles and Macmillan voiced their belief that it was necessary to further strengthen the recently formed Bonomi government in the interest of stability not only of the local situation, but that of the entire Mediterranean region. Dixon, representing the Foreign Office, reiterated the proposal of a preliminary peace treaty that would allow London to place the Italians in an intermediate position between enemies and allies.[27] A similar solution had taken centre stage at Whitehall in the late Spring of 1944 and was strongly endorsed by Macmillan who, adopting one of his ever-articulated metaphors, commented on the armistice provisions which were 'at best a sort of purgatory', while thanks to the Foreign Office plan, the Italians 'should now approach the portals of paradise through a preliminary treaty of peace'.[28]

The conclusions drawn at the end of the meeting portended the opening of a new phase in the history of Anglo-Italian relations. The British, it was agreed, 'should regard Italy as a friendly co-belligerent and no longer as an enemy state'. Several measures – such as the transformation of the Control Commission into an institution meant to support the Italian government rather than constraining it, the appointment of the British High Commissioner in Italy Noel Charles as full ambassador and the transfer of an increasing share of administrative duties to the Italian Government – were to bring these new British policies about.[29] According to Macmillan, London was finally acknowledging that Italy was 'working her passage to the best of her ability'.[30] As neatly summed up by Churchill in a message sent to the Italian people at the end of his visit in the peninsula, the British government 'had no desire but to see Italy free, prosperous and progressive'.[31] Thus, in Rome a different British policy was crafted.

This change, however, did not impact Anglo-Italian relations alone. Even more relevant, from an Allied perspective and in the context of the decision-making process inherent to the Allied occupation, is how this policy ended up being integrated within the framework of the Anglo-American relations with the Italians. Also decisive is how Washington embraced the adoption of a progressive new stance by Britain. A few days before the Hyde Park meeting took place on 26 September 1944, Macmillan asked Churchill for the formulation and dissemination of a clearer directive that would follow the line agreed upon by the British policy-makers in August.[32] On 17 September, the Prime Minister sent to Charles a document basically outlining what would have been presented by the Anglo-American leaders a week later as the new Allied deal for Italy. The two documents would contain similar wording and identical points.[33] The position developed by the British agents over the first half of 1944 sat at the very core of the Allied new course of action.

The implementation of this innovative perspective would follow shortly. Macmillan, meanwhile appointed as new Acting President of the Allied Commission for Italy, in a very detailed memorandum of 4 December 1944, prompted a shift in the Allied emphasis from control to advice, moving in the direction of full restoration of Italian internal sovereignty and initiating the commission's transition to civilian status.[34] The measures imposed by the Combined Chiefs the following January, that finally made good on the 1943 promises to transfer as much control back to the Italians as possible, had been outlined in their entirety in Macmillan's document. If the Italian government decided not to comply with the political directions given by the Allies, Macmillan continued, 'we must shrug our shoulders and allow affairs to take their course'. The Anglo-American governments, in their reconstruction of the Italian institutional system, had to act as 'advisers, not controllers; elder brothers to our weak and errant juniors'.[35]

The course of action advocated by Macmillan would take the form of four concessions granted by the Allied governments: the abolition of the political section of the Allied Commission; permission to the Italian government to establish direct diplomatic relations with foreign powers; the relinquishment of the practice of Allied approval for any main Italian institutional appointments and legislative decrees; and the withdrawal of military officers from the territories under the administration of the Italian government. The work of the commission was reorganized in order to limit its activities to a mere advisory role to the Italian Government. Its functions were only to be exercised in the presence of a specific request originating from the Italians and only in the territories that were yet to be released to Italian control. Following these changes, the Italian government finally regained 'full control over its legislative authority'.[36]

The Combined Chiefs of Staff Directive, put into practice on 24 February 1945 via an aide-memoire presented by Macmillan to the Italian Government, gave the policy enunciated in Hyde Park a concrete form and was a crucial step in the liberal evolution of the Allied policy for Italy. From that moment onwards, the Allied emphasis would be placed on rehabilitation rather than on control.[37] The transformation of Italy into a minor partner in the creation of a new world order needed to start from a radical change in how the British, former senior partners in the Mediterranean, viewed the 'Italian problem'.

Conclusion

The decisive intervention of Macmillan, since December 1944 positioned at the top of not just the British, but the entire Allied decision-making structure in occupied Italy, was an additional element which helps to trace the origins of this new policy back to the British camp. Since the early elaboration of a more pragmatic policy in the Allied Forces Head Quarters of Algiers, marked by an increased attention to the demands and needs of the Italian government and population,[38] Macmillan exerted a moderating and progressive influence on the Allied positions on Italy. Often at odds with the hard line desired by both Whitehall and Downing Street, but in full harmony with Mediterranean Commanders in Chief Dwight Eisenhower, Henry Maitland Wilson and his fellow British agents on the field, the Resident Minister represented the most prominent element in what can be called the group of 'doves' within the multifaceted British articulation of a policy for Italy in late 1943 and 1944.

This is not to say that the Americans blindly followed the British lead. On the contrary, this evolution of the British policy brought the two allies' strategies, conflicting for most of the pre- and post-armistice periods alike, to convergence.[39] Washington's approach to Italian affairs was characterized by a strong emphasis on unconditional surrender during the armistice negotiations and, at a later stage, by a stark refusal to collaborate with Badoglio's post-fascist government. The United States President, and with him American agents in the field in the peninsula, insisted on a harsher handling of Italian politicians and government officers compromised with the Fascist regime, and pushed for fairer treatment of the population instead.[40] The British, on the other hand, adopted a specular position until the radical shift of the Summer 1944. In short, the substantial difference lay in the importance that was given, in the two allied capitals, to the letter of the armistice and to the actions carried out by the Italian government in the phases following the change of alliance. That same shift put the two national policies within the alliance on a similar path and allowed the Allies to present a more united front in the Italian occupation.

A few more points are worth highlighting. Firstly, the analysis of the evolution the British policy experienced during the pivotal post-armistice period shows a deep fracture existing between the politicians in London and Washington and the diplomats and military officers on the ground. The first-hand knowledge of the situation gathered directly in the active theatre of the peninsula clearly led these agents to a better understanding of the delicate balance the occupied country found itself in after the fall of the Fascist regime. Consequently, they pushed for the implementation of a policy that would fully take into account both the harsh realities of war and the prospects for a peaceful post-war transition.

Secondly, and most importantly, Allied policy in Italy followed a 'piecemeal' evolution, adapting to the circumstances in the field and avoiding any rigid top-down decision-making process.[41] In this constant evolution, the balance between the two sides of the Atlantic alliance was shaped by varying stances on different issues, and shifted repeatedly as the international context and the national interests and possibilities changed phase after phase, with the roles of the two allies often trading places. As it has been mentioned earlier, a substantial identity of policies between the United States and the United Kingdom was only reached in the second phase of institutional occupation, during the management of the Italian situation in the aftermath of the crisis that led to the unexpected fall of the Badoglio government in June 1944. Conflict and harmony had long coexisted in the Anglo-American policy for Italy before and after the armistice. In the end, however, because of the military and international situation, the implementation of a more relaxed form of control in Italy had become inevitable, and both parties eventually came to agree on this.

In conclusion, the image of a solely negative British policy in occupied Italy does not, I believe, accurately reflect the evolution it experienced in 1944. This result was not obtained by the Macmillans, the Charles and the Macfarlanes in a vacuum. Churchill too, Eden even, who had been for a long period of time strongly opposed to any openings to the Italians, came in the end to appreciate the value in a change of course. Further, the relevance of this evolution in the British camp within the framework of the joint effort made by the Anglo-American powers to elaborate a coherent policy for Italy is evident. It is possible, then, that the Allied new deal of September 1944 was the combination of two separate but converging national policies and interests, rather than one ally's determinations forcibly imposed upon the other.

'Never in the history of war have conquerors so rapidly and with such sincerity turned from battle to the task of reconstruction'.[42] Perhaps the Resident Minister's words exaggerate the impact the actions of the British government had on the Italian front in the post-armistice period; nonetheless, in the turn of a few years, Italy was transformed from a defeated country into an integral part of the Western Bloc. No small part in this effort was played by the British change of pace in 1944.

Notes

1 The bibliography on Anglo-Italian relations before the war is vast, but particularly relevant are: G. Bruce Strang (ed.), *Collision of Empires: Italy's Invasion of Ethiopia and Its International Impact* (Burlington, VT: Ashgate, 2013); S. Morewood, 'Anglo-Italian Rivalry in the Mediterranean and the Middle East, 1935–1940', in

R. Boyce and E. Robertson (eds.), *Paths to War: New Essays on the Origins of the Second World War* (Basingstoke: Macmillan, 1989), pp. 167–98; D.N. Dilks, 'British Reactions to Italian Empire-Building, 1936–1939', in E. Serra and C. Seton-Watson (eds.), *Italia e Inghilterra nell'età dell'imperialismo* (Milan: Franco Angeli, 1990), pp. 165–94; R. Mallett, *The Italian Navy and Fascist Expansionism, 1935–40* (London and Portland, OR: Frank Cass, 1998); M. Fiore, *Anglo-Italian Relations in the Middle East, 1922–1940* (Farnham: Ashgate, 2010).

2   For a background on the difficult strategic position of the United Kingdom during the years preceding the outbreak of war, and the relevance of the Italian situation in it, see W. Murray, 'The Role of Italy in British Strategy, 1938–1939', *The RUSI Journal*, CXXIV (1979), pp. 43–9; B.J.C. McKercher, 'National Security and Imperial Defence: British Grand Strategy and Appeasement, 1930–1939', *Diplomacy & Statecraft*, XIX (2008), pp. 391–442.

3   For a brief summary on the state of the art related to the formulation and development of an Anglo-American policy for Italy see: J. Hearst, 'The Evolution of Allied Military Government Policy in Italy', unpublished Ph.D. dissertation (New York, NY: Columbia University, 1960); T. Higgins, *Soft Underbelly: Anglo-American Controversy over the Italian Campaign, 1939–1945* (New York, NY: Macmillan, 1968); B. Arcidiacono, *Le 'precedent italien' et les origines de la guerre froide: les allies et l'occupation de l'Italie, 1943–1944* (Brussels: Bruylant, 1984); D.W. Ellwood, *Italy 1943–45* (Leicester: Leicester University Press, 1985); E. Di Nolfo, M. Serra, *La gabbia infranta. Gli Alleati e l'Italia dal 1943 al 1945* (Rome-Bari: Laterza, 2010).

4   W. Reitzel, *The Mediterranean: Its Role in America's Foreign Policy* (Port Washington, NY: Kennikat Press, 1969), p. 26.

5   Letter to Ernesto Rossi, in G. Salvemini, *Lettere dall'America, 1944–1946* (Bari: Laterza, 1967), p. 62. Also see, for references on the British Italian policy in the first years of the war, A. Varsori, 'L'atteggiamento britannico verso l'Italia, 1940–1943: alle origini della politica punitiva', in A. Placanica (ed.), *1944, Salerno capitale: istituzioni e società* (Napoli, 1985), pp. 137–59; D.W. Ellwood, *L'amico nemico. La politica dell'occupazione anglo-americana in Italia, 1943–1946* (Milan: Feltrinelli, 1977); S.J. Woolf, 'La politica inglese nei confronti degli italiani all'inizio della Seconda Guerra Mondiale', *Italia Contemporanea*, 124 (1976), pp. 115–19; A. Varsori, 'Italy, Britain and the Problem of a Separate Peace During the Second World War: 1940–1943', *Journal of Italian History*, 1 (1978), pp. 455–90.

6   Ellwood, *L'alleato nemico*, p. 60.

7   Varsori, *L'atteggiamento britannico verso l'Italia*, p. 147.

8   Reitzel, *The Mediterranean*, p. 26.

9   A. Buchanan, '"Good Morning, Pupil!" American Representations of Italianness and the Occupation of Italy, 1943–1945', *Journal of Contemporary History*, 43:2 (2008), pp. 217–40, p. 240.

10 See Foreign Office's memorandum, 20 April 1944, delivered to Washington on the 24th, in The National Archives, London, Foreign Office (FO) 115/3604; also see Churchill's telegram to Eden, April 26, in which the premature liberation of the Italian government from its armistice shackles was defined a mistake, in TNA, Cabinet Papers (CAB) 120/584.

11 See Sargent's note, May 11, in FO 371/43911.

12 Eisenhower's letter to Badoglio, 29 September 1943, in Archivio Storico-Diplomatico del Ministero degli Affari Esteri (MAE), Segreteria Generale 1943–1947 (SG), vol. II, *Rapporti fra l'Italia e gli Alleati, 1943–1944*. Also see, for wider references to the armistice and the lead-up to it, E. Aga Rossi, *A Nation Collapses: The Italian Surrender of September 1943* (Cambridge: Cambridge University Press, 2006).

13 A clear analysis of the political and military developments of the Allied presence in Italy and the tightening of the Italo-Allied collaboration in 1944 can be found in

B. Arcidiacono, 'The "Dress Rehearsal": The Foreign Office and the Control of Italy, 1943–44', *The Historical Journal*, 28:2 (1985), pp. 417–27; M. Gat, 'Britain and the Badoglio Government, October 1943–April 1944', in P. Artzi (ed.), *Bar-Ilan Studies in History II* (Ramat-Gan: Bar-Ilan University Press, 1982), pp. 211–44; and Ellwood, *Italy 1943–1945*. On the specific issue of the Italian cobelligerency see R. Carrier, 'The Regio Esercito in Co-Belligerency, October 1943–April 1945', in R. Carrier, E. Sica (eds.), *Italy and the Second World War: Alternative Perspectives* (Leiden: Brill, 2018), pp. 95–125.

14 Hyde Park Declaration, 26 September 1944; the full text in U.S. Department of State, *Foreign Relations of the United States Diplomatic Papers (FRUS), The Second Quebec Conference, 1944* (Washington, DC: U.S. Government Printing Office, 1944), p. 494, and H.L. Coles and A.K. Weinberg, *Civil Affairs: Soldiers Become Governors* (Washington, DC: Office of the Chief of Military History U.S. Army, 1964), p. 478. The appointment of Noel Charles, former British High Commissioner in Italy, to the post of British Ambassador to Italy was finally announced to Bonomi on 10 October 1944, while the American representative in Rome, Alexander Kirk, had already been invested of a similar title. At the same time, the Italian government was invited to appoint its own representatives to the British and U.S. capitals. Although the resumption of normal diplomatic relations between London and Rome was not yet possible, direct contact was established with the Italian government for matters concerning political interests between Italy and Great Britain, see Charles' letter to Bonomi, in MAE, SG, vol. XXII, *Rapporti con Gran Bretagna e Stati Uniti*.

15 A. Buchanan, *American Grand Strategy in the Mediterranean during World War II* (New York, NY: Cambridge University Press, 2014), pp. 220–2. Buchanan argues that this progressive change was a factor in the further deterioration of the U.S. relations with Britain: 'every aspect of the "liberal turn" was carried through in the face of British opposition', since 'in Italy, Britain sought to maintain a political setup centered on the King and Badoglio and [...] to block "civilianization" and "rehabilitation"', p. 222.

16 The events, and the relationship between the British Government and the Italian Monarchy, are detailed in M. De Leonardis, 'La Gran Bretagna e la monarchia italiana (1943–1946)', *Storia Contemporanea*, 1 (1981), pp. 57–134.

17 Eden's negative attitude towards Italy and the Italians dated back to the years of the Abyssinian crisis, see R. Mallett, 'Fascist Foreign Policy and Official Italian Views of Anthony Eden in the 1930s', *The Historical Journal*, 43:1 (2000), pp. 157–87; and W. C. Mills, 'The Nyon Conference: Neville Chamberlain, Anthony Eden, and the Appeasement of Italy in 1937', *The International History Review*, 15:1 (1993), pp. 1–22.

18 24 January 1944, Macmillan's telegram to Eden, in FO 371/43909; also in TNA, Prime Minister's Papers (PREM) 3/243/8.

19 Ibid.

20 Cit. Macmillan's telegram to Foreign Office, 2 May 1944, which will be echoed, in the substance and the form, in Charles' telegram to London, 5 May 1944, in FO 371/43911. The High Commissioner believed that, in the absence of significant modifications to the relationship with the Italians, the Allies would risk losing the support and confidence of the Italian population and let the Soviets to take back the initiative in the peninsula.

21 See Macmillan's telegram to Foreign Office, 2 May 1944.

22 On the relevance of the Russian factor in the framework of the Allied policy-making for Italy see M. Gat, 'The Soviet Factor in British Policy Towards Italy, 1943–1945', *The Historian*, 50 (1988), pp. 535–57; B. Arcidiacono, 'La Gran Bretagna e il "pericolo comunista" in Italia: gestazione, nascita e primo sviluppo di una percezione (1943–1944)', *Storia delle Relazioni Internazionali*, 1 (1985), pp. 241–6; B. Arcidiacono, 'The Diplomacy of the Italian Defeat: Italy, the Anglo-Americans, and the "Russian Factor"

(1943–1945)', in M. Dockrill (ed.), *Europe Within the Global System, 1938–1960* (Bochum: Universitätsverlag Brockmeyer, 1995), pp. 55–74.

23 See Charles' telegram to Foreign Office, 13 May 1944, in PREM 3/243/15.

24 See Charles' letter to Churchill, 13 August 1944, in PREM 3/243/15. For a series of references on these themes see M.M. Aterrano, 'Gli uffici di collegamento tra le forze armate italiane e le autorità anglo-americane nella cobelligeranza', in M.M. Aterrano (ed.), *La ricostituzione del Regio esercito dalla resa alla liberazione, 1943–1945* (Rome: Rodorigo Editore, 2017), pp. 83–112.

25 See Foreign Office, *Note on Italian Policy*, 20 August 1944, based on a previous draft of May 11. The position sponsored by Whitehall was then embraced by Macmillan, who integrated the proposal with an analysis of a possible future scenario, in which the organization of the remaining control would be restructured through the abolition of both the Allied Control Commission and the Advisory Council for Italy. The former would, according to this plan, be transformed into a sort of economic council, whereas the latter would be replaced by a council of Allied High Commissioners; see Macmillan's letter to FO, 21 August 1944, in PREM 3/247.

26 See Churchill's speech to the Commons, 22 February 1944, in PREM 3/243/8.

27 The account of the meeting of August 22 can be found in Foreign Office, *Note of Discussion on Italy at the British Embassy in Rome*, in PREM 3/247.

28 See Macmillan's letter to Foreign Office, 31 May 1944, in FO 371/43911. The issue concerning the possible signing of a preliminary peace treaty played a major role in both Anglo-Italian and Anglo-American debate in the first phase of the Allied occupation of Italy, see M. Gat, *Britain and Italy, 1943–1949: The Decline of British Influence* (Brighton: Sussex Academic Press, 1996), pp. 83–7. The same clarification issued by Eden on June 5 to the Foreign Office will be sent to the State Department on June 12, alongside with the aide-memoire *Abolition of Present Armistice Regime in Italy and Conclusion of a Preliminary Peace Treaty with the Italian Government*, FO 371/43911. The proposal for a preliminary treaty with Italy was first put forward by the British between May and June 1944, rejected by the American government and at a later time by the British government itself; in a second occasion, in December 1944, it was the Americans, inspired by the new positions of Macmillan and elaborated by the American members of the CCAC, who find British opposition on the basis that they saw 'no merit in terminating the state of war and not covering post-war questions', and that the present proposal would have only gratified the Italian government without presenting any advantage to the Allies, National Archives and Record Administration, Department of State, European Lot Files, b. 3 (also see the memorandum for the Secretary of State, *Proposal for a Preliminary Peace with Italy*, 23 January 1945, FO 371/49750).

29 Ibid.

30 See Macmillan's note from 26 August 1944, *Plan for Italy*, in PREM 3/247, in which the Resident Minister proposed Allied Commission of Assistance as the new title of the Allied Control Commission.

31 The full text of the message of 24 August 1944, can be found in PREM 3/243/2. The visit seemed to have deeply touched the convictions of Churchill, who confessed to Eden that he had developed ideas that, while not allowing a temporary peace to the Italians, surpassed it in substance in terms of responsibility left to the Italian government, PREM 3/247. On 28 September, Churchill announced to the Commons that he could not feel 'any sentiments of hostility towards the mass of the misled or coerced Italian people', FO 371/43913.

32 Macmillan's telegram to Churchill, 13 September 1944, in FO 954.

33 See Churchill's letter to Charles, 17 September 1944, dating more than a week before the Hyde Park declaration, in which the new policy for Italy was officially announced by the Allied leaders, in PREM 3/247.

34 Macmillan's note, *Allied Policy toward Italy*, 4 December 1944, was drafted in a first version on November 27, in PREM 3/241/7. The same stance, once approved by the British cabinet, was put forward by the British members of the Combined Civil Affairs Committee during the 13 December 1944 meeting, in FO 371/43917.

35 Ibid.

36 See 24 February 1945, Macmillan's *aide-memoire* concerning the new Allied Commission directive to the Italian government, MAE, SG, vol. XIII, *Rapporti con gli Alleati, 1945*.

37 Ibid.

38 On the role played by Eisenhower and his staff in the conduction of political affairs in the Mediterranean theatre see M. Jones, *Britain, the United States and the Mediterranean War, 1942–44* (Oxford: Macmillan, 1996), and N. Barr, *Eisenhower's Armies: The American-British Alliance During World War II* (New York, NY: Pegasus Books, 2015).

39 The evolution of the US policy for Italy during the decade of war is addressed in Andrew Buchanan's chapter, 'American Policy Towards Italy during Its "Decade of War"', in this edited volume. For further references to wartime American strategy for Italy also see W. Reitzel, *The United States in the Mediterranean* (New Haven, CT: Yale Institute of International Studies, 1947); J.E. Miller, *The United States and Italy, 1940–1950: The Politics and Diplomacy of Stabilization* (Chapel Hill, NC: University of North Carolina Press, 1986); J.E. Miller, 'The Search for Stability: An Interpretation of American Policy in Italy: 1943–46', *Journal of Italian Studies*, 1:2 (1978), pp. 246–314; and K. Mistry, *The United States, Italy and the Origins of Cold War: Waging Political Warfare, 1945–1950* (New York, NY: Cambridge University Press, 2014).

40 E.J. Miller, 'The Politics of Relief: The Roosevelt Administration and the Reconstruction of Italy, 1943–1944', *Prologue*, (1981), pp. 193–208.

41 See G. Kolko, *The Politics of War: The World and United States Foreign Policy, 1943–1945* (London: Weidenfeld & Nicolson, 1969), p. 42. Also see, for a reflection on the issue of seniority in the military and political command of the Mediterranean and Italian theatres, A. Varsori, '"Senior" or "Equal" Partner?', *Rivista di Studi Politici Internazionali* (1978), pp. 229–60.

42 Macmillan's telegram to FO, 24 February 1944, in FO 371/49753.

Part II

A fascist warfare?

Military conquest, transnational fighting and the use of violence

5 Blind faith

Rethinking the Italian intervention in Spain, 1936

Javier Rodrigo[1]

Introduction

In the seventh month of 1936, the fourteenth year of the Fascist Era, a coup d'état erupted in Spain. In the days just prior, Benito Mussolini could be found travelling around Italy. From his declarations on the dates when the news first arrived from Africa and the Iberian Peninsula, it would seem the coup resided entirely outside his realm of concern.[2] Though he never mentioned Spain in his public discourses, Mussolini could not claim ignorance. He was promptly informed by his consular network – through the Ministry of Ciano and the Servizio Informazioni Militare (SIM) – of what was happening on the Peninsula and in Africa. Above all, however, Mussolini knew full well that preparations for the July coup had been ongoing for some time, because he and his government helped bring it to fruition.

The Italian one was the largest military contingent of one foreign nation alone in the Spanish Civil War. It was the result of a complex – but not predetermined – succession and juxtaposition of contexts, processes, circumstances and decisions. We already know well Mussolini's conspiracies against the Spanish Republic and the diplomatic moves that led to Italian help for the uprising of 1936. There is general agreement on the size of an intervention which, whether military or not, reached its numerical maximum in February 1937, when Spain had 44,263 Italian soldiers: 18,477 belonged to the Regio Esercito and 25,856 to the Milizia Volontaria per la Sicurezza Nazionale (MVSN), to which the 5,699 men of the Aviazione Legionaria should be added. The resulting total would reach about 79,000 combatants; according to my sources 78,846 – some 45,000 belonging to the regular army, some 29,000 to Fascist militias, some 3,700 died and 11,763 were wounded. The figures match those in all the monographs published since the mid-1970s.[3]

However, the global interpretation of the events is far from conclusive. Paradoxically, it is an intervention devalued by historiography, although it came to accumulate more than twice as many members as the International Brigades: Mussolini was the one who truly internationalized the Spanish Civil War. In this chapter, I am working from a hypothesis contrary to that of the mainstream. Generally, everything surrounding the mass intervention of Mussolini's Italy in

Spain in 1937 is projected onto July 1936 as if it were all pre-arranged from the beginning. I consider and attempt to demonstrate that the massive intervention of 1937 was not the continuation of the original plan from 1936, but the result of its failure, or rather the failure of the entire insurgent plan that the Fascist powers supported from July on. In order to better understand the *what*, the *how*, the *when* and above all the *why* of the whole Fascist intervention in Spain, this chapter examines the period from July to November–December of 1936.

Blind faith

Mussolini had been aware of preparations for the coup d'état since June. The Fascist government knew its definitive form at least a day before the uprising[4] – though the SIM had informed in June of the 'imminent' nature of the 'military and Falangist movement'[5] – and certainly knew its precise features on 18 July 1936. On that day,[6] the Italian Consulate sent Franco's first proclamations: 'glory to the heroic army of Africa. Spain above all else […] Blind faith in victory. Long live Spain with honour'. The Italian ambassador, who just then was on summer holiday with part of his staff in San Sebastian, gave this rather heterogeneous group an even more peculiar name, when seen in perspective: *i rivoluzionari*, the revolutionaries. Based on what the ambassador already knew, their plans would have already been clear on 18 July:

> The plan of the revolutionaries is as follows: uprising of the Foreign Legion in Morocco (this has already happened); the Legion will cross over to Málaga on warships that would have left days ago to receive them and transport them to Spain. The rebels will march on Madrid and at the same time the garrisons of Burgos, Valladolid and Pamplona will rise up under the command of General Mola, right-hand man to Sanjurjo. If the government yields and it would be desirable that command of the country [missing word] the movement would limit itself to this programme, otherwise numerous civilian elements and especially traditional military formations would take action, with the training and disposition for combat in order to take Madrid by force.[7]

This was very precise information, especially if we consider that the formal petition for help from Mussolini's Italy, a few days after, was related to the crossing of the Legion into Andalusia. The canonical narrative on the intervention of fascisms in Spain has almost always started from the idea that either nothing was known of what was going on and the rebellion forced them into immediate decisions, or that if anything was known, it was very little. This telegram discredits both ideas and demonstrates the very high degree of knowledge about the coup d'état: its variables, actors and immediate consequences.[8]

This was obviously not the only information channel for Ciano and Mussolini, and it would seem rather naïve to believe that such a large-scale intervention as that of the Italians reflected the work of a single person or group. The question is certainly important to a better understanding of the 'where' and the 'how'. There were at least four crucial places: Rome, St-Jean-De-Luz, Madrid and Tangiers. On 18 July, the Italian Consul and Minister plenipotentiary in Tangiers, Pier Filippo De Rossi del Lion Nero, sent the consulate military attaché and SIM agent Giuseppe Luccardi to Tétouan to gather information about events as they unfolded. The same day, Franco signed the written petition for air support ('12 bombers, 3 fighter planes with 50 and 100 kg bombs [and bomb releases], 1,000 of 50 [kg] and 100 of 500 [kg]') that Luis Bolín, a correspondent for *ABC* newspaper, carried to Rome. A day later, on 20 July, Pedrazzi confirmed from St-Jean-De-Luz that the uprising was underway, outcomes were unpredictable, and that this was no simple military coup as others had been.[9] That same day, Franco asked Luccardi for ships to transport troops. This telegram reached the SIM on 21 July, and Roatta asked for his opinion: *'la Spagna è come una sabbia mobile'*, Spain is like quicksand, he must have replied in what is now a famous quote. It spoke of how much might be lost and how little gained for Italy in Spain; of the notoriety that would accompany defeat and the parsimony that would accompany victory, in such literal terms that its authenticity must be questioned. In any case, contact continued: on 21 July, Consul De Rossi indicated that it was increasingly difficult to appraise the situation in Spain. At Roatta's instruction, Luccardi related to Franco the difficulties involved with providing him with the air support he had personally requested (which Bolín would ask Ciano for the following day). A day later, Ciano received Franco's first envoy to Rome, Luis Bolín. Unsuccessfully, Mussolini's initial decision was not to provide the help requested. Ciano promised to keep trying and telegraphed De Rossi on 24 July to inquire about the possibility of victory for Franco. Meanwhile, after a decision the previous day (therefore not a consequence of Mussolini's first negative response), General Emilio Mola sent Antonio Goicoechea, Pedro Sáinz Rodriguez and Luis María Zunzunegui to Rome. Goicoechea brought with him another article of persuasion: a letter written from the Modelo Prison on 20 May 1936 and signed by the founder of the Falange José Antonio Primo de Rivera:[10]

> I see, as you do, the tragic situation of Spain and consider it urgent that thought be given to extraordinary remedies. My situation as a prisoner impedes me from much of the management but not from leading the Movement, which grows daily, with efficacy. If in these transactions, concerning persons who cannot come to visit me, you would like to represent me, I would be very grateful, as I have abundant proof of your loyal conduct as a friend.

Meanwhile, information continued to arrive from Tétouan. The future *generalísimo* – the superlative general – indicated to Luccardi that the difficulties had begun to acquire dramatic tones. Franco could not take troops to the continent, and candidly informed Luccardi that this could cause the entire uprising to fail. Whether it was luck, chance or Franco's persuasive capacity that finally tipped the scales remains in the realm of informed conjecture. The decision to support Franco in July determined who would eventually emerge as the maximum authority in Rebel Spain.[11] On 20 July, General Franco was already referred to as '*Generale Franco capo movimento spagnolo*', the leader of the Spanish movement. A day later, Franco declared his intent to establish (opportunistically, according to Heiberg; though I tend to think it sincere) a 'fascist-type republican [government] adapted to the Spanish people', after the 'hard but necessary fight to avoid [a] Soviet state'. In the early days, however, the fight began to take unexpected turns: a telegram received on 23 July indicated that 'for Franco to succeed urgent intervention is needed'.[12] On 21 July, Franco spoke of a fascist-type government; on 23 July, the need for intervention was urgent; on 25 July, the situation was dramatic, and Mussolini held the key that would unlock victory: a handful of aeroplanes. It is difficult not to see in Franco's cornered desperation the real motive for sending the first military aid.

Decision-making involved a complex analysis of European governance, the calculation of probabilities for Fascism, and reports from the Peninsula and Africa of a blocked army and a failed uprising in Madrid. On 25 July, Hitler decided to participate in supporting the Rebels; Mussolini did the same two days later, on 27–28 July. De Rossi reasoned with Il Duce and Ciano that German influence over insurgent Spain would increase in the absence of Italian support. He made it clear that the Third Reich would become the reference power in the attack on an anti-fascist regime, a task that should fall to the Italians. After a request for more information, Ciano received from Tangiers a telegram that specified the Rebel needs and offered assurance that this materiel would guarantee Franco's victory.[13] He urgently needed transport, fighter and reconnaissance aircraft, and a ship, all to move African troops to the Peninsula. Strictly speaking, it was true.[14] The Minister responded on 27 July that twelve cleverly camouflaged planes and a steamer loaded with war materiel were ready to embark for Melilla. However, before committing or promising anything, he needed assurance regarding Franco's situation. De Rossi's answer was immediate and the most conclusive of any he sent to Rome: the supreme struggle between order and Bolshevism that Franco was engaged in required the fresh blood of the Moroccan troops, who were blockaded in Africa by government maritime forces. The fall of Franco's movement could only be avoided, or its success guaranteed, by overcoming this blockade. Consequently, only the help of Fascist Italy could free the '*capo movimento*' from the African death trap.[15] De Rossi acknowledged that the enormous difficulties involved would be trifling by comparison if, under 'the pressure of global uprising', the conflict 'which today remains confined within Spanish borders' assumed 'the character of a battle for the supremacy of social disorder over the order that we represent with our Regime'.[16] In other words: the failure of the coup d'état would radicalize the left and European anti-fascism with it.

In fact, part of the historiography attempts to demonstrate that Italian Fascist intervention in Spain was the 'fruit of the anti-communist duty to stop the Soviet Union from gaining a foothold in the Mediterranean'.[17] However, perhaps they were more concerned about blocking the influence of the anti-fascist Popular Front than that of the Soviets. What Il Duce may have feared more than the almost propagandistic risk of communist expansion was the loss of political hegemony through the possibility of a common French and Spanish popular front in the Western Mediterranean, along with the loss of potential territorial hegemony in the east, which was threatened by the presence of British fleets sent to ensure the 'guarantees' of support to Greece, Turkey and Yugoslavia. For Aristotle Kallis, this also reflected an attempt to expel British power, beginning with their control of the Straits of Gibraltar.[18] John Coverdale argues that it stemmed from rejection of Bolshevik intervention and the conviction that greater Italian intervention would bring a swifter victory for Franco and enormously favour Italian geostrategic coordinates in Europe. Also, it would facilitate the destruction of the anti-fascist Popular Front enemy and guarantee support for a potential subordinate ally – the New Spain.

The ultimate causes for military escalation may remain obscure, but interpretations based on geostrategic calculations regarding the Mediterranean cast more than a few long shadows. In any case, the Fascist war combined diverse factors and had both explicit and preventive defensive interests. In the secret protocol between Italy and Franco's Spain signed on 28 November 1936, the Italian government and army agreed to respect Spanish territorial integrity in the event of continental conflict. In exchange, French colonial troops would not be allowed to cross Spanish territory. Mussolini insisted on preventing any 'black soldier' from being called to defend the metropolis, and his view became canon: De Felice, who has engendered much of the relevant canonical interpretation of Italian historiography (and mentored many of its members), asserted that Italy played no part in the design or preparation of the Spanish military uprising. He argued that Italy's intervention was not even ideological in nature, nor did it seek to install a fascist-type regime in Spain. Rather, motivation essentially corresponded to traditional political-strategic reasoning: Spain – and its Balearic Islands – could not be permitted to ally itself with France and become a bridge for transporting African troops to the metropolis.[19] A victory for Franco had to be ensured in order to gain better control of the Western Mediterranean and block any French influence in Spain. Historiographical quasi-consensus seems to indicate that all motives were defensive. In my opinion, this is an *ex-post* interpretation that projects both 1937 escalation and 1938–1939 maintenance in war to 1936 decisions.

What cannot be denied is that in the summer of 1936, Mussolini broke the tie for the first time. A squadron of twelve Savoia-Marchetti S-81 bombers left for Morocco from the aerodrome at Elmas, on Sardinia. From that moment, events accelerated. Two days later, the cargo ship *Morandi*, filled with fuel and munitions, also left the island for Spanish territory.[20] However, only nine planes arrived: two crashed and one had to make an emergency landing in French

Morocco. Strong headwinds had caused them to run out of fuel. The secrecy of the intervention lasted exactly four days. None of this, however, stopped the sending of arms and support.

Why? Between 1936 and 1937, Mussolini sent a full expeditionary army of 45,000 soldiers to Spain. In my opinion, an entire army was not created to defend a geostrategic position. It was on the ground to attack, conquer and vanquish, whether the aim was to annihilate the enemy or pre-emptively defend the Fascist political system and the regime itself. As Ciano put it: Italy was at war to defend Fascist civilization and revolution. For this reason, in the summer and autumn of 1936, the Italians redoubled their efforts to influence and even determine the evolution of insurgent Spain. Ciano must have explained to Cantalupo, the first ambassador of Fascist Italy to Spain after Italy formally recognized the Franco government in November, how at first they only thought about sending aeroplanes to assist in troop transport, but with 'pressure from every side [...] we have jumped in with both feet'. In theory, they were simply assisting a plan by which Franco would take Madrid via Jarama, while the Legion attacked Valencia and would then support the liberation of the capital from Guadalajara. The North would then fall, and the war would be reduced to a siege of Barcelona, 'in a matter of weeks'.[21] On 7 August, Italy sent 27 Fiat fighter planes, 5 Fiat-Ansaldo light tanks, 40 machine guns and 12 cannons to Spain, along with 3 hydroplanes and 6 fighter planes to Mallorca on 13 and 19 August, respectively. In the same period, Germany sent 46 machines. Roatta would take Málaga and Valencia, Orgaz would take Jarama and Madrid, Roatta again in the Sierra and Guadalajara, then from San Sebastian to Barcelona. In no time, there would be 'general peace and game over', as if it were a table game. But the game would drag on for many more months.

No turning back

Franco's requests for support and weapons from Italy continued and increased, especially after Wilhem Canaris and Mario Roatta, who were responsible for the intelligence services of the Reich and Italy, completed the transactions for sending their military missions to Spain. Roatta himself would direct the *Missione Militare Italiana in Spagna* (MMIS, Italian Military Mission in Spain). Fascist intervention in the Spanish Civil War began with the sending of weapons. The arrival of foreign help – the transport of more than 15,000 men from Africa to the Peninsula in a space of ten days – enabled the rebels to initiate two campaigns that considerably improved their situation. However, getting beyond Guadarrama to take Madrid would require more help. It might also, as De Rossi said to Ciano, put the autonomy of the rebel command and possibly even territorial integrity in question. In the agreements of August 1936, Roatta and Canaris clearly stipulated that Franco was obliged to accept the military counsel of them both, since he was receiving substantial military aid from both countries. Ciano valued the materiel at 55,000,000 lire, for which repayment had not been requested, in addition to the 12 pilots who had been lost in what he saw as a 'conflict [...] of direct concern to anti-communist states'.[22] The game was being played out on multiple chessboards, and ended with the massive and practically unreserved entry of Fascist Italy in the war. One of the chessboards was evidently the League of Nations, which had just lifted sanctions on Italy for its invasion of Ethiopia. Its Non-Intervention Committee served as a screen for double diplomacy, half-truths and the construction of a narrative in which Fascist Italy was not participating in any Spanish war.

All this multiplied the relevance of the Balearic Islands exponentially. Control of Mallorca was especially fundamental, and here is where we find a key to understanding Mussolini's decision to enter the war: he sought control of maritime traffic in the western Mediterranean. Leaving Arconovaldo Bonaccorsi and the summer missions of fascistization aside, the islands were so strategically important, and weighed so heavily in official opinion, that Mussolini was obliged to state in the *Daily Mail*, as early as 9 September 1936, that he had no intention of trying to take them. A stable Italian force was soon present in Mallorca to prevent the islands from falling into Republican hands and being used by the government as a bargaining chip to secure French support. From the establishment of the first air base on the island in August 1936, and especially from December of the same year, when the *Aviazione Legionaria* became nominally dependent on the MMIS, Italian fighter and bomber aviation was fundamental to wartime control of the Spanish skies. In 1936, it was crucial in controlling the Straits of Gibraltar and in the subsequent bombing of Cartagena, Alicante and Almería. Seeking to control the ports of Barcelona and Valencia, with the coast and inland from France to the Cape of San Antonio as the objective, flights from the Balearic Islands served to experiment with new military techniques.

In Spain, the *Aviazione Legionaria* discovered the tremendously useful damage that could be inflicted by bombing in port waters, even if they could not reach the ships.[23] The Civil War hosted an intense experimentation campaign for aviation warfare tactics – the most Fascist of weapons. Italian naval control was fundamental too. Achieved in summer, in anticipation of a massive sending of troops, on 10 August, ten Italian submarines were already deployed in the Mediterranean.[24] Two days later, Italian planes bombed and sank a Danish cargo ship off Barcelona; the next day they destroyed a Spanish cargo ship, the *Conde de Albasola*.[25] In November, with air assistance, the Italian submarine *Torricelli* incapacitated the light cruiser *Miguel de Cervantes*, which was anchored in the port of Cartagena, placing it out of commission until 1938. Submarine warfare played a key role in the beginning of hostilities. In acts of flagrant piracy, Italian forces supporting the rebellion attacked the French ship *Parame*, the Panamanian oil tanker *MacKnight*, the Russian ships *Timiryasev* and *Blagoiev* and the British ship *Havock*, preventing them from providing any help to the legitimate government. Thus, Italian participation proved decisive in everything related to maritime warfare. In his own words, the military envoy Ferretti, who commanded the *Missione Navale Italiana* (MNI, Italian Naval Mission) between 3 October 1936 and 22 November 1938, had been given orders to place the sea at the disposition of the insurgents, in a delicate balancing act between the need to not compromise official Italian neutrality while effectively supporting the *Motoscafo Armato Silurante* (MAS, Torpedo Armed Motorboats) and Italian Legion submarines (Onice, Iride, Ferraris, Galileo), which completed at least thirteen war operations along the 'Red' coast.

The international situation limited and indefinitely postponed a large-scale action to sink enemy ships in Mediterranean waters through a combined attack from the air and from Italian submarines. It had been planned and approved; Ciano supported it with 'enthusiasm and decision'. The problem was not lack of enthusiasm, but lack of opportunity. However, no one could accuse Mussolini of a lack of commitment. In late September, fifteen tanks and thirty-eight 65 mm anti-aircraft guns arrived in Spain, along with radio and telegraph equipment and a group of one-hundred sixty volunteer instructors, who were incorporated directly into the Spanish regiment that was engaged in combat around Navalcarnero.[26] This completed the first phase of aid in the form of armament and initiated the next phase of tactical and combat intervention. To prepare for it, Roatta boarded the *Leone Pancaldo* for Spain on 1 September, accompanied by Emilio Faldella, Carlo Sirombo and the Germans Walter Warlimont and Lucan, who entered Spain with Italian passports. Their objective was to meet Franco and present their credentials, which they did on 6 September. Following military help, acknowledgement of the Franco regime originated in the meeting between Ciano and Von Neurath on 21–22 October, from which a nine-point bilateral pact emerged. They formalized the strengthening of relations between the two powers, mutual support in the League of Nations (especially if Italy abandoned it), recognition of communism as the great threat to European peace and security, and above all for our interests, *de facto* recognition in anticipation of *de jure* recognition of the Spanish national government, confirmation of the principle of non-intervention and respect for Spanish territorial sovereignty and integrity. They laid the diplomatic foundations for future military escalation.

That came soon. The idea that they were already planning their intervention, and would implement it between November 1936 and early 1937, is in fact the most coherent perspective with respect to how the Spanish conflict developed into a civil war. It is no coincidence that many of the November initiatives were designed with a long war in mind. Harsh and heavy Fascist military escalation began in that month, as Italy and the Third Reich officially recognized the Franco government in Burgos. On 22 November, Mussolini reminded Roatta to indicate to Franco that this measure obligated him to continue operations with maximum energy. In Mussolini's own words, it was absolutely inadmissible that, in being too confident of Italian and German material and moral solidarity, '*codesta gente si metta sull'imbraca*': that 'these people rest on their laurels' and evade their obligations and responsibilities. Though Il Duce only said it to his right-hand man in Spain, not in public, the admonition was clearly aggressive. Behind it were both the offer of mass entry into the war that had been presented in the favourable context of September and the reiteration of the help that had been offered, under the same precepts (sending volunteers under the Italian flag and Fascist control) but in an extremely more complex moment: the onset of a long civil war.

This was when the insurgent army was closest to taking the capital, as all the reports from Italy to Spain conclusively indicated. The Madrid offensive planned by Mola and approved by Franco would, as in Toledo, facilitate rapid entry into the capital from the west; it even included Falangist details regarding which radio stations and newspapers would be immediately occupied in Madrid.[27] Not everyone was equally optimistic, however. Roatta was very critical of the military capabilities of the rebel troops, and expressed his doubts regarding the general military situation in a report. He judged that poor organization, scarce armament and lack of coordination above the battalion level impeded organic use beyond these units. His opinion of the rebel command was even worse, except for Franco. It extended to the Africanists in general, and Varela especially, who gave orders like an old Napoleonic general from his command centre (in Leganés, of all places), surrounded by filth, sherry bottles and coffee, with a single telephone line to connect him to the world. The insurgents had scarce means (the best of which had been supplied by the Italians and Germans, but were not always used correctly) and were cruel in combat; mass shooting of prisoners caught alive became their wartime standard. Roatta had enormous doubts about the capacity of the 'revolutionaries' to finish what they had started and recommended doubling efforts to support them.[28]

The idea was that the war would be brief, lasting to the end of the month at most. However, this was not the impression of Ettore Muti: 'our flights create more destruction in Madrid every day. But for weeks now, nothing is happening on the ground'. At that pace, he calculated 'sometime in the first half of the twenty-first century, we will have taken Madrid'.[29] Even that, in his opinion, would not imply the end of the war, or the Republic. The Italian command itself acknowledged that the reorganized and reinforced Republican Army, with its greater capacity for resistance, combined with the fact that the insurgents were trained in slow combat (which was diametrically opposed to Fascist tactics), made it impossible to even remotely foresee an immediate victory with the occupation of Madrid. According to Roatta, the Spanish military considered it their destination, as though the enemy would simply dissolve. He thought that with luck on their side, it would be an intermediate step in a long war.[30] At this point, the tactical and strategic differences became evident between Spanish and Italian generals: the latter advocated the very Fascist idea of *guerra celere*, a swift, motorized war accompanied by the equally Fascist weapon of aviation. These differences would fill Italian military reports for the next two-and-a-half years.

In fact, the plan to take Madrid quickly was soon frustrated. The coup d'état and the column war derived from it ended immediately and the long, exhausting war to totally destroy the enemy began. In this context, Mussolini made his own decisions. Instead of withdrawing from the 'quicksand' situation, he recognized the Franco government on 8 November, and sent a chargé d'affaires to Spain as head of the Italian diplomatic mission. The Hispano–Italian Secret Protocol was signed, based on solidarity in the fight against communism, the development of reciprocal relationships, and Italian support to preserve the integrity and assist the re-establishment of the political and social order. The *de facto* reality of the preceding months became official. According to Antonio Magaz, the unofficial envoy who soon became the insurgent government's official delegate in Rome, this had not happened earlier, when they were waiting for the Francoist troops to enter Madrid, because it would have been considered premature and might have 'exposed Italy's play in our favour'. However, in his opinion the 'advance of our troops, and perhaps Russia's brazen support of the Government of Madrid' had tipped the scales to favour the new situation.[31] Magaz, however, was mistaken: in the space of a month, Mussolini abandoned his public image of caution and limited risk in order to assume unconditional implication in the war. This authentic military escalation soon brought 10,000 men to the Peninsula, who crossed at night in civilian clothes and with false passports.

There was no going back: the birth of the Axis in October and the recognition of the government of Burgos in November were followed by the 6 December meeting in Palazzo Venezia where Mussolini, Roatta, Ciano, the under-secretaries of the military ministries and Canaris, the head of German intelligence, discussed how to increase support to Franco. The Spanish Office was created with officials from the *Milizia* and the three branches of the armed forces, under the control of Count Luca Pietromarchi; but it remained separate from the military ministries. From 6 to 18 November, Hitler sent 92 combat airplanes with more than 3,800 pilots and technicians to Spain. Soon after, the air division boasted 140 aircraft, with a support battalion of 48 tanks, 60 anti-aircraft cannons and 5,600 men. On 7 November, Mussolini gave Brigade General Roatta (who would be promoted to Division General after Málaga) command over 50,000 men in four divisions. Roatta asked that no non-career troops or officers be sent. From the outset, he had to demonstrate the absolute supremacy of Italy in the war and in Spain.[32] Small, urgent, timely shipments were no longer in order; this was the moment for 'a direct and intense intervention'.[33]

Conclusions

Preceded by the will to destroy the Republic, decided in July, and planned in September, the 'how' and the 'when' of the large-scale intervention in Spain materialized in October and November of 1936. Prior to that, involvement had been limited to the sending of untraceable materiel to Spain, along with a few specialists via Cádiz and Vigo in September, who were incorporated into Italian–Spanish units. Did Mussolini have to do this? Admiral Giovanni Ferretti, the first head of the Italian Naval Mission in Spain, explicitly acknowledged that the idea behind intervention in the Spanish Mediterranean was above all to lay the material, spiritual and informational groundwork for the future maritime military influence of Italy in Spain, based on fascist 'supremacy'.[34] Between supremacist allegories of a united Mediterranean bloc held in the iron tongs of two 'brother' nations on the same path to glory, balance, peace and common civilization, Francesco Belforte insisted time and again how the affinity among Italian Fascism, the 'national' Spain and German national socialism should 'logically' lead to a common political platform involving 'healthy autarky'.[35]

Its grand objective would be to aggressively defend its common interests in a manner coherent with military collaboration in matters of arms and the proud shedding of blood.

In any case, I am inclined to think that Mussolini appropriated the Spanish conflict for himself: first in the coup d'état against the Republic and then in full-scale open war. Though Italy had been an implicit power in July–August of 1936, it did not fully engage until October–November of that year. Il Duce saw no contradiction – and in fact there was none – between the 'gentlemen's agreement' with the British government regarding the western Mediterranean in November 1936 and entry in the war. As a result of the Italian–German agreements of 6 December, Mussolini transferred command of all Italian troops to Roatta, and asked him to meet with Faupel and Franco to organize the Chiefs of Staff as agreed and to inform of the creation of the Spanish Office in the Ministry of Foreign Affairs. Troop transport to Spanish soil began immediately. Many of these first volunteers were ex-combatants from Abyssinia and had enlisted with the MVSN, which received 'constant petitions from volunteers seeking the 300 lire recruitment bonus and 20 lire per day in pay'.[36] Troops were sent in November to innervate and fill national formations, while a contingent of 1,500 prepared men awaited transfer in Italy.[37] They left from an enclosed pier in Gaeta, far from curious eyes, though they spent the hours required for boarding shouting '*viva!*' to Il Duce. They set off in 'absolute secrecy', unarmed throughout the entire voyage aboard the *Lombardia*. They flew no flag on that risky journey, and the first contingent disembarked in Cádiz on 22 December. All of this, together with other actions such as Major De Blasio's activation of a counter-espionage plan, corresponded to much more than simple support for a natural ally. It was the intervention of a third warring party. More than help for a friendly nation, it identifies and implicates Fascism as a front-line contender.

Now, Italy was not *officially* at war with Spain. But the war it entered *de facto* generated income, entailed rights and created orphans, widows, medals for valour, and sentences for treason or self-mutilation. In 1936, there was no apparatus in place to address such issues. The opening of the Spanish Office in December, so that Ciano and his Ministry could coordinate everything relevant to intervention in Spain, was a first step in that direction. It ratified centralized control of all Spanish affairs, to the point of making the military dependent on diplomatic and political spheres in 1936. Thus, on 15 December, the MMIS was declared operative, with headquarters in Seville. On 22 December, the first contingent of 3,000 soldiers disembarked from the *Lombardia* in Cádiz, and on 15 January 1937, the second contingent arrived, for a total of 10,000 soldiers within one month. Among Mussolini's papers, we find he insisted on underscoring the voluntary nature of the support offered, both in the specific sphere of the fascist *Milizia* and in the military, emphasizing that the troops and officials destined for Spain would be selected from among those who volunteered.[38] A lottery system was developed to fill compulsory service quotas for each regiment, under penalty of arrest and trial for lack of discipline.[39]

1936 was hardly a year for Italy to harbour more doubts than assurances with respect to participating in an open war. The total Italian aeronautical contribution that year involved bringing down 105 aircraft, executing 150 bombing runs and dropping 170,000 kg of explosives. At sea, they provided general support and submarine action. On land, they directly intervened in the actions of Navalcarnero on 23 October, the occupation of Esquinas and Seseña on 24–25 October and the action on Torrejón.[40] All of this generated important expenditures: approximately 110,000,000 lire in aeronautics, 16,575,460 in naval activity, 42,000,000 in combat and 85,961 in 'foreign expenditures'. Altogether, it amounted to 168,661,421 lire, a fraction of which (5,533,407 lire) would have been covered by the aforementioned gold deposited in the Foreign Ministry account of the *Banca de Italia*, along with deposits of francs and sterling equivalent to 5,750,115 lire in the SIAT account of the *Banca Commerciale* on 20 August, for a total of 11,283,522 lire. Thanks to that, Franco could obtain arms and buy them on credit, without putting up any security.

In sum, the intervention in Spain was much more multi-faceted, then, and had much more content than has usually been attributed to it by Spanish historiography (an unimportant aspect within the civil war) and by Italian (one more element in the analysis of Mussolini's foreign policy). And perhaps it is not an enigma, but its interpretation is undoubtedly far from being satisfactory. In my view, an intervention which involved so much military, economic and human effort, which spilt so much blood, which broke so many lives, could not simply be the result of the Duce's desire to control the western Mediterranean. It could not be merely defensive. And it cannot simply be detached from the political, ideological and identitarian nature which sustained Fascist power. Vital for the rebels' victory, the sending of troops and supplies as well as the open participation by Fascist armed forces in the conquest of territory, the bombing of military and civilian targets or the naval war indicate for good measure central elements of the civil war from the Spanish perspective and also the Italian. Fascist Italy became a *de facto* third belligerent party in an internal war. Moreover, the experience of war clearly marked a new chapter in the use of diplomacy and propaganda within the framework of Europe's fascistization and its expansion on the back of total war.[41] The Spanish experience was thus the war which most and best situated Italian Fascism's ambitions in Europe, in the Mediterranean, in Spain, or in relation to the foreign policies of its neighbouring countries, at least before World War II. But, above all, it already marked in a definitive way the inseparable relation between Fascism and war, between expansion, penetration and violence, obedience, combat and belief. 'We want a Franco victory', Ciano said: swift, conclusive, over Madrid.[42] They wanted guarantees that maximum effort would be exerted to ensure it. Almost 49,000 Italian military personnel in Spain at the end of the winter of 1937 legitimized their demand for it. However, he neither won the war when he could have in November, nor did he win it later with the massive transfer of troops and supplies to Franco's army. Embedded in this logic, we find the bellicose progression of Italian intervention in the Spanish Civil

War: a year that began with strength and success in Málaga and ended in exhaustion, literally sunk in the mud, the snow and the ice of Guadalajara.

Notes

1 This work is supported by the Spanish Ministerio de Ciencia, Innovación y Universidades by means of the Research Project Posguerras civiles: violencia y reconstrucción nacional en España y Europa, 1939–1949 (PGC2018-097724-B-I00). It builds on my book *La guerra fascista. Italia en la Guerra Civil española, 1936–1939* (Madrid: Alianza, 2016).
2 The most convenient way of knowing the Duce's thinking and movements is D. and E. Susmel (eds.), *Opera Omnia di Benito Mussolini*, 44 volumes (Florence and Rome: La Fenice, 1951–1963 and 1978–1981).
3 An excellent review of some of the big debates stirred up in the 1970s is D. Smyth, 'Duce Diplomatico', *The Historical Journal*, 21:4 (1978), pp. 981–1000. J. Coverdale, *La intervención en la Guerra Civil Española* (Madrid: Alianza, 1979), is the Spanish edition and the one that I use of 1975 *Italian Intervention in the Spanish Civil War* (Princeton, NJ: Princeton University Press). My work is strongly linked to M. Heiberg, *Emperadores del Mediterráneo. Franco, Mussolini y la guerra civil española* (Barcelona: Crítica, 2004). More for their reconstructions than for their interpretative aid, A. Rovighi and F. Stefani, *La partecipazione italiana alla guerra civile spagnola* (Rome: Ufficio Storico dello Stato Maggiore dell'Esercito, 1992). From Spain, I. Saz and J. Tusell (eds.), *Fascistas en España. La intervención italiana en la Guerra Civil a través de los telegramas de la 'Missione Militare Italiana in Spagna' (15 diciembre 1936–31 marzo 1937)* (Madrid: CSIC-Escuela Española de Historia y Arqueología en Roma, 1981); I. Saz, *Mussolini contra la Segunda República. Hostilidad, conspiraciones, intervención* (Valencia: Alfons el Magnànim, 1986); *Italia y la Guerra Civil española (Simposio celebrado en la Escuela Española de Historia y Arqueología de Roma)* (Madrid: CSIC, 1986); J.L. Alcofar Nassaes [José Luis Infiesta], *CTV. Los legionarios italianos en la Guerra Civil Española* (Barcelona: Dopesa, 1972); J.L. Alcofar Nassaes, *La aviación legionaria en la guerra española* (Barcelona: Euros, 1976); J.L. Alcofar Nassaes, *La marina italiana en la guerra de España* (Barcelona: Euros, 1975).
4 Ministero degli Affari Esteri, *I Documenti Diplomatici Italiani (DDI)*, Serie 8, vol. IV, 16 July 1936, p. 607.
5 Heiberg, *Emperadores*, p. 51.
6 Archivio Storico Ministero Affari Esteri (ASMAE), MinCulPop, b. 230.
7 Saz, *Mussolini*, p. 212.
8 The same conlusion in M. Heiberg and M. Ros Agudo, *La trama oculta de la Guerra Civil. Los servicios secretos de Franco 1936–1945* (Barcelona: Crítica, 2006), p. 34.
9 ASMAE, Gabinetto, b. 785, s. n.
10 Archivio Centrale dello Stato (ACS), Ministero dell'Interno, PolPol, Segreteria Particolare del Duce, Carteggio Riservato, f5.
11 P. Preston, *Franco 'Caudillo de España'* (Barcelona: Grijalbo, 1994), p. 201.
12 Ministero, *DDI*, p. 652.
13 ASMAE, Gabinetto, b. 796.
14 Ministero, *DDI*, pp. 690–691.
15 ASMAE, Gabinetto, b. 796.
16 ASMAE, Gabinetto, b. 795.
17 P. Preston, 'La aventura española de Mussolini. Del riesgo limitado a la guerra abierta', in P. Preston (ed.), *La República asediada. Hostilidad internacional y conflictos internos durante la Guerra Civil* (Barcelona: Península, 1999), p. 43.

18 P. Pastorelli, 'La politica estera fascista dalla fine del conflitto etiopico alla seconda guerra mondiale', in R. de Felice (ed.), *L'Italia fra tedeschi e alleati. La politica estera fascista e la seconda guerra mondiale* (Bologna: Il Mulino, 1973).

19 ASMAE, UC, b. 46. R. de Felice, *Mussolini il duce. II. Lo Stato totalitario (1936–1940)* (Turin: Einaudi, 1996 [1981]), p. 359.

20 Coverdale, *La intervención*, pp. 21–2; Saz, *Mussolini*, pp. 184–6; S. Attanasio, *Gli italiani e la guerra di Spagna* (Milan: Mursia, 1974), p. 42.

21 R. Cantalupo, *Fu la Spagna. Ambasciata presso Franco. Febbraio-Aprile 1937* (Milan: Mondadori, 1948), p. 63.

22 Ufficio Storico dello Stato Maggiore dell'Esercito (USSME), F6, b. 327.

23 ASMAE, Ufficio Spagna, b. 23.

24 J.M. Campo Rizo, 'El Mediterráneo, campo de batalla de la Guerra Civil española: la intervención naval italiana. Una primera aproximación documental', *Cuadernos de Historia Contemporánea*, 19 (1997), pp. 55–87; Alcofar, *La marina*.

25 F. Olaya, *La intervención extranjera en la guerra civil* (Madre: Tierra, 1990).

26 E. Faldella, *Venti mesi di guerra in Spagna (luglio 1936-febbraio 1938)* (Florence: Le Monnier, 1939), p. 122.

27 Preston, *Franco*, p. 257.

28 USSME, f. 18, b. 5.

29 ASMAE, Gabinetto, f. 792.

30 USSME, f. 6, b. 327.

31 Archivo del Ministerio de Asuntos Exteriores (AMAE), Archivo de Burgos, Legajo 1459, Carpeta 3.

32 USSME, f. 18, b. 9.

33 Ibid.

34 USSME, f. 6, b. 280.

35 F. Belforte, *La guerra civile in Spagna* (Milan: ISPI, 1938), vol. IV, p. 237.

36 Attanasio, *Gli italiani*, pp. 167–8.

37 USSME, f. 18, b. 9.

38 USSME, f. 9, b. 1.

39 AMAE, Archivo Burgos, Caja RE101, C27.

40 ASMAE, Ufficio Spagna, b. 1.

41 For the concept of fascistization and its application, F. Gallego, *El evangelio fascista. La formación de la cultura política del franquismo (1930–1950)* (Barcelona: Crítica, 2014). From a general point of view but paying little attention to the opportunities to understand the Spanish case, A. Kallis, '"Fascism", "Para-Fascism" and "Fascistization": On the Similarities of Three Conceptual Categories', *European History Quarterly*, 33:2 (2003), pp. 219–49.

42 ASMAE, Ufficio Spagna, b. 1207.

6 The conquest of Albania

The real beginning of World War II in Italy

Valentina Villa

Introduction: Fascist Italy's approach to Albania

Italian expansionism in Albania has gone largely unmentioned in national, and European, historiography, due to a range of factors: its temporal proximity to the official beginning of World War II, whose tragic nature obscured the events that preceded it; the large number of idiosyncrasies surrounding the final attack and its aftermath; probably a desire to avoid what represents an inglorious chapter in Italy's past.[1] Mostly, Albania is remembered as the bridgehead for the invasion of Greece more than one year later and not as a political and military enterprise on its own.[2] However, retracing the tumultuous events of April 1939 and trying to understand the reasons that prevailed in the unfortunate decision to invade the so-called 'Land of the Eagles' is not a waste of time – first, because the Albanian conquest represented for the Kingdom of Italy the true start of the military conflict that ended in 1945, and second, because it helps us to understand the European situation before the war (the conquest took place just five months before Hitler invaded Poland, which marked the official start of the conflict), enables us to analyse the clashes between the King and his Head of Government regarding military decisions and provides critical information on the state of the Italian Army in 1939.

Italy's relationship with the Balkan region dates back to the early nineteenth century and, according to the plans of Italian Prime Minister Francesco Crispi, was to be strengthened in 1896 by the marriage of Crown Prince Vittorio Emanuele to the King of Montenegro's daughter, Elena. However, for Vittorio Emanuele III, who was crowned King in 1900 after the assassination of his father Umberto I, his happy marriage was more of a family affair and he was never particularly interested in seizing opportunities to expand in the region.[3] Therefore, the Italian presence in Albania was initially limited and unregulated. During World War I, under the secret Treaty of London, Italy briefly occupied part of the southern half of Albania, along with France, Greece and Serbia, which took the rest of the country. After the conflict, Albania only avoided formal loss of sovereignty with support from the United States, yet by that point the unstable country, exhausted by war and foreign occupation, was already in need of foreign capital and protection.

Unfortunately in the mid-1920s, after the refusal of the League of Nations, the only European state willing (and able) to lend money to Albania was Fascist Italy, though by no means was it an act of charity.[4] Mussolini had always been obsessed with the notion of expansionism, drawing inspiration for his colonial plans from a supposed and dubious link between his government and the Roman Empire, and he was constantly in search of opportunities. Political instability and easy access to Albania – Vlorë's harbour is only 40 miles away from the coast of Otranto, in Apulia – made the country a perfect target for his imperial ambitions.

Moreover, on the other side of the Mediterranean, the Fascist regime found in Ahmet Bej Zogu an eager and corruptible partner. Zogu, a former landowner, was Prime Minister of Albania from 1922 to 1924, President of the Albanian Republic from 1925 to 1928, and then crowned himself monarch as Zog I, King of the Albanians, echoing the myth of the Albanian national hero George Skanderbeg.[5] Italy was the only country to officially recognize the self-proclaimed monarchy, and Zog gladly accepted Italian interference in Albanian political and economic affairs (and the resulting limitations on sovereignty) because he desperately needed money to maintain his power against his many tribal rivals. He allowed Italy great concessions, such as exploiting Albanian mineral and natural resources and imposing preferential tariffs for Italian goods. In addition, he committed to signing two friendship treaties in 1926 and 1927, which some considered the beginning of a 'protectorat deguisé'.[6] Italian infiltration in Albanian economy in the 1920s was slow but significant. Italian capital was essential in establishing the National Bank in 1925; the following year, the two countries founded the Society for the Economic Development of Albania, an Italian agency for managing and directing Fascist loans; and in 1930, Italy had already become Albania's principal trading partner.

However, it is important to note that, despite the large flow of capital from Italy to Albania, the situation of the country did not improve at all. In fact, loans were mainly used for the construction of roads and infrastructure – both very useful for mobilising the Italian army, less so for the daily lives of the poorest people in Europe – and some were used for bribes and payoffs to keep construction from being stopped. Moreover, from the Italian point of view, Albania proved to be a bottomless pit with absolutely no economic return for its Fascist lender. From this perspective, the subsequent territorial occupation seemed like a form of compensation for years of financial losses.[7]

This deep involvement in Albanian affairs was not limited to the country's economy. At King Zog's approval, Italian advisors were appointed in many government departments and the weight of Italian influence was particularly heavy in the education and the army. Indeed, the military instructors sent to Albania with the official task of training Albanian soldiers and supplying modern equipment also canvassed extensively, and by the end of the 1930s the sympathies of most of the Albanian army were with the Italians.[8] Studying the Italian language, which Mussolini vainly tried to require by law, was widely encouraged, especially among the youngest, and Albania's national identity suffered from this rough attempt at Italianization.

Meanwhile in Italy, the government launched a campaign to promote resettlement in Albania.[9] Entire families from the poorest regions of Italy received money to relocate to the other side of the Adriatic Sea. This policy, which was used also in the African colonies of Libya, Eritrea, Somalia and Ethiopia, had the double advantage of relieving poverty in Italy and more deeply penetrating the colonies. Even in the 1930s, it was predicted that 'the history of the two nations will soon merge [as] Albania must become the safe bridge for the expansion of Italian activity in the near East'.[10] In the end, the independence of the Land of the Eagles was so jeopardized that when Italian troops landed on the Albanian coast in 1939, the country was already a colony in all but name.

The appointment of Count Galeazzo Ciano as Minister of Foreign Affairs in 1936 caused a dramatic shift in relations between Italy and Albania, eventually becoming one of the most decisive factors in determining the country's fate. Indeed, Mussolini's son-in-law made Albania his personal hunting ground, where he could satisfy his aspirations and his desire for expansion, and he was pivotal in triggering the military attack against it.[11] Ciano devoted himself to cultivating his self-interested friendship with Ahmet Zogu, mostly by depositing money in his personal bank account in hopes of taking full possession of the government. One of the many prospects the Italian Foreign Minister dangled in front of Zog was marrying one of King Vittorio Emanuele's daughters, which would form a permanent link between the oldest Royal House in Europe and the small fictitious monarchy of Albania. The Italian king, appalled by the scenario, rejected the Count's idea.[12] Zog – who would soon need a wife to have an heir to his newly created dynasty and secure a line of descent – resentfully settled for a Hungarian countess; yet, he did not forget that humiliating event, and started to suspect Ciano's loyalty.

The frantic arrangements for a military action

Zog's fears were in fact justified, because during 1938 the possibility of military attack started to appear on the horizon. In a diary entry on the day of Zog's wedding, Ciano, who was the best man and most prominent political figure among the guests at the ceremony, wrote of a 'complete solution' for the Albanian question.[13] That same evening he also composed a memo for Mussolini in which he discussed three possible options for taking over Albania. The first option was to tighten their economic bonds (but the impatient Foreign Minister stated that he found this strategy too slow); the second explored the idea of a partition of Albania between Italy and Yugoslavia (but the fall of the Yugoslavian government of Ciano's ally, Stojadinovic, soon afterwards made the plan unfeasible); and the third alternative, clearly the choice of Mussolini's son-in-law, was direct annexation of the country. In order to gain the head of government's support, Ciano also attached a report detailing Albania's strategic value and how they would benefit from the invasion. However, the economic figures presented to Mussolini were dubious and inaccurate. The majority of the profits were said to derive from some alleged oil reserves, but during the many years of Italian presence in the country no serious geological studies were ever conducted.[14] Also, the hypothetical project of attaining complete economic autarky – one of Mussolini's greatest claims during the Great Depression of the 1930s – by combining the import of raw materials from Albania with the export of manufactured goods from Italy was a failure because the Albanian market was practically non-existent. Moreover, the foreign minister suggested that up to two million Italians could relocate to Albania, even though the Albanian population already amounted to more than a million people in a mountainous and rugged region nearly as big as Sicily. In the end, despite the fact that the project had no real utility for Italian prosperity, Albania was described as a worthwhile object for the glorious expansion of the Fascist Empire.

The overconfident count wrote in his diary that 'there is no longer an independent Albania',[15] and was even ready to lead an immediate attack. However, he had not considered opposition from Mussolini. Indeed, the Duce, never a decision-maker, kept delaying the attack because he was assailed with doubts and worried about the international community's reaction and possible complaints in the event of a military action, especially from the United Kingdom. The idea of expanding eastwards, in any case, was rather appealing to him, especially because the Italian conquests in Africa had already proved to be hard to maintain, very expensive and quite unsuccessful. The Albanian endeavour could finally give the dictator the possibility of conquering a country in Europe and at the same time supporting the Italian economy.

The main argument that eventually took root in Mussolini's mind and persuaded him to endorse the project was the Nazi invasion of Czechoslovakia. After annexing Austria in 1938, Hitler managed to invade Prague in March 1939 and proclaim the region a German protectorate, all without informing his lesser ally. It was now obvious that the alliance between the Duce and the Fuhrer was no longer one between equals; Mussolini needed a quick conquest somewhere in order to counterbalance relentless German expansion, and he needed it as soon as possible.

However, as with many other important political issues (for instance, macroscopically, their alliance with Hitler), Vittorio Emanuele III and the Duce did not agree on the advisability of the intervention. The king, sceptical about permanently occupying Albania with a military operation, kept repeating that a war in order to 'seize a few rocks'[16] was not a sensible decision, whereas Mussolini's desire to oppose the monarch after many years of silent tensions played a great role in his determination to move forward with the plan. Indeed, Mussolini's anger and frustration about Vittorio Emanuele's indecisiveness became so great that he declared to have returned to his original, lingering republicanism, angrily remarking to Ciano that 'if Hitler had to deal with an idiot of a king, he would never have been able to take Austria and Czechoslovakia'.[17] The fact that after twenty years of authoritarian command Mussolini still lacked the power to order an invasion and actually open fire against a foreign country alone without the king's consent created enormous bitterness in the Prime Minister and made him fully convinced of the necessity to obtain supreme command of the army, which he did after the beginning of World War II.

Nonetheless, even though it looked like Mussolini forced the situation and ordered the attack against the king's will, his solution to the crisis was not only the result of a Fascist misuse of power, but of the monarch's silent neutrality. Indeed, Vittorio Emanuele, who had not changed his mind about the attack, left Rome for his country house in the days before the vote on the military operation. He was perfectly aware that his absence from the capital would give Mussolini absolute latitude, and therefore he essentially authorized the invasion without making himself vulnerable. In a certain sense, very conveniently, he turned a blind eye. This outside-the-box solution was symptomatic of the strange relationship between the two members of the diarchy. It closely recalls Vittorio Emanuele's behaviour on the day before the March on Rome in 1922 when he refused to sign the military order for Rome's state of siege presented by Prime Minister Luigi Facta, thus giving Mussolini the green light to take the government.[18]

Therefore, after the king's tacit consent, the military invasion was hastily set for the spring of 1939. The Fascist propaganda machine immediately went to work, emphasizing the strategic importance of Albania's location in the Balkans and the history of Rome's great Mediterranean power: on the radio and in the newspapers, Albania was continuously referred to as 'la quinta sponda' [the fifth shore].[19] It was fairly clear then that the ambiguous policy of recent years was coming to an end and a drastic change in Italy's relations with Albania was forthcoming.

In order to avoid other leaks about their plans, Count Ciano decided to attack in the first week of April. In addition, Zog's wife, Countess Geraldine, was pregnant with his heir and Ciano, well informed about the queen's pregnancy, thought that the imminent birth would prevent Zog from reacting to the invasion forcefully. Under the pretence of signing a new international treaty, the Fascist government sent a proposal that was actually an ultimatum, demanding the full Italian takeover and colonization of Albania.[20] The conditions were unacceptable; Albania would have voluntarily become an Italian protectorate in exchange for money, and King Zog, despite the vulnerability of his power, rejected the agreement twice.

Meanwhile, similarly to what had happened with Austria and Czechoslovakia, the international community remained more or less silent and preparations for the attack were undertaken amid the general indifference of other European countries towards Albania's fate. This was partly due to Italian diplomacy lying to hide the truth from the foreign offices (as late as the end of March, the British ambassador, Sir Andrew Ryan, was told that Italy would respect Albanian independence),[21] and partly due to many politicians still underestimating the aggressiveness of the Fascist power, and, lastly, because some governments nonetheless considered Albania expendable for the sake of overall peace. Great Britain, for instance, was one of them: on 6 April 1939, the day of the assault, when Chamberlain was asked in the House of Commons whether Great Britain had any interest in Albania, he closed the matter bluntly by replying: 'no direct interest, but a general interest in the peace of the world'.[22] Indeed, without realising the inevitable links between the two scenarios, Chamberlain was more interested in avoiding Italian expansion in Greece than challenging the invasion of Albania, and Mussolini's promise to withdraw Italian troops from the Spanish Civil War was enough to appease him. Mussolini reciprocated by sending the British Prime Minister a message in which he confidently assured him that 'the resolution of the Italo-Albanian question will take place in such a form as not to provoke a crisis in Anglo-Italian relations or the international situation in general'.[23]

The attack, its aftermath and its significance

The Oltremare Tirana (Overseas Tirana) Operation started at 6:30 p.m. on 6 April 1939, and ended a few hours later, on the morning of the 7th, Good Friday, when after a series of minor fighting and a clear demonstration of inadequacy, the Italian troops entered the capital virtually without firing a shot. Even though the military relevance of the entire operation was minimal, the attack was indicative of the state of the Army and should have been taken into consideration by Mussolini. In fact, the Fascist army showed the substantial faults that would contribute to its defeat during World War II: a lack of training, the complete absence of coordination among the units, unbelievable inaccuracy in knowledge of the territory and wrong or unusable equipment supplies. Such episodes were almost innumerable: there were, for example, bicycles that quickly got stuck in the muddy Albanian streets and motorbikes shipped with diesel instead of petrol; there were telegraphists who did not know how to use a telegraph and soldiers who could not drive a motorcycle in formation and got into numerous accidents (thus wrecking the vehicles or leaving them with expensive damage).[24] One episode, in particular, was symptomatic of the state of the army and should have been taken into consideration: during the landing at San Giovanni di Medua [Shëngjin] some of 'the Bersaglieri [light infantry corps] shuddered at the thought of putting their feet in the water' as they had never seen the sea in their lives before crossing the Adriatic. Therefore, it was necessary to build extemporary landing platforms, all the while wasting precious time in case of an attack.[25]

The only reason that explains Italian victory was the weakness of the military response from the Albanian army. Indeed, contrary to the fake reports appeared on some European newspapers,[26] there was virtually no fighting – no large-scale resistance materialized and only small groups of patriots, especially in the city of Durres, briefly tried to defend their harbours. After the invasion, King Zog tried to broadcast a message to the nation declaring that he would resist the invasion, but in a country where radios were virtually unknown, the call went largely ignored and Zog, with his wife and their two-day-old son Leka, was forced to flee, leaving the country and seeking refuge in Greece. When this odd invasion was over, the government, through the words of a satisfied Count Ciano, used a recurrent theme in totalitarian warfare and colonial expansionism, stating that the Italian act was nothing but a response to the calling of the Albanian people, allegedly vexed by the wrongdoing of their former friend Zog: 'Zog's tyrannical and wasteful government and the insidious attitude he took towards

Italy brought about the revolution of the Albanian people and the Italian inter-vention. [...] Repeated messages were sent to the Italian government requesting help to break free from Zog's oppression'.[27]

The conquest concealed as a rescue was definitively completed a few days later. On 12 April, a provisional national assembly formed by delegates from all the Albanian provinces voted to willingly offer the crown to Vittorio Emanuele; during the formal ceremony, which took place at Quirinal Palace in Rome, it was quite clear that neither the king nor the Albanian ministers believed in that farce.[28] Moreover, according to Ciano, still far from his July 1943 realization, most of the Albanians' resentment was caused by the king's timid attitude in contrast with Mussolini's martial strength.[29] The next day, though, the Grand Council of Fascism 'greeted the historic event with virile joy' and approved the law sealing the union of the two crowns, the Italian and the Albanian.[30] Ciano's discourse before the Camera dei Fasci e delle Corporazioni was a powerful example of vacuous Fascist rhetoric:

> *Camerati* [brothers in arms], in this historic event that brings the destiny of the Albanian people together with that of the Italian people, twenty-two centuries of fruitful and peaceful bonds find their propitious epilogue under the sign of the *Littorio* [Lictor].[31]

Mussolini's speech, on the contrary, was fairly clear; indeed, it unmistakably showed the dictator's dangerous intentions and should have been considered an alarm bell by other heads of state, who unfortunately were too used to his boastful talk to take necessary measures: 'We approach peoples who are friends with a friendly attitude; with hostile peoples we will have a clear, decisive, resolute hostile attitude. We ask the world to leave us in peace, intent on our great, everyday efforts. In any case, the world must know that we, tomorrow as yesterday, as always, will stand tall'.[32]

Conclusion: a smaller version of the World War?

On 22 April 1939, the former Italian ambassador in Albania, Francesco Jaco-moni di San Savino, was officially appointed as general lieutenant of the king, and on 2 June,[33] the Albanian Fascist Party was founded, making the Land of the Eagles a full part of the Italian state.[34] However, the annexation of Albania was such a juridical anomaly that an eminent Fascist professor of international law hastily justified Vittorio Emanuele's possession of the crown by maintaining that the Albanian crown did not disappear in 1939 with the illegitimate Italian invasion, but still existed after the attack, and therefore it was lawful for the Italian king to receive it.[35] The situation was even more absurd though, because the Albanian crown came from Zog's personal invention and not from a royal bloodline (a national assembly stated in 1928 that 'the illustrious crown of the historical Albanian throne is offered to the saviour of the nation under the title Zog I, King of the Albanians').[36] Professor Angelo Sereni, an Italian Jew who fled Italy after the passing of the racial laws, was of a different opinion: the Albania, he stated, 'that existed prior to April 1939, now remains only an empty shell. Albania, in fact, is only an annex of Italy'.[37] However, the Italian fiction 'of the separate existence of the two states' gave Italy a dangerous set of advantages: for example, Sereni argues, it could control two votes in an international union or keep Albania neutral in the event of a conflict in order to use its territories and resources without risk of an attack.[38] Pointing out these possibilities, the scholar underlined the problem of the occupation by the Axis powers of apparently independent states; indeed, from a legal point of view, the Albanian invasion was not much different from Hitler's annexation of Czechoslovakia, even though it received so much less attention from the international community.

The Albanian conquest was the last military operation before the official start of the conflict; also, it was the last victory of the Fascist regime, albeit an empty one. However, the attack already showcased all the characteristics of the Fascist war in embryonic form. Indeed, the specific nature of the invasion makes it a powerful example of Mussolini's confused foreign policy and his problems relating with the head of state; the Albanian question certainly provides meaningful insight into the dynamics of the diarchy, the anomalous institution that ruled Italy throughout the twenty-year dictatorship.[39]

The assault also provides us with a dramatic vision of Europe in the fateful months before World War II, when the continent was ruled by the British appeasement policy and the underestimation of the Italian potential for war. Actually, in the frantic months that led to the outbreak of the conflict, the invasion of Albania – along with the *Anschluss* the year before, the incorporation of the Sudetenland and the brutal occupation of Prague – was by all means the most evident sign of the impending tragedy and the real menace to peace posed not only by Hitler but also by his seemingly less frightening ally, Mussolini, a sign that the European Chancelleries purposely chose to ignore, with devastating consequences for the world.

Finally, the brief military assault sheds new light on the extraordinary lack of organization and means of the Italian Army in the lead up to 'the hour of irrevocable decisions'. For all these reasons, the Fascist venture in Albania still deserves more attention from scholars and could act as an interesting frame of reference for understanding the military politics of the regime. Indeed, the dynamics that surrounded the attack had a distinctive resemblance with those that brought Italy into World War II and the conquest marked the fire of the first shots in the Balkan powder keg.

Notes

1 Even though the Albanian question has not been considered extensively in Italy, some scholars have recently produced innovative analyses, suggesting renewed interest in the topic. See, for instance, P. Rago (ed.), *Una pace necessaria. I rapporti italiano-albanesi nella prima fase della Guerra fredda* (Rome and Bari: Laterza, 2017); P. Sakja, 'Così vicina, così lontana: visioni fasciste dello sviluppo dell'Albania negli anni Quaranta', *Nuovi annali della Scuola speciale per*

archivisti e bibliotecari, 30 (2016), pp. 169–89; A. Becherelli and A. Carteny (eds.), *L'Albania indipendente e le relazioni italo-albanesi (1912–2012): Atti del Convegno in occasione del centenario dell'indipendenza albanese* (Rome, 22 November 2012) (Rome: Nuova Cultura, 2013); G. Villari, 'Il sistema di occupazione fascista in Albania', in L. Brazzo and M. Sarfatti (eds.), *Gli ebrei in Albania sotto il fascismo: una storia da ricostruire* (Florence: Giuntina, 2010), pp. 93–124; and M. Borgogni, *Tra continuità e incertezza. Italia e Albania (1914– 1939). La strategia politico-militare dell'Italia in Albania fino all'Operazione 'Oltre Mare Tirana'* (Milan: Franco Angeli, 2007). For a general view on the Italian presence in the Balkans during the war, the reference book is the recent work of E. Aga Rossi and M.T. Rossi, *Una guerra a parte. I militari italiani nei Balcani 1940–1945* (Bologna: il Mulino, 2017). Last, researchers who want to approach the Albanian question cannot overlook this fundamental guide: S. Trani, *L'Unione fra l'Albania e l'Italia: censimento delle fonti (1939–1945) conservate negli archivi pubblici e privati di Roma* (Rome: Ministero per i beni e le attività culturali, Direzione generale per gli archivi, 2007).

2 According to Ciano, Mussolini started considering the Albanian conquest in order to attack Greece as early as one month after the invasion. He recorded in his Diary on 12 May 1939: 'The entire road-building programme has been directed towards the Greek border. And this is by order of the Duce, who is thinking more and more of attacking Greece at the first opportunity'; G. Ciano, *Diario. 1939–1943* (Milan: Rizzoli, 1946), p. 109.

3 The happy marriage between the two monarchs has been extensively described in G. Artieri, *Il tempo della regina. Appunti per una biografia di Vittorio Emanuele III* (Rome: Sestante, 1950).

4 B.J. Fischer, *Albania at War. 1939–1945* (West Lafayette, IN: Purdue University Press, 1999), p. 7.

5 For an in-depth examination of the controversial figure of Zog, see J. Tomes, *King Zog: Self-Made Monarch of Albania* (Sutton: Stroud, 2003).

6 A. Giannini (ed.), *I trattati di conciliazione e di regolamento giudiziario del Regno d'Italia* (Rome: A.R.E., 1928), p. 25.

7 An interesting analysis of the economic relationship between the two countries is included in A. Roselli, *Italy and Albania: Financial Relations in the Fascist Period* (London: Tauris, 2006).

8 P. Crociani, *Gli albanesi nelle Forze armate italiane. 1939–1943* (Rome: Ufficio Storico dell'Esercito, 2001).

9 'The country is close and promising for those who bring their enterprising spirit, untameable will and serious preparation. There is every kind of resource; the weather is not different from ours; security nowadays is guaranteed', declared one of the many Fascist propaganda publications. F. Tajani, *L'avvenire dell'Albania* (Milan: Hoepli, 1932), p. 11.

10 *Il nuovo Stato. Quindicinale fascista* (Rome, 1932), p. 8.

11 Most of the information regarding Ciano's endeavour is taken from his personal account of the events, the diaries written between 1939 and his death, and G. Ciano, *L'Europa verso la catastrofe. 184 colloqui con Mussolini, Hitler, Franco, Chamberlain, Sumner Welles, Rustu Aras, Stojadinovic, Goring, Zog, Francois-Poncet ecc. verbalizzati da Galeazzo Ciano. Con 40 documenti diplomatici inediti* (Milan: Mondadori, 1948).

12 'The House of Savoy is at the country's service, not at the latecomer's', comments the king with irritation'. R. Bracalini, *Il re 'vittorioso'. La vita, il regno e l'esilio di Vittorio Emanuele III* (Milan: Feltrinelli, 1980), p. 191.

13 Ciano, *Diario*, p. 33.

14 Fischer, *Albania at War*, p. 11.

15 Ciano, *Diario*, p. 79.

16 Ibid., p. 273.

17 Ibid., p. 274.

18 It is interesting to notice that, despite his personal hesitations about the invasion, Vittorio Emanuele did go to Albania; he spent in the country nine days (9–18 May 1941), but the visit was not very auspicious from the start, as a few minutes after landing in Tirana, the King avoided an assassination attempt. Moreover, it was the last time that he set foot outside Italy before going into exile. P. Puntoni, *Parla Vittorio Emanuele III* (Milan: Palazzi, 1958), p. 56.

19 P. Bondioli, *Albania – Quinta Sponda d'Italia* (Milan: Cetim, 1939). To support the link between the Fascist expansionism and the Roman tradition, Bondioli even recalls a prophecy written by Virgil in the poem *Aeneid* in which Rome and Buthrotum will become sister cities, pp. 10–11.

20 O. Pearson, *Albania and King Zog: Independence, Republic and Monarchy. 1908–1939* (London: Tauris, 2004), p. 429.

21 Fischer, *Albania at War*, p. 19.

22 The National Archives, Foreign Office, FO 371, *Albania*, file 23716.

23 A. Puto, *From the Annals of British Diplomacy: the anti-Albanian Plans of Great Britain during the Second World War according to Foreign Office Documents of 1939–1944* (Tirana: 8 Nëtori, 1981), p. 24.

24 An extract of the long and detailed report written by Badoglio is included in Borgogni, *Tra continuità e incertezza*, p. 375.

25 Ibid., p. 398.

26 According to Eichberg, European fake news about the fighting was based on misinformation provided by Zog's government during the invasion. See F. Eichberg, *Il fascio littorio e l'aquila di Skandeberg. Italia e Albania 1939–1945* (Rome: Apes, 1998), pp. 40–1.

27 G. Ambrosini, *L'Albania nella comunità imperiale di Roma* (Rome: Istituto nazionale di cultura fascista, 1940), p. 54.

28 Newsreel *Giornale Luce B1499* (19 April 1939) by Istituto Luce. Available from www.youtube.com/watch?v=cLFF_r6tV8l [Accessed on 18 September 2017].

29 Ciano, *Diario*, p. 463.

30 B. Mussolini, *Scritti e discorsi. Vol. 12* (Milan: Hoepli, 1939), p. 168.

31 *Bollettino Parlamentare*, 1939, vol. 13, p. 64.

32 Mussolini, *Scritti e discorsi*, p. 168.

33 Ironically, 2 June is the day on which, seven years later, the Italians would reject the monarchy and choose a republican form of state; even more ironically, moreover, by that time, the king was already in Egypt where Zog and his family were also living in exile.

34 To read his personal recollection of the events, see F. Jacomoni di San Savino, *La politica dell'Italia in Albania* (Bologna: Cappelli, 1965).

35 G. Cansacchi, 'La luogotenenza generale per l'Albania', *Jus. Rivista di Scienze Giuridiche*, II:2 (1941), pp. 1–55.

36 B.J. Fischer, *King Zog and the Struggle for Stability in Albania* (Boulder, MA: East European Monographs, 1984), p. 141.

37 A.P. Sereni, 'The Legal Status of Albania', *The American Political Science Review*, 35:2 (1941), pp. 311–17, p. 316.

38 Ibid., p. 317.

39 On this theme, see D. Fisichella, *Dittatura e monarchia. L'Italia tra le due guerre* (Rome: Carocci, 2014), and P. Colombo, *La monarchia fascista 1922–1940* (Bologna: Il Mulino, 2010).

7 'The despicable fighting qualities of the Wops'

The East African campaign and the British Commonwealth's victory over Fascist Italy

Andrew Stewart

Introduction

A lack of balance has shaped popular assessments of how the Italian military fought during World War II.[1] A narrative was established during the wartime years of poor performance and this quickly became fixed once the conflict had ended. The British wartime leader Winston Churchill was one of the voices reinforcing such sentiments. In his 'unofficial' post-conflict history, he adopted an often-sympathetic voice towards his counterpart Benito Mussolini and his inter-war achievements in preventing a Communist takeover of the country. It was only when war came that he had chosen the wrong side and 'marched to ruin'.[2] A result of what his close aide General Hastings 'Pug' Ismay later described as Churchill's 'contempt of the fighting qualities of the Italian Army', there was, however, scant positive reference to his opponent's military forces and the role they played.[3] This, for the most part, was an approach which endured until the important corrective works produced by MacGregor Knox and James J. Sadkovich. More recently Richard Carrier, and his examination of the fighting in North Africa, has provided a sophisticated interpretation noting that, as this campaign wore on, a gradual increase in 'fighting power' actually allowed Italian troops to 'learn, adapt, and improvise'.[4]

Within the failure to produce reliable assessments, the Italian military's experience of the campaign it fought against British and Commonwealth forces in Italian Somaliland, Ethiopia and Eritrea has received a particularly distorted review.[5] In his otherwise authoritative 1989 article 'Understanding Defeat', even Sadkovich misrepresents the strategic position as it appeared at the time. He referred to the East Africa campaign as being 'like a siege, and the Italian defeat not unlike those suffered by the British in Hong Kong, Malaya and Singapore'.[6] In reality it was their opponent who, at least initially, faced an apparently hopeless position. When Italy declared war in June 1940, General Sir Archibald Wavell in Cairo, in charge of the Middle East Command, feared a lightning strike, particularly once France had been forced to surrender that same month increasing the defensive commitments required of his already scattered garrisons. There were simply no reserves and little chance that an attack in Kenya or the Sudan could be beaten back. But whilst there seemed to be considerable enemy forces in the region it would become apparent that, as was also the case elsewhere, these were 'shamefully ill-equipped to conduct a major war'.[7] As one historian has noted, Mussolini had 'neglected to prepare the strategic plans that would have been necessary'.[8] For the Italian military commanders in East Africa, this eroded any desire on their part to use their initial advantage and pursue a basic tenet of military strategy: the attacking force holds the initiative and determines the pace and tempo of battle. Such a critical failure undoubtedly shaped how their opponents viewed them at the time and how they were remembered later.

The view from the front

There were two strands to the discussion of how the Italian military had fared in East Africa during this 18-month campaign. The first, unsurprisingly, was delivered by eyewitnesses, more specifically those who had fought against them, although there were actually few detailed comments provided by British and Commonwealth troops. Where there were these tended to be written hurriedly by men who had already moved on to their next campaigns in North Africa or the Far East or after the war as part of a much more expansive accounts in which their experiences in East Africa formed only a brief part. What references were made tended to portray an opponent that had never really wanted to fight and so had not performed well. Typical of such writers was Colonel Frank Messervy who commanded the mobile striking column 'Gazelle Force', a mixed force of infantry and armoured vehicles carrying out operations from the Sudan. He later wrote 'the "Itie" showed himself to be an unenterprising foe' with a lack of aggression which allowed for much greater risks to be taken in terms of preparing and conducting offensive operations. This even extended to his men being able to disregard basic security considerations and driving in full view of enemy observation posts. Indeed, Messervy, who described his opponent as being 'most gullible', made a point of driving at night with full headlights on to exaggerate the strength of his forces.[9]

Another who reached a view based on first-hand experience, albeit from his position as a relatively junior intelligence officer in the British Indian Army, concluded that the mystery of why, ultimately, the Italians collapsed was not a particularly profound one. In George Young's account:

> The generals were rather old perhaps but well versed in the history and lessons of war. There was nothing wrong with their actual ability to handle masses of men according to a plan. They were well up in the science of what is now called logistics. But they did not want the war, they had made up their minds that war would mean the loss of their Empire, if they did

have a war then Mussolini and his German friends could do the fighting. They proposed to content themselves with putting prepared plans into effect.[10]

In what was a far-reaching post-conflict assessment, he listed four critical areas in which the enemy had failed identifying these as poor morale, a lack of confidence in their cause, superior British training, determination and initiative shown amongst junior officers, NCOs and the ordinary ranks and, finally, a more successful use of the bayonet.[11] To these could perhaps be added the degree to which more generally the Italians were found to be unprepared for the battles they would have to fight, with their previous regional military campaigns largely involving irregular warfare leaving them lacking in a knowledge of more modern techniques and, specifically, an inadequate anti-tank capability. This meant they had no real answer to fast advancing columns and well-trained and highly motivated professional troops. Young also noted that, at least theoretically, Ethiopia was an easy country to defend against an invasion, with the near impossibility of movement except on the very few primitive roads, the almost total lack of communications and the great distances involved. These serious restrictions, however, applied equally to the defenders as well as any invading force but it was the British and Commonwealth troops who proved far more adept at overcoming the resulting logistical challenges. Time and again they showed themselves to be better able to move over poor terrain at great speed and keep their opponent uncertain of their strategy.

Discussions such as these, contained within letters and diaries, often also made some reference to race and other forms of prejudice in determining how assessments were reached. And it was not only the British participants who were sharing critical opinions about their opponents. Writing home from Mogadishu, one young South African gunner told his parents:

The Italians seem to be a peace-loving people – not very warlike at all. They build fine roads, beautiful houses and lovely towns. However, they do not seem to be very clean nor care much about hygiene and, by and large, the soldiers are a dirty lot. Maybe this is because they have been out here for some time and have picked up indigenous habits and women.[12]

The idea that the enemy had been in some way weakened by the locals may well have reflected the racial tensions under-pinning South African society, but it also pointed to an attempt to mitigate for why a European power had performed so badly on the battlefield. Some of the eyewitnesses went further and were far more critical. Undoubtedly the most severe – and persistently hostile – commentator to emerge from the archives examined was a young Royal Artillery officer who, in December 1940, arrived in Nairobi to assume a highly important role. Having been commissioned as a regular officer less than two years before, James Blewitt's first assignment had been to act as military assistant to

General Sir Alan Cunningham and he accompanied him when he took command in Kenya of British and Commonwealth forces. Having been given the acting rank of major, he had set out from England travelling by boat, aircraft and train to reach East Africa.

In the months that followed, Blewitt did not see much fighting first-hand but instead the immediate aftermath of battle as he accompanied the general following the rapid advance of his troops. Despite only witnessing one part of the war fought in East Africa – there were two distinct pincers to the British and Commonwealth strategy and he witnessed none of the fighting which took place in the north in Sudan and Eritrea – he nonetheless clearly held the enemy in the lowest regard. By March 1941, it already appeared to him as if the Italian garrison in Ethiopia would not hold on much longer and he wrote to his sister: 'I haven't words to express my contempt for the Italians, they're dirty, lazy and frightened out of their wits if you say boo to them, frightened even if you don't say boo but only pull a bit of a face'.[13] With Addis Ababa liberated the following month and Haile Selassie restored as Emperor, everything Blewitt saw of the retreating enemy made him 'more and more contemptuous of them. They can put on a good show superficially, but there is nothing ever behind it all and invariably if you look into anything of theirs it is always inefficient and dirty'.[14] Much later in the campaign, when one of the last major garrisons at Gimma was eventually reached on 21 June, 8,000 Italians surrendered with barely any fight. Blewitt could not hide his contempt writing 'the place was lousey with Wops both prisoners and civilians who were giving themselves up wherever they could'.[15] Half were women and children but amongst those captured were a colonel and two staff officers who came down from the town to see what was going on and wandered straight into an enemy patrol, the clearest reminder of the 'despicable fighting qualities of the Wops'.

It is not clear how representative this young British officer was of views held by the European soldiery now deployed to the region, but his letters demonstrated a starkly racist outlook and considerable contempt for many of those he encountered. Blewitt complained that the local population were the most unpleasant people he thought he had met, 'dirty, cruel and lazy in anything except making sure that they have enough to eat'.[16] Opposing forces were rarely referred to as 'Italians' but instead nearly always 'Itis' or 'Wops'. The largely Eritrean colonial troops fighting alongside them were 'the filthiest natives'. Even the Ethiopians, who were working with the British and Commonwealth forces, were described as 'real gollywogs'. This language led ultimately, however, to him displaying a contradictory stance as he questioned British regional policy and whether it was sensible to remove the Italians – for once referred to more positively as 'the white man' – who had replaced a backwards and feudal form of government and had been doing their best to civilize the country. In his comments, he seemed to doubt whether it was possible to train 'the black man' and provide a level of education so that he could rule himself, albeit whilst others still took what was wanted from the country.

In his final letters written during the campaign, Blewitt also made some more specific reference to comments made by Cunningham who he referred to as also having 'a most terrific hate against Wops and loathes seeing any of them at all'.[17] The only apparent exception to this was the Duke of Aosta, the Italian Viceroy who had commanded the failed defence in East Africa. He had been educated in part in England and was apparently found to be quite charming by those British officers he encountered following his eventual surrender. Whilst there is no formal evidence within letters written at the time by Cunningham of him holding any such views or indeed of there being an institutional disapproval of the Italian military, Blewitt spent most of his time with the general and the other senior commanders and it is difficult to believe that he formed his judgements solely on what he himself saw. The reality seemed to be that there were not many within the British and Commonwealth forces who had anything positive to say about the enemy they were fighting.

The 'armchair generals'

The other – and much more vociferous – contemporary contribution to the narrative of failure came from elements within the British media and its conclusions were more certain in dismissing the Italians as an entirely inadequate military power. There was no doubting that the battles fought against Italy offered a considerable propaganda benefit: as Max Hastings has argued recently, the British leadership in fact 'owed a perverse debt of gratitude' to Mussolini for declaring war, as the battle against the Italians presented something for the British Army to do following its defeat in France and 'the only realistic opportunity for British land engagement'.[18] Operation 'Compass', the campaign which began in North Africa in December 1940, initially delivered outstanding results helping reinforce a popular image of the enemy's incompetence. A two-page photo-spread on 21 February 1941 in *The War* focussed on the results of the fighting with pictures showing huge quantities of captured vehicles and ammunition along with vast numbers of prisoners.[19] As the writer noted, 'our casualties have been amazingly light. Italian casualties have given our medical services most of their work'.[20] The same edition of this popular weekly magazine also reported the challenges facing the Italian Armistice Commission in Tunis where 'snubbed by the Germans, ignored by the French, [the Italians] spend much of their time writing letters [...] and protesting when [local] newspapers play up the British communiqués or the American war effort'.[21] These reports included a cooking column with 'recipes of two dishes much appreciated by Greeks – spaghetti à la Macedoine and macaroni à la Grecque'. Such criticism had an effect and the British public's perception of the enemy worsened.

With the arrival of German forces in Libya to bolster their allies, and a rapid decline in the British and Commonwealth position, newspaper attention switched to East Africa. In the growing commentaries produced by the popular media throughout January 1941 detailing the collapse of the Italian defences, the message was, once again, the same. One report concerned the small and remote garrison at Gubba on the border between Ethiopia and the Sudan which was described as having 'lost their nerve and bolted into the jungle'.[22] This was a very minor event in the much broader context of the campaign but as this particular writer put it,

I do not envy the lot of the Italian officers and men who are marooned in the outlying positions of the Italian African Empire. They are stuck in a savage and hostile land, thousands of miles from their native vineyards and olive groves, without supplies, without reinforcement and without the faintest hope of rescue.

As this analysis revealed, however, it was not so much how poorly these troops had performed but the propaganda value that could be gained from spreading news of the success being enjoyed by British and Commonwealth troops:

In Africa, prestige is almost more important than in almost any other part of the world. When the Abyssinian and the Eritrean and the Sudanese and the fighting tribes of Kenya see that the RAF ranges wherever it wishes, and sees that the British attack the Italians wherever they meet them, it is bound to have enormous repercussions amongst the natives of Africa. And once the wheel starts turning in our favour and the natives in the jungle armed with rifles and cartridges and inspired by a deep hatred of the Italians, then I think we shall see a very speedy end to Mussolini's famous empire.

It was certainly a popular line for the correspondents to suggest that Wavell's success in Africa was having a huge regional impact with 'news of this great disaster now flying from one small village to the next, across the forests, swamps and deserts, transmitted sometimes by throbbing drum and sometimes by runner' confirming the extent of the Italian military failure.[23]

There were few dissenting voices. The correspondent for *Time* wrote in June 1940, 'although it is fashionable to belittle Italian soldiering (Aduwa, Caporetto, Guadalajara), Italy has many troops whose valour and ability should not be underrated'.[24] And in December, as General Richard O'Connor's Western Desert Force appeared to brush aside the massed Italian armies, a *Daily Express* editorial had warned of 'the armchair folk [...] who talk of "riffraff" and "cowardice"' amongst the Italian troops. Instead of listening to retired military commentators, it preferred to quote from an officer who had fought in the battle and who chose to commend the bravery of the Italians.[25] The Scottish writer, journalist and broadcaster Archibald MacDonell was perhaps the most objective commentator and keen also to stress that Britain's opponent in Africa was not entirely lacking in merit. He had told his readers that:

While estimating the likelihood of any part of the Italian army to stand and fight, it must always be remembered that the temperament of the Italians varies very much according to the locality from which they come. Thus, probably the worst soldiers in Europe are the Sicilians and the southern Italians and the Neapolitans. The men from the north, however, from Piedmont and Lombardy and the Alpine provinces, are a very different calibre. It was they who followed Garibaldi and made Italy a united nation.[26]

His death in mid-January 1941 put an end to comments from one of the more unbiased reviewers of the fighting but, by then, even he had noted, 'it has not yet been decided by historians whether an Italian General is of more value to the Italian army before he has been captured or after'.[27]

MacDonell's replacement was Sir Hubert Gough, a celebrated retired general from the previous world war, and he seemed much less willing to find any positives; by the middle of February he was writing that

> the situation of the Italian soldiers and civilians in Abyssinia is most precarious and unless the Duke of Aosta, who is at present governing that country, surrenders shortly and throws himself and his people on our mercy it is to be feared that their fate will be a terrible one at the hands of the Abyssinians.[28]

By this stage, it was almost impossible to find any correspondent who was willing to say a positive word about the performance of the Duce's military forces. William Connor, who wrote as 'Cassandra' in his *Daily Mirror* column, was particularly critical of the Italian leadership. As the defeats in East Africa gathered pace, an especially harsh example was a March 1941 diatribe in which he referred to Mussolini, who he often called 'Bullfrog', as 'suffering from delayed drop deflation, punctured pride and busted bombast'.[29]

There was, however, a danger throughout these first months of 1941, as at least one British magazine noted, of the popular press comparing the fight in Africa against the Italians to a 'pleasure-trip [...] which it clearly was not'.[30] By the beginning of March, as the Italian forces completed their evacuation of Italian Somaliland and continued their rapid retreat through Ethiopia heading for Addis Ababa, the same writer provided the following devastating assessment:

> Down, tottering down, comes the proud Empire of Rome; 'records' are being created in its dismantling. It may have had good masons here and there, but its architecture was not inspired. For some months after the war began, Humpty-Dumpty sat on a wall: now he has had a great fall, and not all the Boche Stukas nor all the Boche men will ever put Humpty-Dumpty together again. Long is the night ahead of Italy, a night to be lit only by such illuminations as may be reflected from her northern neighbour and master. Her own stars are in eclipse, her own empire is in ruins.[31]

The rapidly worsening derision seemed in large part to have been driven by the frustration amongst at least some within the British establishment that 'decent' Italians had yet to 'take their fate into their own hands, rid themselves of their present leaders and stand once more for the freedom that their grandfathers won at so heavy a price'.[32] Until such time as they did there would be no choice 'but to continue the piecemeal destruction of the Italian empire'. This was, in fact, another increasingly familiar argument which had been made before to the public. In December 1940, one of the columnists for the weekend newspaper *The Observer* had written that

> the Italian people know that we had no quarrel with them. The insane struggle to overthrow the British Empire was forced upon them and the iron answer on us. [...] Their good instinct told them that it could only make them either the victims of Nazi defeat or the jackals of Nazi success.[33]

This message was repeated by Winston Churchill in a pre-Christmas broadcast to the Italian people in which he reminded them both of the long friendship the two countries had enjoyed and once again pointed to their leadership never having consulted with them about the war into which they had then been committed.[34] And now, within the 'ramshackle Fascist system', eastern Africa was the remotest part and vulnerable to attack and here the level and manner of the defeat was the most severe.

The battle of Keren: a different tone

The one exception, for both the military eyewitnesses and the media writers, was what remains today the little-known battle of Keren (or Cheren as it is referred to locally). This was an epic struggle fought by British and Indian troops and 30,000 Italians, including many elite forces trained in mountain warfare. The defenders exploited the terrain, used their equipment well and displayed great skill and considerable courage in what was one of the most effectively conducted Italian military operations of the war.[35] Unable to break through the defences, the British and Commonwealth forces were forced to conduct frontal attacks at great cost and the repeated and increasingly frenzied attempt to recover Fort Dologoro-doc made by the Italians should have been enough to convince any observers of their resolve. The final engagements involved bitter hand-to-hand fighting and, at the battle's eventual conclusion, 356 of the attackers were dead with more than 3,000 men wounded, almost half of them front line troops; it had taken a total of 53 days between the first and last attempts for the attacking forces to capture the position.[36] The Italians suffered even greater losses, more than 3,000 men were killed and 4,500 wounded before the white flag was seen flying from their key defensive position at Mount Sanchil.[37] As one of the British brigadiers involved later wrote, 'the enemy had fought well and bravely, but our men had fought better and had been infinitely better directed'.[38]

A similar more generous assessment, one which recognized a robust quality to the Italian performance which had not been witnessed previously, had been evident during a review of the campaign which took place in May 1941 in the House of Lords. One of the speakers acknowledged that at Keren, enemy forces had 'fought stubbornly and bravely in a series of counter attacks, all the time suffering heavy casualties', with another giving special praise noting that 'alpine climbing at a snail's pace and then to assault at the summit again and again demands great physical strain and determination'.[39] One government speaker also gave 'great credit' to the Italians for how they had performed during this battle and the manner in which they had conducted an organized retreat following their defeat. This brief speech went on to add the view that,

> although we might not have a very good opinion of the fighting qualities of the Italian forces, we must all of us realise what extraordinarily clever, astute and resourceful engineers and miners they are, especially in work connected with fortifications and demolition.[40]

Returning once again to the question of where responsibility lay for Italy's military woes, there was also praise for Aosta who 'made a terrific effort to save the honour of his country so tarnished by the Dictator who calls the tune in Italy'.[41]

It was a hard-fought victory which received considerable popular acclaim as a high point of the British Commonwealth war effort to that point and proved to be the critical moment in the East Africa campaign.[42] Wavell himself was so impressed by what his men had achieved that when he was later ennobled he chose as one of the additional titles 'Viscount of Keren in Eritrea'.[43] Indeed, at least one of the post-war writers who studied the campaign concluded that this could 'claim to be considered as one of the truly decisive battles of the world'.[44] Another commentator agreed explaining that the ultimate loss of the Keren position had precipitated the collapse of the entire Italian East African Empire.[45] It allowed General Sir William Platt, the Northern Front commander, the opportunity to accomplish the objectives given to him by Wavell, securing the Sudanese border and protecting the Middle East Command's southern flanks. He also, just as importantly, cleared the Italians from Red Sea coast which opened this critical maritime supply route to international vessels including the then neutral United States.[46] And, after this defeat, the remaining Italian forces were left weary and discouraged and for the first time even Eritrean soldiers, who had previously been their most loyal colonial troops, deserted in large numbers.[47]

In describing the battle of Keren, even the British media had something more positive to say in the descriptions and comments they offered their readers. Both the military correspondents reporting back to London and the commentators in Fleet Street were in agreement that the Italian resistance during this one battle was 'more obstinate and better directed' than anything which had been experienced during the entire African campaign up to that point. This had resulted in 'an extremely difficult' struggle and some of the writers were even prepared to grudgingly recognize for the first time that the Italians had mounted a brave defence.[48] This view was strengthened by the prominent reference made in the post-battle accounts to comments from experienced Indian Army officers that the terrain at Keren as having been worse than anything that could be found on the North-West Frontier. Whilst few readers would have any familiarity with conditions in East Africa, some of them knew something about this hostile part of

India.[49] This helped ensure that at least some respect was shown for the performance of the Italians and that, briefly, it was recognized as a battle which proved the enemy was capable of considerable bravery.

Conclusion

Mussolini apparently referred to his East African territories as 'the pearl of the fascist regime'.[50] However, as one of the official histories summarized the outcome of the campaign fought there in 1940 and 1941, 'the Empire which Italy took seven months to gain was lost in four [...] [and] resulted in the complete destruction of an Italian army of 300,000 men'.[51] For the men who fought in its defence, the defeat they suffered was disastrous. Whilst the Italian leader reached the view that too many of his troops had surrendered and too few had been killed, Sir Ivone Kirkpatrick, who had served in the British Embassy in Rome in the 1930s, wrote post-war that, as a result of the defeat, 'the prestige of the Fascist system at home and abroad had sunk and discontent was rife'.[52]

Within Carrier's excellent reflections about 'fighting power' he explains this concept as 'the capacity to engage the enemy and to sustain combat'.[53] He also agreed with the conclusions offered by Israeli academic Martin von Creveld who has argued that it has (and, implicitly, needs) 'mental, intellectual and organizational foundations' which are critical to its ability to function.[54] Without the addition of resolute political will – and the version offered by Mussolini was never more than stuttering and uncertain – it might more accurately be described as only representing 'potential fighting power'. It was certainly true that in early 1940 the direction provided by the leadership in Rome was that, at the earliest, it would be two years before war broke out. When orders came well ahead of schedule to begin the fight the commanders on the ground in East Africa and elsewhere were not ready physically or mentally and could not respond.[55]

It was certainly the case that the British military who were present at the time in Kenya, the Sudan, Ethiopia and the Somalilands reached the consensus that their opponent often appeared not to want to fight a war for which it believed itself to be hopelessly unprepared.[56] This reluctance was, in turn, reported by the English-speaking media and became a narrative of failure based on a lack of ability. For the most part, modern historians still accept this assessment and remain unforgiving. In his brief discussion of the subsequent wartime military performance – typical in its brevity of most recent accounts of the war – Hastings accepted that not all of their 'generals were incompetents, [and] not all Italian formations fought feebly'. But, at the same time, he still concluded:

> Never for a moment were Mussolini's warriors in the same class as those of Hitler. North Africa, and the Mussolini's pigeon-chested posturing as an Axis warlord, offered British soldiers an opportunity to show their mettle. If the British Army was incapable of playing in a great stadium against world-class opposition, it could nonetheless hearten the nation and impress the world by a demonstration in a lesser league.[57]

The reality is that in East Africa, whilst the Italians often fought bravely at the tactical level, poor decisions, inactivity and incompetence at the operational and strategic level lost them those engagements in which they did stand and fight.[58] The inability to make better use of the advantage which, to a beleaguered British public facing the threat of imminent invasion in the summer of 1940 they appeared to hold, was as much as anything else what helped influence how the campaign was reported at the time and has been subsequently remembered.

Notes

1 For an excellent review of the literature, see E. Griebling, 'Broken Fasces: Historical Perceptions on the Failure of Fascist Italy', Master of Arts in Diplomacy and Military Studies, Hawaii Pacific University, 4 December 2009.

2 W.S. Churchill, *The Second World War* (London: Pimlico, 2002), p. 688.

3 Hastings Ismay to John Connell, 13 September 1961, Ismay Papers, Liddell Hart Centre for Military Archives (LHCMA), Ismay 4/9/39.

4 R. Carrier, 'Some Reflections on the Fighting Power of the Italian Army in North Africa, 1940–1943', *War in History*, 22:4 (2015), p. 528.

5 A. Stewart, *The First Victory: The Second World War and the East African Campaign* (London: Yale, 2016), pp. X–XIV.

6 J.J. Sadkovich, 'Understanding Defeat: Reappraising Italy's Role in World War II', *Journal of Contemporary History*, 24:1 (1989), p. 39.

7 C. Hibbert, *Mussolini: The Rise and Fall of Il Duce* (Basingstoke: Palgrave Macmillan, 2008), p. 127.

8 D. Mack Smith, *Mussolini* (London: Weidenfeld & Nicolson, 1994), p. 247.

9 F. Messervy, 'The East African Campaign', n.d. (1950), The National Archives (TNA), CAB 106/912.

10 'The Role of British Forces in Africa', George Young, Oxford Development Records Project, Bodleian Library (Oxford), b. 19, no. 309, MSS.Afr.s.1715.

11 Capt. S. Hyat, 'The Battle of Ambar Alagi or The Fall of an Empire', *The Journal of the United Service Institution of India*, LXXII:306 (1942), pp. 92–4.

12 K. Ford, *From Addis to the Aosta Valley: A South African in the North African and Italian Campaigns 1940–1945* (Solihull: Helion & Company Limited, 2012), p. 52.

13 James Blewitt to Miss Annie Blewitt, 17 April 1941, Major James Blewitt Papers, Imperial War Museum, London, 08/88/3.

14 Ibid., Blewitt to Family, 18 May 1941.

15 Ibid., Blewitt (Jakes) to Family, 30 June 1941.

16 Ibid., Blewitt to Colin (??), 2 August 1941.

17 Ibid., Blewitt (Jakes) to Family, 14 July 1941.

18 M. Hastings, *Finest Years – Churchill as Warlord 1940–45* (London: Harper Press, 2009), p. 117.

19 This had started out as the *War Weekly* in October 1939 and, until August 1941 when shortages of paper led to its closure, it was published by Newnes and edited by R.J. Minney.

20 'How Italy's African Empire was Shattered', *The War Incorporating War Pictorial*, 21 February 1941, pp. 1658–9.

21 'Tunisia Jeers at the Italians', *The War Incorporating War Pictorial*, 21 February 1941, p. 1660.

22 A.G. MacDonell, 'The Week's War on Land: How We Are Breaking Up Mussolini's African Empire', *The War incorporating War Pictorial*, 21 February 1941, p. 1572.

23 'Wavell's Master Stroke', *The Observer*, 15 December 1940.

24 'Southern Theatre – Italy in Arms', *Time*, 24 June 1940.

25 'Opinion – Our Foes', *Daily Express*, 18 December 1940.
26 A.G. MacDonell, 'The Week's War on Land: Wavell's Brilliant Operations in Libya', *The War incorporating War Pictorial*, 21 February 1941, 17 January 1941, p. 1551.
27 A.G. MacDonell, 'Obituary', *The War incorporating War Pictorial*, 21 February 1941, p. 1596; Id.,'Should We Send Them Home?', *The War incorporating War Pictorial*, 7 February 1941, p. 1615.
28 H. Gough, 'The Week's War on Land: We Must Clear Africa and Albania by March for the Next Move', *The War Incorporating War Pictorial*, 21 February 1941, p. 1551.
29 'Prominent Invalids' (Cassandra), *The Daily Mirror*, 25 March 1941.
30 K. Williams, 'Cordon Closing in on East Africa – What the Colonists Think of Mussolini', *Great Britain and the East*, 13 February 1941, p. 126.
31 K. Williams, 'The Italian Stars Go Down – A Jerry-Built Overseas Empire', *Great Britain and the East*, 6 March 1941, p. 186.
32 'Italy's Plight', *Great Britain and the East*, 27 February 1941.
33 J.L. Garvin, 'The Boldest Measures', *The Observer*, 8 December 1940.
34 'Mr Churchill Speaks to Italy', *The Manchester Guardian*, 24 December 1940.
35 W.E. Crosskill, *The Two Thousand Mile War* (London: Robert Hale, 1980), p. 136.
36 Ibid., p. 122.
37 A.J. Barker, *Eritrea 1941* (London: Faber and Faber, 1957), p. 174.
38 Brig. H. Charrington, 'Notes on the Operations in Eritrea and Northern Abyssinia, Jan-Mar. 1941', 10 June 1941, Harold Charrington Papers, LHCMA, 3/7.
39 Ibid.
40 'East African Campaigns', House of Lords Debate, 28 May 1941, *Hansard*, vol. 119 cc. 297–311.
41 Ibid.
42 H.E. Raugh Jr., *Wavell in the Middle East, 1939–1941 – A Study in Generalship* (London: Brassey's, 1993), p. 183; Stewart, *The First Victory*, pp. 165–90.
43 Raugh, *Wavell in the Middle East*, p.181.
44 C. Mackenzie, *Eastern Epic: Vol.I, September 1939–March 1943 – Defence* (London: Chatto & Windus, 1951), p. 64.
45 W.G. Hingston, *The Tiger Strikes* (Calcutta: J.F. Parr, 1942), p. 92.
46 Gen. Sir W. Platt, *The Campaign against Italian East Africa 1940/41*, Lees Knowles Lecture 1951, Camberley, Army Staff College, 1962, Lecture II, p. 19.
47 A. Mockler, *Haile Selassie's War: The Italian–Ethiopian Campaign, 1935–1941* (Oxford: Oxford University Press, 1984), p. 335.
48 Brig. Gen. J. Charteris, 'Keren Resistance', *The Manchester Guardian*, 21 February 1941; 'Italian Counter-Attacks Fail at Keren', *The Manchester Guardian*, 19 March 1941.
49 'The Final Assault on Keren', *The Manchester Guardian*, 28 March 1941.
50 Mack Smith, *Mussolini*, p. 267.
51 J.S., 'The Rise and Fall of the Italian African Empire', 21 January 1943, TNA, CAB 106/404.
52 Mack Smith, *Mussolini*, p. 267; Sir Ivone Kirkpatrick, *Mussolini – A Study of a Demagogue* (Long Acre, London: Odhams Books, 1964), p. 469.
53 Carrier, *Some Reflections on the Fighting Power of the Italian Army in North Africa*, p. 509.
54 M. van Creveld, *Fighting Power: German and U.S. Army Performance, 1939–1945* (Westport, CT: Greenwood Press, 1982), p. 3.
55 M.A. Bragadin, *The Italian Navy in World War II* (Annapolis, MD: Naval Institute Press, 1957), p. 3.
56 Barker, *Eritrea 1941*, p. 24.
57 Hastings, *Finest Years*, p. 117.
58 A. Sbacchi, 'Haile Selassie and the Italians 1941–1943', *African Studies Review*, 22:1 (1979), p. 26.

8 From occupiers to comrades-in-arms
Italian fighters in the ranks of the Greek People's Liberation Army

Ioannis Nioutsikos

Introduction

On 11 September 1943, the commander of the 24th Infantry Division *Pinerolo*, General Adolfo Infante, arrived at the village of Porta in Thessaly. There, he met with the representatives of the Joint Guerrilla Headquarters and the representative of the British Military Mission, Colonel Christopher Woodhouse. After discussions, they agreed that all units of *Pinerolo* Division would pass to the lines of the guerrillas and would be placed under the protection of the Greek People's Liberation Army (ELAS).[1] As a result of this agreement, *Pinerolo* Division became the very first Italian unit that officially passed to the Allied side, in fact, more than a month before Badoglio declared war on Germany.[2] This massive passing of Italians to the Allied side was an astonishing development indeed. Nevertheless, it does not summarize the experience of the Italian fighters in the ranks of the Greek resistance. The present chapter demonstrates that the participation of Italians in the guerrilla campaign of ELAS is mostly the story of individual people, whose political and ethical beliefs led them to become partisans in the Greek mountains.

The Italian Resistance has already been examined through the prism of the individual protagonists and their personal convictions that motivated them to participate in the Resistance. The most significant study was that of Claudio Pavone, who traced how people chose their allegiance in such critical moments by focusing on the notion of *moralità*, which he defined as an amalgam of political and ethical beliefs.[3] Pavone argued that between 1943 and 1945, three interconnected wars took place in Italy simultaneously: a patriotic war, a civil war and a class war. This perspective is not confined to Italy, but it can actually be expanded to the broader conflict through the notion of the 'European civil war'. Pavone adhered to the view that the Second World War was much more than a conflict between states, and focused on its dimension of a 'civil and ideological war' that 'crossed the borders of the various countries'.[4] Another Italian scholar, Enzo Traverso, elaborated on the concept of the 'European Civil War'. In his mind, Italy and Greece represent emblematic cases of how a war of national liberation, a class war and a civil war blended together. In the same way as Pavone, Traverso also emphasized the atomic character of the Second

World War. According to him, this is highlighted by the important role played by the partisans, who embodied the fusion of the liberation and political fighter.[5] The innovative perceptions of the Second World War and of the Resistance suggested above underline that the dichotomy between Fascism and anti-fascism was an integral aspect of the war, and provide us with a scope for further research.

The present chapter is an attempt to apply these analytical tools to an overlooked subject that is the participation of Italians to the guerrilla campaign of ELAS. By weaving together the stories of individual people, it demonstrates that the Italians stationed in Greece faced the same moral dilemmas as their compatriots did in Italy, and many joined the forces of the Greek Resistance driven by their own *moralità*. In fact, the chapter argues that the Italian guerrillas in ELAS also fought in three interwoven conflicts as the Italian partisans did: a liberation struggle, a civil conflict and a revolutionary fight. The common denominator in these conflicts was Fascist ideology, either as the main cause that dragged the Mediterranean countries into the war, or as a factor that cemented the unity of those determined to prevent it from sweeping across Europe.[6] In that sense, the examination of the Italian partisans in Greece can provide us with useful insights with regards to the role and impact of Italy in World War II and, most importantly, shed light on the nature of the broader conflict.

Occupiers become comrades-in-arms

Greece belonged to the Fascist *spazio vitale*, but it had a low priority on the German strategic plans. As a result, Hitler acknowledged the Italian advantage (*preponderanza*) in the occupation of the country and the largest part of its territory (around 70%) was allotted to the Italians. The Ionian Islands were *de facto* annexed, and most of mainland Greece and the Cyclades fell under the control of the Italian 11th Army, which was under the command of General Carlo Geloso and consisted of three *Corpi d'Armata*, including two to three divisions each.[7]

The Italian advantage in the occupation meant that the Italians were also primarily responsible for dealing with the resistance. Yet, despite the abundance of troops that the 11th Army had at its disposal,[8] it failed miserably in its task. The main reason was the adoption by the Italians of a passive method of occupation. This was based on placing sentries on large towns and places of military interest (ports, railway lines, mines, etc.), in addition to pillaging the countryside and conducting atrocities against the civilian population. The rationale behind the concentration of the Italian forces in towns and the destruction of villages was to cut off the supply line of the guerrillas.[9] In practice, this method of passive defence meant that large, mountainous areas, remained outside the reach of the occupation forces, something that allowed space for the development of the armed resistance.

The most important resistance organization in occupied Greece was the National Liberation Front (EAM). EAM was founded in September 1941 at the initiative of the Communist Party of Greece. The armed wing of EAM was ELAS, which grew to become a massive guerrilla army that carried out the bulk of the armed resistance against the Axis forces. The struggle of

EAM-ELAS was not confined to achieving national liberation, but also had revolutionary aspects, based on a programme of social and political reforms. Its dual nature of a liberation and a revolutionary movement brought EAM-ELAS in a civil strife against armed collaborationist formations and rival resistance organizations that culminated in the 'December Events'. This was a violent revolt that broke out in Athens on 3 December 1944, after the police killed twelve unarmed demonstrators. For 33 days, the capital turned into a battlefield, with ELAS on one side and the government forces, former Nazi collaborators and the British on the other. The victory of the latter marked the end of ELAS and allowed the establishment of a post-war regime that engaged into political repression and widespread discrimination against the leftists.

In spite of the eventual defeat of ELAS in the Battle of Athens, the very creation and activity of such a massive guerrilla army was a remarkable achievement in Axis-occupied Europe. According to British sources, in December 1944, ELAS included 53,350 regular guerrillas.[10] Among them were many foreign nationals, such as Italians, Soviets, Poles and Germans. The most interesting example of a multi-national unit in ELAS was the International Company of the 2nd Battalion of the 30th Regiment, comprising Italians, Russians, Poles, Austrians and Moors. As a gesture of gratitude, the commander of the unit had put on his garrison cap next to the ELAS insignia, the insignia of all their countries.[11]

The largest foreign ethnicity in the ranks of ELAS was the Italians, and their recruitment can be divided into two phases. First, were those few who defected to the guerrillas long before the official capitulation of Italy. The most famous among them was Giancarlo Matteotti, serving in ELAS's 'Death Battalion'. Giancarlo was the 28-year-old son of Giacomo Matteotti, leader of the United Socialist Party, and the first prominent victim of Fascism in Italy. Giancarlo Matteotti had taken part in the Spanish Civil War and had fought in Guadalajara, Valencia and Catalonia. His participation in ELAS was publicized by the Communist Party of Greece through an interview he gave for Rizospastis, its official newspaper. Matteotti mentioned that he had fought Fascism in Italy, Spain, France and Greece, and that he joined the guerrillas of ELAS only a month after his arrival in Greece.[12]

In addition to Matteotti, there is also the documented case of an Italian lieutenant, who passed to the guerrillas in 1942. He was a doctor and particularly valuable, as he offered his services to both the fighters and the civilian population.[13] Another early Italian defector had the nickname 'Rosso' (Red). He had defected to ELAS a year before the Italian capitulation, and because of that, he was highly regarded by the guerrillas. Rosso was in his fifties and, along with his band, he attacked Italian quartermaster officers who had looted the Italian supply storages and sold the material on the black market. He called himself 'proletarian punisher' and he used to carry with him a pass signed by Aris Velouchiotis, the founder of ELAS himself.[14] Last but not least, was Italian Sergeant Antonio Partini who served in the 8th Regiment of ELAS. Before the war, Partini was a student at the University of Naples and a member of the student anti-fascist movement. When he arrived with his unit to Gytheio before the armistice, he established contact with EAM and left for the mountain of Tayge-tos. As a Sergeant, he soon assumed the command of a guerrilla group, and later he became Platoon Commander. He took part in all the battles that his unit fought, and he was seriously injured in the second Battle of Anogeia on 24 April 1944.[15]

Other early Italian defectors passed to the lines of the partisans in groups. Such was the case of three soldiers who were stationed in Tripoli, in the area of the Peloponnese. In August 1943, they took their equipment and left their gar-rison for the 11th Regiment of ELAS.[16] Many Italian soldiers also took refuge in the 30th Regiment. One of them was called Domenico, and another, due to his amusing character had the nickname Rigoletto. An Italian military tribunal had condemned them to imprisonment, but they jumped off the train which was transferring them to Italy. They both joined the ELAS band in Paiko Mountain. Another Italian partisan in the 30th Regiment was Mario, who was described as a 'fiery revolutionary'. His father was a veteran socialist in Italy and had been prosecuted by the Fascist regime. Mario had escaped from Thessaloniki where he had a Greek girlfriend who taught him Greek. It seems that Mario had genu-ine feelings for her, as he constantly pleaded with his commanders to bring her to the mountains and make her a partisan.[17]

The largest influx of Italians in the ranks of ELAS came with the capitulation of Italy on 8 September 1943. This was a watershed moment for all Italians, including those who were part of the occupation forces abroad. The armistice created an 'institutional void' and confronted individual Italians with 'a clear and difficult choice': the freedom of having to choose their own allegiance.[18] Still, for the vast majority of the Italian troops stationed in Greece, the war was over and their only concern was to return back home. Believing that the safest way to do so was by surrendering to the German forces, most Italian units allowed themselves to get swiftly disarmed. In reality, the destination of the sur-rendered Italians was usually the German Reich or the Eastern Front to be used as forced labour. In three weeks, 135,000 Italian soldiers and 5,500 officers were cramped into trains and evacuated from Greece.[19]

A number of Italians chose to remain loyal to the Axis. The Germans divided them into two categories: those 'who were willing to fight' (Kawis) and those 'who were willing to help' (Hiwis). In order to discern who remained loyal, the Germans focused on the individual soldiers instead of whole units. For those who were only willing to be posted in auxiliary services, ideology was not as important as their technical skills. Until the end of October, 15,000 Italians joined German forces in posts such as horse keepers, drivers, mule drivers or cooks.[20] Even fewer, although more fanatic, were those who assumed armed service. Ideology was an important factor for their choice as most of them were Blackshirts.[21] They were highly regarded by the Germans, not least because some of them 'assured the Ger-mans that they would have killed their officers, if they had ordered them to turn against the *Wehrmacht*'.[22] In Crete, when the Fascist Major Fernando Casini was informed that his superior General Carta had fled, he formed a unit named *Legione Italiana di Creta 'Giulio Cesare'*, and he even attempted to secure the support of

Mussolini. On the island of Rhodes, the Blackshirt Captain Mario Porta was supported by the Germans in his futile plans to transform the Blackshirts into the nucleus of a Fascist army. In Athens and Thessaloniki, supporters of the Italian Socialist Republic attempted to revive cells of the Fascist Party.[23] In Evoia, although the commander of the local Italian division surrendered to ELAS, the notorious Fascist officer Marazzi did not lay down his arms replying to the partisans that 'the fascists do not surrender and they will crush you!'.[24] Italians loyal to the Axis could be found even in Cephalonia. Some officers were transferred to Mesolongi, where they reaffirmed their allegiance in front of the commander of the 36th Blackshirt Battalion. Afterwards, they were transferred to Münsingen and joined the *Monterosa* Division, a military unit of the Italian Socialist Republic.[25] Other Italians remained on the island, where 300 of them manned artillery units in German service.[26] In total, approximately 10,000 Blackshirts assumed armed posts, and three Italian battalions along with a company were formed with, nevertheless, strong German presence in them.[27]

Some Italian units stationed on islands decided not to surrender to the Germans. Even before the capitulation, the organizations of EAM in Cephalonia had established connection with Italian anti-fascist soldiers and officers inside the 33rd *Acqui* Division. When the news of the armistice reached the island, two opposing views appeared within *Acqui*. The intention of the pro-German commander of the Division, General Gandin, was to surrender its arms; however, he was opposed by a group of officers and soldiers who wanted to resist.[28] The negotiations took place with an artillery battery turned to the headquarters of the Division and a heavy armed platoon ready to arrest Gandin.[29] Eventually, it was decided to fight back the Germans with the help of volunteers from ELAS who were attached to the Italian units.[30] In spite of their efforts, the German forces prevailed and massacred 5,000 Italians. The Italians in Corfu were also in touch with EAM, but as in Cephalonia, their resistance was futile.[31]

In mainland Greece the pattern was reversed, with whole Italian units passing to the side of the partisans. The most distinctive example was that of the 24th Infantry Division *Pinerolo*, that was stationed in Thessaly. The British Military Mission and the Joint Guerrilla Headquarters had already commenced negotiating with the Italians in Thessaly since early August. *Pinerolo* Division was under the command of General Adolfo Infante, who had served as a military attaché in the Italian embassy in London and Washington and was considered to be sympathetic to the Allies.[32] In contrast, the command of *Pinerolo* did not trust the guerrillas of ELAS and preferred surrendering to the resistance organization of the National Republican Greek League (EDES). The Military Commander of ELAS, Major-General Sarafis, objected to that, since *Pinerolo* was stationed to an area controlled by ELAS; thus, the negotiations were fruitless.[33] Nevertheless, the armistice sped things up, and on 11 September it was agreed that all units of *Pinerolo* Division would switch sides and pass to the lines of the guerrillas under the guarantee of the British Military Mission.[34] The troops of the *Aosta* Cavalry Regiment followed those of *Pinerolo* to the mountains, in addition to other garrisons and individual troops, and as a result, the Italians reached a number of 7,000 men.[35] The agreement between the resistance and the Italians was on the basis that those who wanted to fight would retain their arms and be considered equal to the guerrillas. Those who did not wish to fight would be detained in camps. Since the Italian soldiers had no experience in guerrilla warfare, they were attached to ELAS's units in small separate units, with the prospect of being assigned their own territory.[36]

In practice, the events turned out much differently, and proved how difficult it was for the former occupiers to be accepted as comrades-in-arms. First, ELAS was more interested in the Italian arms stockpile than in the fighters themselves, who would strain its scarce food supplies.[37] Second, the memories from the Italian atrocities and retaliation measures were still fresh and put a strain on the relationship between the Italians and the guerrillas.[38] A characteristic example of this mistrust and vengefulness took place during the battle of Aspropotamos, when an Italian who had fought for ELAS tried to have a sip of raki from a flask that was looted from the enemy. His commander fired his pistol without hitting him, and shouted 'Leave it! No, you can't, you damned Italian!' Then he took the flask and smashed it on the floor shouting 'Not you Italian, you can't!'[39] Third, according to a British liaison officer, 'the contrast between the well-pressed uniforms and thick-soled boots of the Italians and the ragged, bare-footed partisans was too great' for the latter to ignore.[40] Fourth, the Italian declaration of war to Germany meant that the status of the Italian fighters in ELAS would be upgraded. ELAS was unwilling to allow the existence of an independent armed force whose allegiance would be questionable in case of civil strife. Furthermore, Italian Communist Party cells that were active within *Pinerolo* promoted disobedience to Fascist officers, and the early Italian defectors to ELAS pressed for the disbandment of the unit.[41] Finally, the fighting morale of the Italians who took *en masse* to the mountains was particularly low. On 26 September 1943, an Italian detachment following British orders attacked the Larissa airport, but the operation ended up in a fiasco, with the Italians abandoning the demolition equipment.[42]

This gave EAM-ELAS the excuse it was seeking, in order to disband the separate Italian units. On 15 October, under the pretext of the limited fighting capabilities of the Italians and an alleged conspiracy of Fascist officers within *Pinerolo*, the I Division of ELAS disarmed *Pinerolo* without resistance, and following brief fighting, the *Aosta* Cavalry Regiment was disarmed as well. After their separate units were disbanded, the majority of the Italians were considered prisoners-of-war and suffered terrible hardships due to the lack of supplies, since the British ceased paying for their support. Eventually, they secured the provision of food and shelter when they were allowed to become employed in the villages, and the British agreed to resume payments.[43]

The truth was that most of the Italians who passed to the side of the resistance after the armistice did so in order to save, not risk their lives.[44] In contrast to them, those who wished to continue fighting retained their arms and were admitted to the existing units of ELAS as partisans.[45] Indeed, there were several Italians, not only from *Pinerolo* Division but from other units as well, who remained in the ranks of ELAS and distinguished themselves, or even lost their lives, in battle. The Italians were familiar with the equipment of ELAS, as this was mostly of Italian origin, and thus, they often served as machine-gun and mortar users. The most famous of them was 'Renato' who served as a machine-gunner and mortar user in the 7th Regiment of ELAS in Evoia.[46] The Artillery Company of the 8th Regiment included a whole platoon of 30 Italian mortar users, who were considered 'good fighters'.[47] The courage of the Italian volunteers is highlighted by the example of two Italian machine-gunners, who fought through the ranks of the 34th Regiment in the battle of Porta, during the German anti-guerrilla operations in October 1943. In the third day of the battle, the guerrillas were presented with a machine-gun that no one knew how to use. Yet, in the day before the battle begun, an Italian Sergeant Major, along with an Italian regular soldier had arrived to the guerrilla unit. The Sergeant inspected the gun, moved the bolt and made sure that the weapon was in good condition. Then, he humbly turned to the guerrilla commander and offered his help by saying: 'since no one knows how to use it, can I take it? Where do you want me to set it?' The commander reluctantly agreed and showed him the location. The Italian Sergeant turned to the Italian soldier and prompted him by saying: 'Avanti Francesco!' The two Italians picked up the machine-gun, and amid dense enemy fire, they set for the designated spot. They deployed the machine-gun and started firing to the German forces. Nevertheless, the Germans soon pinpointed their location, and shelled them with artillery, killing them both.[48]

One of the best-known cases of Italian fighters in ELAS was that of Romolo Galimberti, who initially was a soldier of *Pinerolo* Division. Galimberti described in his memoirs the divergence of allegiance between the Italians after the armistice, and how difficult it was for them to be accepted as comrades-in-arms by the partisans. As he noted, he joined the forces of ELAS due to his 'passion for communism' and actually, his only fighting experience as a guerrilla was in the battle of Aspropotamos, that was part of the civil strife between the rival resistance organizations of ELAS and EDES. After the war was over, Galimberti attended Bocconi University and became a journalist for *L'Unità*, the official newspaper of the Italian Communist Party.[49]

Large concentrations of Italian fighters were found in III, VIII and IX Divisions, the 9th Brigade and the 42nd Regiment of ELAS.[50] After the armistice, 100 Italian soldiers arrived to the 6th Regiment and asked to become partisans. Yet, their Blackshirt officers had forbade them to retain their firearms, and ELAS did not have any spare weapons. As a result, only five of them were armed by the guerrillas and fought in the first line of all the battles that the regiment gave.[51] The only known exception to the absence of any exclusively Italian units was the 'Guerrilla Group of the 18' (*Banda dei Diciotto*). This belonged to the 3rd Battalion of the 5th Regiment of ELAS in Elassona and it was formed by Lieutenant Giacomo Amati, and Second Lieutenants Massimo Tantilo, Emanuele Curatolo, Di Pristera and Pascuale, who denounced their ranks and fought along with 13 of their compatriots. Still, it is uncertain how long this unit lasted.[52] Finally, many Italians served in the Greek People's

Liberation Navy (ELAN), the naval branch of ELAS.[53] In mid-July 1944, a ship of the Independent Flotilla of Maliakos attacked two German patrol vessels and stormed one of them. During the hand-to-hand combat, Filippo Marzocco was killed and Danilo Davolio was injured. Both Italians had been sailors in ELAN for a long period of time.[54]

In addition to the Italians who became partisans on the mountains, there were some who participated in the urban resistance. In Athens, the organization of EAM at the district of Vyronas sheltered three Italian soldiers. The first of them was named Armando. He was from Southern Italy and when he defected, he brought with him his firearm. In 1944, Armando received a certification from EAM that he was indeed a defector from the army and he managed to return back home. The second was Mario, who brought with him his accordion and taught his Greek comrades the song '*Bandiera Rossa*', which became their favourite. He took part in the battles of the Athenian ELAS, and he was killed near the church of Analipsi in Vyronas. He was buried along with the rest of the fighters of ELAS at the church of Agia Triada. The last Italian was Alessandro, who came from Bologna and whose father had been sent into exile by Mussolini. Alessandro had defected from the Italian army in 1943, and while in ELAS, he managed to learn Greek. In the summer of 1944, during the final battles with the Germans, Alessandro climbed up a church in order to snipe at the enemy. When his comrades-in-arms started to withdraw, he remained at his place to cover their retreat and was killed.[55]

The organizations of EAM on the island of Cephalonia also sheltered some men from the 33rd *Acqui* Division and transferred them to mainland Greece, where they joined the forces of ELAS. One of them was Captain Amos Pampaloni, who was a partisan in ELAS for 14 months and fought against the Germans in the battles of Pontolovitsa, Ai Vlassis and Amphilochia. Captain Pietro Bianchi and Lieutenant Giuseppe Triolo were also transferred to mainland Greece and served as cavalry commanders in the 1st Cavalry Regiment of ELAS. Other Italians remained on Cephalonia and joined the forces of ELAS on the island, such as the Carabinieri Scanga and Calvagno, and Sergeant Major Walter Gorno who served as a radiotelegraph operator.[56]

In fact, many Italians contributed to the guerrilla campaign of ELAS from non-fighting posts. As the equipment of ELAS was mostly of Italian origin, they were quite skilful in repairing weapons. Others served as nurses,[57] while an order by the General Headquarters made explicit that Italian doctors could be used for the Medical Service of ELAS.[58] Indeed, several Italian doctors practiced medicine at the facilities of EAM-ELAS, such as Rocco Rotundo in Thessaly, Eduardo Ardito in Western Macedonia and surgeon Romeo Rubini. Furthermore, the surgeon at the hospital of ELAS in Megalo Chorio and the doctor at the sickbay in Larisa were also Italians.[59] In addition to the doctors, an Italian chef prepared the meals for the patients at the hospital of ELAS in Tzena.[60] Finally, the radio communications of ELAS's General Headquarters benefited from the services of the former director of the 'Radio Marelli' factory.[61]

A particularly interesting, yet unexplored, category of Italian fighters were those who remained in ELAS even after the liberation of Greece and fought along with the guerrillas in the uprising that took place in Athens in December 1944 against royalist forces, former collaborators and the British. A document from the Hellenic Ministry of Interior to the Directorate General of the Urban Police, dated 27 March 1945, listed the foreign nationals who were prosecuted by the post-war Greek state as 'war criminals'. Among them, we can find the names of three Italians who were accused of fighting in Athens through the ranks of ELAS during the 'December Events'. The first name was that of the 29-year-old Mimi Turiano, who was born in Messina and was a former soldier of the Italian Army. Turiano was arrested and accused of serving as a machine-gunner in ELAS during the fighting in Piraeus. After the end of the battle, he had followed the defeated guerrilla forces to their retreat towards Lamia. The second name was that of the 22-year-old Mario Castellani, who had also served as a machine-gunner in ELAS during the street fighting, but his whereabouts were unknown. The third Italian was Giuseppe Abia, who was arrested for being a member of ELAS.[62]

Conclusion

In September 1944, the guerrillas of ELAS fought against Nazi collaborators and harassed the German forces during their retreat from Greece. During the Battle of Achladokampos, an Italian fighter of ELAS was mortally wounded. His final request to his comrades in ELAS was 'to send a letter to the partisans of Italy to tell them that I am dying for the same cause in Greece'.[63] The last words of this Italian partisan encapsulate the notion that World War II was more than a war between nations. It was also a struggle against Fascism on a European scale, with the bonding force between people from different nations being the notion of *moralità*; the Italians who remained in the ranks of ELAS and took part in its guerrilla campaign did not simply jump on the victor's bandwagon. Instead, their allegiance was driven by their political and ethical beliefs, something that is highlighted by their participation in three interconnected wars – identical to those that were taking place in Italy. The first was a liberation war against the German occupation forces. The second was a revolutionary struggle against royalist forces and rival resistance organizations. The epitome of Italian revolutionary fighters was represented by those who remained in ELAS after the liberation of Greece and fought even against the British during the Battle of Athens in December 1944. The third was a civil war, fought against their compatriots of Fascist ideology who remained loyal to the Axis. In other words, Fascism and the opposition to it were not incidental to the war. Instead, it was the criterion on which the Italians, and the other peoples dragged into the conflict, chose their allegiance. The experience of the Italian partisans in ELAS is a prime manifestation of the rift created by Fascism and a reflection of the wider conflict that 'crossed the borders of the various countries'.[64]

In sum, the present chapter suggests that the participation of Italians in the Greek resistance emphasizes the nature of World War II as a 'European Civil War', and that the examination through the prism of the individual protagonists can provide a new perspective of the conflict. As it has been pointed out, it was a war fought for 'the most noble or the most abject' causes, such as 'liberation, justice, equality, human dignity, freedom from oppression, but also vengeance, racism, exacerbated nationalism, religious fanaticism'.[65] Choosing sides in this 'Fascist decade of war' was a clear, yet, difficult choice. Indeed, despite the massive influx of Italians in ELAS, only those who shared the same ethical and political convictions managed to overcome the understandable mistrust of the guerrillas and transform themselves from occupiers to comrades-in-arms.

Notes

1   S. Sarafis, *ELAS: Greek Resistance Army* (Atlantic Highlands, NJ: Humanities Press, 1981), p. 182.

2   C. Woodhouse, *To Milo tis Eridos* (Athens: Exantas, 1976), p. 246; H. Fleischer, *Stemma kai Swastika* (Athens: Ekdoseis Papazisi, 1995), vol. 2, pp. 170–1.

3   C. Pavone, *A Civil War: A History of the Italian Resistance* (London-New York: Verso, 2014), pp. 1–2.

4   Ivi, p. 364.

5   E. Traverso, *The European Civil War 1914–1945* (London-New York: Verso, 2017), pp. 57–60, 77–80.

6   Pavone, *A Civil War*, p. 365; Traverso, *The European Civil War*, p. 263.

7   H. Fleischer, 'Katochi kai Antistasi, 1941–1944', in E. Kofos (ed.), *Istoria tou Ellinikou Ethnous* (Athens: Ekdotiki Athinon, 2000), vol. 16, pp. 8–57, see pp. 8–12.

8   On the day of the armistice on 8 September 1943, the 11th Army comprised of 12 divisions that incorporated 172,000 troops and 7,000 officers, S.G. Gasparinatos, *E Katochi* (Athens: I. Sideris, 1998), vol. 1, p. 529.

9   I. Chandrinos, *ELAS: O megalyteros stratos tis Ethnikis Antistasis* (Athens: Gnomon Ekdotiki, 2011), vol. B, p. 14; L. Santarelli, 'Muted Violence: Italian War Crimes in Occupied Greece', *Journal of Modern Italian Studies*, 9:3 (2004), pp. 280–99.

10   The National Archives, HS5-624, Resistance Groups and Partisan Forces: Secret Armies (Mainly EAM/ELAS), July 1944–August 1945.

11   T. Mitsopoulos, *To 30o Syntagma tou ELAS* (Athens: Ekdoseis Odysseas, 1987), pp. 117–8.

12   *Tagma Thanatou*, Newspaper '*Rizospastis*', 20 October 1943.

13   C.U. Schminck-Gustavus, *Oi Itimmenoi tis Kephalonias* (Athens: Smili, 1994), Narration of Amos Pampaloni, 4 December 1991, pp. 21–2.

14   R. Galimberti, *Trypia Arvyla, Apo ti Merarchia Pinerolo stous Antartes tou ELAS* (Athens: Filistor, 1999), pp. 41–3.

15   L.I. Kapellakos, *Antartis ston Taygeto: Sto 8o Syntagma tou ELAS* (Piraeus: 1995), pp. 313–4.

16   G. Asouras, 'Italoi fantaroi ston ELAS', *Ethniki Antistasi*, 44 (March 1985), pp. 35–6, see p. 35.

17   Mitsopoulos, *To 30o Syntagma*, pp. 84, 105.

18   Pavone, *A Civil War*, pp. 5–75.

19   Fleischer, *Stemma kai Swastika*, vol. 2, pp. 172–3.

20   Ibid., pp. 171–2; The Liddell Hart Centre for Military Archives, Prentice/Wickstead Files, File 2/4, Interrogation of Oberget. Franz Brandl (1 Mtn Div.), 11 October 1944.

21   Fleischer, *Katochi kai Antistasi*, p. 29.

22 Fleischer, *Stemma kai Swastika*, vol. 2, pp. 171–2.
23 M. Mazower, *Stin Ellada tou Hitler: E Empeiria tis Katochis* (Athens: Alexandreia, 1994), pp. 176–7.
24 D.K. Nikolis, *Istoriki Poreia tou Ellinikou Ethnous: E Ethniki Antistasi kai e metadekemvriani Ellada (1941–1982)*, 2nd ed. (Athens: Siagkris, 1990), vol. 6, pp. 1203–4.
25 H.F. Meyer, *Aimatovammeno entelvais: E li Oreini Merarchia, to 22o Oreino Soma Stratou kai e egklimatiki tous drasi stin Ellada, 1943–1944* (Athens: Viviliopoleion tis Estias, 2004), vol. A, p. 563.
26 Schminck-Gustavus, 'Oi Itimmenoi tis Kephalonias', *Narration of Amos Pampaloni*, 4 December 1991, p. 24.
27 Mazower, *Stin Ellada tou Hitler*, p. 177; Fleischer, *Katochi kai Antistasi*, p. 29.
28 S. Loukatos, *Ta Chronia tis Italikis kai Germanikis Katochis kai tis Ethnikis Antistasis stin Kephalonia kai Ithaki*, 3rd ed. (Athens: Novoli, 2011), vol. 2, pp. 54–5; Fleischer, *Stemma kai Swastika*, vol. 2, p. 161.
29 Schminck-Gustavus, 'Oi Itimmenoi tis Kephalonias'*, Narration of Amos Pampaloni*, 4 December 1991, p. 13; G. Moscardelli, *Cefalonia* (Rome: Tipografia Regionale, 1945), p. 45, quoted in Meyer, *Aimatovammeno entelvais*, vol. A, p. 436.
30 Loukatos, *Ta Chronia tis Italikis kai Germanikis Katochis*, pp. 152–6.
31 V. Georgiou (ed.), *Istoria tis Antistasis 1940–1945* (Athens: Aulos, 1979), vol. 2, pp. 895–6; Fleischer, *Stemma kai Swastika*, vol. 2, pp. 163–4.
32 Woodhouse, *To Milo tis Eridos*, pp. 244–6.
33 Sarafis, *ELAS*, pp. 172–173; Fleischer, *Stemma kai Swastika*, vol. 2, p. 170.
34 Sarafis, *ELAS*, pp. 181–6; Woodhouse, *To Milo tis Eridos*, pp. 245–6.
35 Sarafis, *ELAS*, p. 183; Fleischer, *Stemma kai Swastika*, vol. 2, p. 171.
36 Sarafis, *ELAS*, pp. 181–4.
37 Fleischer, *Stemma kai Swastika*, vol. 2, p. 170; S. Grigoriadis, *Istoria tis Sychronis Elladas 1941–1974* (Athens, 2011), vol. 2, p. 187.
38 Fleischer, *Stemma kai Swastika*, vol. 2, p. 213.
39 Galimberti, *Trypia Arvyla*, p. 111.
40 J. Mulgan, *Report on Experience* (London, 2010), p. 131.
41 Grigoriadis, *Istoria tis Sychronis Elladas*, vol. 2, pp. 186–7; Fleischer, *Stemma kai Swastika*, vol. 2, pp. 213–4, 231; Sarafis, *ELAS*, pp. 198–9.
42 Grigoriadis, *Istoria tis Sychronis Elladas*, vol. 2, p. 187; Sarafis, *ELAS*, p. 186.
43 Fleischer, *Katochi kai Antistasi*, p. 35; Fleischer, *Stemma kai Swastika*, vol. 2, pp. 231–3; Sarafis, *ELAS*, pp. 198–9; 201–2; 228–30.
44 D. Eudes, *Oi Kapetanioi* (Athens: Exantas, 1974), p. 136.
45 Sarafis, *ELAS*, 199.
46 Chandrinos, *ELAS*, vol. A, pp. 75–6.
47 A. Petroulas, *E odysseia enos ametanoitou kommounisti* (Athens: Kedros, 2012), p. 49.
48 F. Grigoriadis, *To Antartiko: ELAS-EDES-EKKA (5/42)* (Athens: Ekdoseis Kamarino-poulou, 1964), vol. 4, pp. 353–68.
49 Galimberti, *Trypia Arvyla*, pp. 39, 56, 69–79, 98–9, 111, 129–31, 157–9.
50 Nikolis, *Istoriki Poreia tou Ellinikou Ethnous*, vol. 5, p. 143.
51 Asouras, *Italoi fantaroi ston ELAS*, p. 35.
52 Chandrinos, *ELAS*, vol. A, p. 76.
53 L. Skamparinas, *O Ypaspistis tou Stratigou Sarafi thymatai kai grafei* (Athens: Sygchroni Epochi, 2005), p. 56.
54 M. Kailas, *ELAN: Elliniko Laiko Apeleftherotiko Naftiko* (Athens: Nea Synora, 1975), pp. 38–9.
55 X. Fileris, *Oi saltadoroi tou Vyrona*, 2nd ed. (Athens: Kastaniotis, 2005), pp. 83–90.
56 Loukatos, *Ta Chronia tis Italikis kai Germanikis Katochis*, pp. 181–2.

57 Chandrinos, *ELAS*, vol. A, p. 75.
58 The Contemporary Social History Archives (ASKI), KKE Archive, b. 493, Φ 30 January 128.
59 Chandrinos, *ELAS*, vol. A, p. 75; G. Tsitouris, *Oi giatroi stin Ethniki Antistasi* (Athens: 2012), pp. 79, 87, 160, 199.
60 Mitsopoulos, *To 30o Syntagma*, p. 327.
61 F. Geladopoulos, 'E Eurytania stin Antistasi', in K. Koutsoukis (ed.), *E Ethniki Antistasi stin Eurytania: 50 Chronia apo tin idrysi kai to Ethniko Symvoulio tis P.E.E.A. (1944–1994)* (Athens: Epistimoniki Viviliothiki EKPE, 1995), vol. A, pp. 25–53, see p. 45.
62 Historical and Diplomatic Archive of the Hellenic Ministry of Foreign Affairs (IAYE), 1946, Subfolder 23.3 'War Criminals', Ministry of Interior to Directorate General of the Urban Police, No. 2480, Φ 366/1, 17 April 1945.
63 Asouras, *Italoi fantaroi ston ELAS*, p. 35.
64 Pavone, *A Civil War*, p. 364.
65 Traverso, *The European Civil War*, p. 73.

Part III

Ideology and propaganda for the empire at war

9 A new navalism for a Fascist empire

Navy, geopolitics, propaganda and radicalization (1934–1940)

Fabio De Ninno

Introduction

The origins of Italy's decade of wars are traceable in the ideological-political project to build a new Fascist civilization, capable of dominating a vital space that stretched from the gates of the Mediterranean, Gibraltar and Suez, down to the Red Sea and the Indian Ocean.[1] During the 1930s, in order to prepare the Italians for the realization of this project, the regime enveloped the entire Italian society with militarism.[2] The increased importance of military propaganda was part of these developments, but studies have focused mainly on the Fascist 'aviation ideology',[3] in particular the use of air force to support myths about the 'youth and modernity' of the regime.[4] However, in the broader context of Fascist propaganda, these themes were more common before 1933; thereafter, propaganda switched to more imperialistic and geopolitical arguments, following the regime's radicalization.[5]

In the Mediterranean and the Red Sea, Italy had to face the strongest maritime power of the time, the British Empire. Thus, military propaganda had to adopt maritime-naval topics as part of its message, involving the Italian Navy in this aspect of Fascist militarism. Indeed, MacGregor Knox identifies the importance of the Italian Navy's geopolitical vision as a primary source for the Fascist theory that Italy was a prisoner in the Mediterranean.[6] Robert Mallett has shown the inclination of Italian admirals, in particular of the Undersecretary of the Navy Domenico Cavagnari (1933–1940), to support the expansionist policies of Mussolini.[7] Finally, Paolo Frascani underlines how naval officers published works characterized by a strong political commitment, contributing to the build-up of the myth of *mare nostrum*.[8] Despite this, no analysis of Italian navalism during the Fascist period yet exists.

This aspect is interesting if we consider the current studies of the role of navies as 'think tanks' for geopolitical and strategic perspectives during the age of imperialism,[9] or their role in mobilizing widespread support in pre-1914 internal politics of the major global powers.[10] After 1918, the 'navalist frenzy' calmed down, but the major navies continued to use propaganda as part of the application of sea power, both for internal purposes and for external affirmation.[11] Finally, Italian naval power reached its height during the interwar period, giving the Navy a growing importance in Fascist propaganda.

Navy and fascist geopolitics

After World War I, the major experts on the Italian Navy were convinced that the country was vulnerable because of its dependency on seaborne trade. Between 1919 and 1922, the chiefs of naval staff, Paolo Emilio Thaon di Revel and Alfredo Acton, argued that Italy needed to secure control over the Adriatic in order to project its naval power over the Mediterranean against France to defend national communications.[12] At the same time, a pro-British attitude persisted because, as the Minister of Navy Giovanni Sechi argued, 'Britain can bring us to our knees in one month, without employing a single infantryman. We might as well have good relations with England and save us from the French danger'.[13]

Sechi was not alone in this belief. Romeo Bernotti, the most prominent Italian naval strategist of this period and chief of the Istituto di Guerra Marittima (Institute for Maritime Warfare – IgM), argued that the Italian situation resembled that of 1870, a time when the country was threatened by French naval superiority and was seeking an alliance with Britain.[14] In 1921, even Enrico Millo, an actively filo-nationalist admiral, suggested that Italy needed 'secure and powerful allies on the sea'.[15] He was referring to the British. Finally, in a secret memorandum prepared for the IgM concerning the 'maritime potential of Italy', Italy's leading expert on submarine warfare Vincenzo De Feo expressed the same opinions.[16]

The Navy's ideas about Italian vulnerability and dependency on the sea influenced the Fascist movement from its beginning. Mussolini's rhetoric about the necessity to acquire control of the *mare nostrum* was a direct consequence of this influence. Although the Duce had been convinced of the need to expel the British from the Mediterranean since 1919,[17] his admirals were more prudent, as their attitude during the Corfu crisis of September 1923 demonstrated.[18] However, between 1925 and 1926, significant changes occurred in the Navy and in Italy as a whole, when the Duce was finally able to establish a real dictatorship over the country. Key figures who had a deep-seated respect for the Royal Navy and for British sea power were pushed aside, and younger officers, exemplified by the new Undersecretary of the Navy Giuseppe Sirianni, took control of the institution, soon demonstrating their receptiveness to the imperial message that Mussolini was promoting.[19]

In July 1925, the Duce argued in front of the Admirals' council that Italy might hope to acquire control of France's colonies in North Africa, thanks to the demographic decline of that country.[20] One year later, at the end of the fleet's summer manoeuvres, he delivered a speech on the deck of the dreadnought *Cavour*, declaring that in the future the Mediterranean would once more be under Roman control.[21] In the same period, he declared that Italy needed to gain free access to the oceans, and in October, during a conference held in Perugia, he envisaged Roman expansion in the Mediterranean as a model for future Italian maritime expansionism.[22]

Unlike in 1923, no naval officers contested his point of view. Instead, the *Rivista Marittima*, the official journal of the Navy, reproduced the text of the conference. It was a clear sign that this way of thinking was breaching the intellectual core of the Navy.[23] Already in 1926, Giuseppe Fioravanzo, a major Italian naval thinker of the Fascist era, in a textbook for the Naval Academy argued that Mussolini's Italy had started a process of expansion in the *mare nostrum* by establishing its influence in Spain, Egypt and the Balkan states.[24] He also envisaged the possibility of war in the Mediterranean against France, Yugoslavia and Britain, or a combination of these countries.[25]

The confidence to face such eventualities grew during the period 1926–1934. The Regia Marina went through a phase of significant expansion, which, in combination with naval disarmament, enhanced its position among the world's major fleets. In theory, Italy could now count on battleship parity with France, with the ability to build a fleet slightly inferior to the Marine Nationale in tonnage, but larger in terms of units.[26] At the same time, the parity established between the United States and Britain convinced Italian admirals that a significant shift was happening in the global maritime balance of power. In 1929, in a top-secret memorandum, the naval staff stated that Britain 'had lost for the first time in history its supremacy'.[27] The main consequence for Italy, argued a second report prepared in 1930 for the incoming London naval conference, was that 'the English factor had to be considered with less importance [bilancia di scala] than in the past'.[28]

In the early 1930s, at the start of the regime's radicalization, the idea grew in the Navy that the stage was set for a possible Italian expansion in the Mediterranean. It was not the base for a realistic naval policy, which instead was characterized by constant financial problems.[29] However, now Italian naval thinkers were sure that the country was at the dawn of a new age of economic and military expansion. Indeed, some publications from key Navy experts expressed these opinions openly. Among them, there were Fioravanzo, Oscar Di Giamberardino, probably the most pro-fascist thinker within the Navy,[30] Guido Vannutelli, vice chief of naval staff during the Ethiopian crisis, and Francesco Bertonelli, a major expert on colonial problems. Also, some navalists who had expressed prudence during the 1920s now switched their position, as Bernotti did.[31]

According to their theories, Italy was at the beginning of its ascendancy in the Mediterranean and the Red Sea, thanks to the Fascist regime.[32] These areas constituted a single geopolitical entity, which was rising at the centre of global politics and economy, thanks to its position at the junction between Asia, Africa and Europe. Even more importantly, this entity could be an alternative powerhouse to the Anglo-American-dominated Atlantic.[33] Italy needed to dominate these areas by acquiring control of the choke points of the region: Suez, the Dardanelles, Gibraltar, the Maltese Channel and the Bab-el-Mandel strait.[34]

Naval officers claimed that Italy effectively had the possibility to acquire this vital space, thanks to the decline of its imperial rivals: France and Britain. Indeed, the first was a sort of modern Carthage: a wealthy nation with a declining population, which required the racially inferior soldiers of its colonies to wage war.[35] Meanwhile, Di Giamberardino described the British Empire as an organism that 'suffers from countless diseases'.[36] In particular,

Imperial unity was in peril, thanks to the 'centrifugal' tendencies of the dominions and the weak political control of London over the Middle Eastern mandates. Italy could eventually exploit these weaknesses to gain influence in these areas.[37] The Italian Navy was interested in these propaganda efforts also to counter French control of the Lebanon and its Beirut naval base, which was a constant threat for Italian communications in the Eastern Mediterranean.[38]

Finally, they identified the importance of an alliance with Germany and its Navy, wherein the sympathy for the Fascist regime and its fleet was high.[39] Already by 1932, Di Giamberardino stated that two groups of nations existed in Europe: the first was composed of 'rich and egoist' states (France and Britain) and the second by 'oppressed and unsatisfied' nations (Italy and Germany). He also concluded that the 'clear and continued hostilities' by some nations against Italy 'indicated without a doubt our position'.[40] Later, Fioravanzo argued that Italy and Germany shared the problem to 'maintain open their communications with the rest of the world and to intervene even in the oceans'.[41] Finally, in 1937, the naval staff encoded these common objectives into the motivations that stood in favour of an alliance with Germany:

> 1) affinity of political ideology; 2) similar demographic problems; 3) necessity of territorial expansion; 4) problems [to acquire] raw materials; 5) building a political bloc to counter other European or extra-European blocs; 6) fighting the spread of Bolshevism.[42]

Italy's acquisition of its new world power status would have required generations to reach fruition. Thus, for the moment, Italy needed to exercise the power of interdiction in the areas it aimed to control by blocking the possibility for other powers to use the sea lanes of the Mediterranean and the Red Sea without its permission.[43] From this came the necessity to build an offensive fleet, powerful in submarines and land-based airpower, conventional sea denial weapons and eventually capable of projecting itself in the nearby oceans to disturb enemy communications.[44] These theories explained much of the Italian naval policy in the 1930s.

Italian intellectuals of this period shared the idea that Western powers were in decline.[45] However, during the second half of the 1930s, the Navy's experts exercised a direct influence on other prominent authors. For example, the historian Pietro Silva, author of an acclaimed book on the history of the Mediterranean, often quoted Fioravanzo and Vannutelli to explain the growing strength of the Italian position in the Mediterranean.[46] Another example is *Politica marinara e Impero Fascista*, the most important navalist book wrote by a civilian during the Fascist era, Edoardo Squadrilli, General Commissar of the Navy League.[47]

In the works of these officers, we can find a foreshadowing of the themes dominating Fascist expansionism: demographics and the necessity of securing an adequate 'vital space'.[48] Moreover, they also reinforced Mussolini's view that demography dictated the power of nations instead of economic and military considerations.[49] Thus, before the Ethiopian war, which marked a turning point in the history of Fascist expansionism, the Navy had already contributed to strengthening the intellectual bases used by the Duce to legitimize the geopolitical claims that stayed at the very basis of the Italian wars of 1935 to 1943.

Navy, radicalization and propaganda

In the second half of the 1930s, the Navy contribution to Fascist navalism shifted to more direct forms of propaganda. These efforts were part of the regime's build-up of credibility for its radical policies and increasing warmongering, as seen in the racial segregation that followed the conquest of Ethiopia and the promulgation of the racial laws in 1938.[50] This mobilization included a 'call to the sea', to allow the Italians to perceive the Mediterranean as an Italian lake.[51] After 1933, the regime fostered the credibility of its fleet, claiming that Fascist spirit had rebuilt it.[52] Later, the conquest of Ethiopia allowed propagandists to claim, at least on paper, that the Italian Navy was able to hold in check the Royal Navy.[53] Finally, with the victory in Africa, Italy had reached an 'Imperial' status, and soon Bernotti argued: 'the conquest of the empire, for Italy, marked the passage from the Mediterranean to global politics', testifying to the rise of a 'new cycle' in Mediterranean history.[54] These claims showed the adherence of the Navy to the radicalization of the regime.

Mussolini now wanted navalist propaganda to form part of the everyday life of Italians.[55] Soon the high-ranking officers of the fleet followed his suggestions, as did Admiral Silvio Salza when he claimed that navalism was 'the ethical base of the maritime power'.[56] Thus, the Navy had the task of providing 'vulgarization of the questions of naval policy, as we and other navies see them'.[57] Indeed, after 1935, the Navy's propaganda activities increased, thanks to the new Undersecretary Domenico Cavagnari, selected by the Duce also for his close attention to this aspect of Navy activity.[58]

Propaganda involved the use of history. The Navy historical branch started the publication of an official history of the naval operations of the Great War to show the fleet's efforts during that conflict and its ability to win.[59] Meanwhile, in 1936, when plans for an oceanic fleet were underway, it also published a series of books dedicated to the oceanic cruises of Italian warships.[60] The Navy also established an active cooperation with the Lega Navale Italiana (Italian Navy League). Founded in 1897, until World War I, the League remained a tiny political pressure group.[61] In 1927, it passed to the direct control of the Fascist party, and grew steadily in the following years: in 1929 it had 18,000 members, 38,000 in 1931[62] and 147,000 in 1940.[63] Finally, two laws of 1933 and 1936 promoted the League as the only State institution for naval propaganda.[64] Thirty years after Britain and Germany, Fascist Italy finally had a mass organization for this purpose.

The League could count on direct support from the Navy Ministry. The secretary of the Fascist party was its president, but retired admirals were vice presidents: Ernesto Cuturi from 1931 to 1940 and Bernotti from 1940 to 1942.[65] Officers in active service were involved in the social life of the association on an everyday basis, participating in banquets and ceremonies held by the local sections, punctu-ally reported by the LNI review *L'Italia marinara*:

> Brilliant and characterized by the maximum intimacy [schietta familiarità] has been the gala offered by the Genoese section His Excellency Fleet Admiral Giuseppe Cantù to the Admirals Miraglia and De Feo and to a large delegation of the First Naval Squadron general staff [...] The presi-dent of the section cav. Uff [Knight Officer] Parini welcomed S.E. Cantù, which responded with brilliant words exalting the identity of perspectives that moved the Navy League and the Regia Marina.[66]

Traditional forms of propaganda involved key intellectuals of the Navy giving lectures, organized in cooperation with the League sections all over the penin-sula. The topics of these encounters were a vulgarization of the naval experts' works: Bernotti discussed the problem of 'sea domination' at the University of Pisa in 1936, Fioravanzo 'The Navy and the Empire' at Taranto in 1937.[67] Also, the rare public speeches of Cavagnari fostered the credibility of the Italian fleet. For example, in his last speech to the Chamber of Deputies before World War II, in March 1938, he maintained that Mussolini was right to renounce the construction of aircraft carriers and that thanks to Fascist naval policy, Italy now had the strongest submarine fleet of the world.[68]

The cooperation with the League also embraced various manifestations: 'sea weeks', 'sea festivals', the launch of ships and battle flag consignments. These events existed already during the Liberal period and were similar to those of other major Navy leagues.[69] However, during the late 1930s, for the first time they reached mass and widespread dimensions, precisely a consequence of the Italians entering the age of mass politics promoted by the Fascist party.[70] Key figures from local authorities and the party were usually involved. Fascist organizations were fully mobilized under the coord-ination of the local sections of the Navy League.[71] For example, during the battle flag consignment, defined by the Luce newsreel as a 'religious and warring ritual', the young members of the Gioventù Italiana del Littorio (GIL) passed the flag to the commanding officer of the ship involved in the ceremony.[72] Often, ships selected for these events recalled local maritime traditions: the city of Torre del Greco, famous for its coral jewellery produc-tion, offered the flag to the submarine 'Corallo'.[73] Everything was designed to instil the importance of naval tradition in the Italians, a project that had some parallels with similar activities of the German and British navies during the age of imperialism.[74]

Naval propaganda was also an instrument of external affirmation. During the interwar period, naval diplomacy was an integral part of the application of sea power, using the Navy to define one country's sphere of influence and demon-strate its operational capacity. Comparisons are possible with the presence of the Royal Navy in South America or with the British, French and Soviet pres-ence in the Baltic.[75] Fascist naval diplomacy aimed to show the presence of the

Regia Marina in waters claimed by Fascist Italy, to establish a 'bridge' with the Italian emigrants and to impress potential allies and enemies.

A major expedition set sail between September 1933 and February 1934. Two submarines (Sciesa and Toti) circumnavigated the African continent, navigating for 15,946 miles in 'full war conditions' and proving their capacity to operate in the Indian Ocean. Meanwhile, they visited ports, established contacts with the local Italian colonies, and exercised influence, arousing 'among the locals the greatest interest and admiration for our Navy and Fascist Italy'.[76] The visit of the cruiser Diaz to Australia, between September 1934 and February 1935, had similar objectives. It showed the 'renewed face of the motherland and modern efficiency of the Italian Navy', both to the Australians and the Italian emigrants, at a moment when Italy was on a collision course with the British Empire.[77] In 1938, the cruisers *Montecuccoli* and *Colleoni* went to Japan, visiting the ports of Nagasaki, Kobe, Yokohama and Aomori, at the same time as an important delegation of the Fascist party was visiting the country.[78] Clearly, this was part of the tightening relations between the two countries, within the framework of the future Tripartite Pact, which now included Germany, Italy and Japan.[79]

The two tendencies of Fascist naval propaganda, internal and external, found their most accomplished embodiments in the great naval reviews of 1936, 1937 and 1938, held in the Gulf of Naples.[80] These mass parades involved a huge mobilization of the Neapolitan population and the fleet in impressing potential allies visiting Italy: the Hungarian regent Miklos Horthy, the German War Minister Werner Von Blomberg and finally Hitler himself. The last one, the 'H' (Hitler) review, was held on 5 May 1938, as part of the visit of the German dictator to Italy. A crowd of thousands filled the entire route travelled by the Fuhrer from the railway station of Mergellina to the maritime station. Here Hitler and King Vittorio Emanuele boarded a motorboat that reached the dreadnought *Cavour*, the same ship from which in 1926 the Duce had announced his project to make the Mediterranean a Roman sea. Almost the entire Italian fleet – over 200 units supported by 48 seaplanes and 72 aircraft – was at sea. The simultaneous surfacing of 90 submarines concluded the review, which was the largest held in the Mediterranean up to that time.[81]

The entire parade occupied the lion's share in the Luce's documentary about Hitler's visit.[82] Newspapers acclaimed the review with resounding headlines like La Stampa's 'The phantasmagorical parade of 200 ships in the Gulf' or, even more symbolic, Córriere della Sera's 'The great day of the Imperial Navy'.[83] Meanwhile, during its preparation, execution and aftermath, Cavagnari was in constant contact with the Minister of Popular Culture, Dino Alfieri, paying close attention to foreign delegations, by meticulously organizing their presence and carefully observing their reactions.[84]

Some historians and writers have argued that this parade was particularly unpopular among the Italian naval officers or that it was just a standard move of diplomacy and propaganda, like the British coronation review at Spithead, held in 1937.[85] These are misunderstandings, because the review was part of the more general propaganda effort set up by the Navy and was the product of an institutional tendency supported by the Italian Admiralty to insert naval propaganda among the liturgy of 'collective harmony' developed by the regime.[86]

Hitler and Mussolini were at the centre of the review, and with them the ideological relationship between Fascist Italy and Nazi Germany. Also, the importance bestowed to the submarine arm of the Navy was a clear message for the British because it was considered a leveller against their superiority in battleships and aircraft carriers.[87] Indeed, this parade came at a moment of growing tension in the Mediterranean: the Spanish Civil War was still in progress, and Italian submarines had just ceased their secret and illegal blockade operations against the Spanish Republic. Italy had just agreed to reinforce the patrolling operations in the Mediterranean, against 'piracy' and the shipment of weapons to Spain, after that Britain and France decided to treat it on equal footing regarding the control of Mediterranean waters.[88]

The 'H' fleet review was a way to assert Italy's capability to dominate the Mediterranean with its fleet. Moreover, the nature of this propaganda, like all Fascist propaganda, was primarily ideological. On the one hand, it aimed to indoctrinate the Italian masses to the militaristic-navalist spirit that the regime was trying to build, while on the other, it wanted to impress Italy's allies and enemies by enhancing the credibility of the Italian armed forces. However, more than anything else, the review was an expression of Italy's siding with Nazi Germany, an alliance which had at its very basis common ideological motivations. All these aspects made the review the pinnacle of Fascist navalism.

Conclusion

The effectiveness of Fascist propaganda in militarizing Italian society has been contested by Paul Corner.[89] Moreover, for a full understanding of Fascist navalism, it is important to analyse the contribution of civilian experts and the activities of the Navy League. Despite this, the conclusion emerges that, during the interwar period, the Regia Marina was a 'think tank' for geopolitical perspectives and a powerful instrument for both internal and external propaganda. The rise of Fascism contributed to radicalizing its political and strategic designs, leading the Navy to anticipate and cooperate in the construction of the ideological vision that shaped Fascist foreign policy in the second half of the 1930s.[90] The doyen of Italian military historians, Giorgio Rochat, defined the objectives of Fascist foreign policy as 'science fiction',[91] but this does not change the fact that their existence allowed Mussolini to claim that Italian war aims in World War II were 'free access to the sea, a window on the ocean'.[92]

The problems analysed raise the question of how much the armed forces managed independently to adhere to the imperial and warmongering ambitions of the regime.[93] Here the remarks made by Enzo Collotti concerning another Italian institution, the diplomatic corps, are useful. The existence of a 'potential for cooperation' developed into an active support for Fascist foreign policy.[94] The same scheme is relevant for the Navy, because the propaganda disseminated by the Italian Admiralty supported the regime's radicalization in the name of a shared geopolitical vision. In the end, the involvement of the Navy in the construction of Fascist navalism reminds us that this institution (and the other two branches of the armed forces) held part of the political-ideological responsibility for the beginning of the Italian decade of war.

Notes

1 M. Knox, *Destino comune, Dittatura, politica estera e guerra nell'Italia fascista e nella Germania nazista* (Turin: Einaudi, 2003), pp. 73–4; D. Rodogno, *Il nuovo ordine mediterraneo. Le politiche di occupazione dell'Italia fascista in Europa (1940–1943)* (Turin: Bollati Boringhieri), p. 69.

2 E. Gentile, 'L'uomo nuovo del fascismo, Riflessioni su un esperimento totalitario di rivoluzione antropologica', in E. Gentile (ed.), *Il fascismo. Storia e interpretazione* (Rome and Bari: Laterza, 2002), pp. 251–3.

3 M. Isnenghi, 'Italo Balbo, ovvero il volo fascista', in *Italia moderna, Immagini e storia di un'identità nazionale*, vol. 2 (Milan: Electa, 1982–1986), pp. 111–26; for the Army see N. della Volpe, *Esercito e propaganda tra le due guerre* (Rome: Ussme, 1992).

4 G. Rochat, *Italo Balbo aviatore e ministro dell'Aeronautica* (Ferrara: Bovolenta, 1979), pp. 69–81; M. Di Giovanni, 'L'aviazione e i miti del fascismo', in P. Ferrari (ed.), *L'aeronautica italiana, Una storia del Novecento* (Milan: Franco Angeli, 2005), pp. 203–28; E. Lehman, *Le ali del potere, La propaganda aeronautica nell'Italia fascista* (Turin: UTET, 2012).

5 R. Ben-Ghiat, *La cultura fascista* (Bologna: Il Mulino, 2006), pp. 165–75.

6 M. Knox, 'Foreign Policy, Ideology and War', in A. Lyttelton (ed.), *The Short Oxford History of Italy, Liberal and Fascist Italy, 1900–1945* (Oxford: Oxford University Press, 2002), pp. 109–11.

7 R. Mallett, *The Italian Navy and the Fascist Expansionism* (London: Frank Cass, 1998), p. 4.

8 P. Frascani, *Il mare* (Bologna: Il Mulino, 2008), p. 132.

9 See D. Bonker, *Militarism in a Global Age. Naval Ambitions in Germany and the United States before World War I* (Ithaca, NY: Cornell University Press, 2012); R. Hobson, *Imperialism at Sea, Naval Strategic Thought, the Ideology of Sea Power, and the Tirpitz Plan, 1875–1914* (Leiden: Brill, 2002).

10 See for Britain and Germany: J. Ruger, *The Great Naval Game: Britain and Germany in the Age of Empire* (Cambridge: Cambridge University Press, 2008); for Japan: J.C. Shencking, *Making Waves Politics, Propaganda, and the Emergence of the Imperial Japanese Navy, 1868–1922* (Stanford, CA: Stanford University Press, 2005).

11 C. Bell, *The Royal Navy, Seapower and Strategy between the Wars* (Stanford, CA: Stanford University Press, 2000), pp. 138–79; C.S. Thomas, *The German Navy and the Nazi Era* (Annapolis, MD: Naval Institute Press, 1990), p. 144.

12 W. Polastro, 'La marina militare italiana nel primo dopoguerra', *Il Risorgimento*, III (1977), pp. 141–6.

13 Archivio Storico del Ministero degli Affari Esteri (ASMAE), Affari Politici 1919–1930, b. 1289, Sechi to Sforza, 3 February 1921, p. 3.

14 R. Bernotti, *Il potere marittimo nella Grande guerra* (Livorno: Giusti, 1920), p. 545. On the necessity of an alliance with Britain: M. Gabriele and G. Friz, *La politica navale italiana dal 1885 al 1915* (Rome: Usmm, 1982), p. 45; on the importance of Bernotti see: P. Ramoino, *Romeo Bernotti* (Rome: Usmm, 2006); L. Donolo, *Storia della dottrina navale italiana* (Rome: Usmm, 1996), pp. 226–31, 302–3.

15 Archivio dell'Ufficio storico della Marina militare (AUSMM), Registri del comitato degli ammiragli, Meeting of 10 October 1922, p. 4.

16   AUSMM, DG, DG-1, B, C, D, box 12, folder 2, D-1, V. De Feo, *Studio sulla potenzialità marittima dell'Italia* (Istituto di guerra marittima, 1921), p. 46.

17   M. Knox, *To the Threshold of Power: Origins and Dynamics of the Fascist and National Socialist Dictatorship* (Cambridge: Cambridge University Press, 2007), p. 300.

18   M. Pizzigallo, 'L'incidente di Corfù e la politica estera italiana nel Levante', *Storia e politica*, 13:3 (1974), pp. 427–35; E. Ferrante, 'Un rischio calcolato? Mussolini e gli ammiragli nella gestione della crisi di Corfù', *Storia delle Relazioni Internazionali*, 5:2 (1989), pp. 221–44.

19   E. Pellegrini, *Giuseppe Sirianni, Ministro della Marina* (Rome: Usmm, 2001), p. 74.

20   AUSMM, Registri del comitato degli ammiragli, Meeting of 11 August 1925, p. 5.

21   'Mussolini ai comandanti della squadra navale', 5 July 1926, in *Opera Omnia di Benito Mussolini*, E. Susmel and D. Susmel (eds.), vol. XXI (Florence: La Fenice, 1951–1980).

22   E. Canevari, *La guerra italiana retroscena della disfatta* (Verona: Tosi, 1948), p. 212; for the Perugia conference see L. Canfora, *Ideologie del classicismo* (Turin: Einaudi, 1980), p. 91.

23   B. Mussolini, 'Roma antica sul mare', *Rivista marittima*, October 1926, pp. II–XVI.

24   Biblioteca dell'accademia navale di Livorno (BAN – Library of the Italian Naval Academy), D. Fioravanzo, *Schemi di arte militare marittima per il corso superiore*, vol. II (Livorno: Tipografia dell'Accademia navale, 1926), p. 1618.

25   Ibid, pp. 1231–3.

26   B. Sullivan, 'Italian Naval Power at the Washington Conference', in E.J. Goldstein and J.H. Maurer (eds.), *The Washington Conference 1921–1922: Naval Rivalry, East Asian Stability and the Road to Pearl Harbor* (London: Frank Cass, 2003), pp. 220–48.

27   AUSMM, Raccolta di base (Rdb), b. 1718, f. 2, Ufficio del Capo di stato maggiore della R. Marina, *Il problema della limitazione degli armamenti nei suoi aspetti tecnico-pratici*, Roma, 1929, Riservatissimo, pp. 24–5.

28   AUSMM, Rdb, b. 3181, f. 23, *Conferenza navale di Londra 1930, aspetti del problema navale italiano*, pp. 2–3.

29   On the financial and building limitations see J. Gooch, *Mussolini and his Generals: The Armed Forces and Fascist Foreign Policy, 1922–1940* (Cambridge: Cambridge University Press, 2007), pp. 47–50, 88–91, 141–52.

30   He was also author of two politological essays about Fascism: O. Di Giamberardino, *Il fascismo e gli ideali di Roma* (Florence: Vallecchi, 1931); O. Di Giamberardino, *L'individuo nell'etica fascista* (Florence: Vallecchi, 1940).

31   See the encyclopedic entry 'Marina' in which the authors compare the Italian position to that of Britain: R. Bernotti, P. Fraccaro, and G. Ingianni, *Marina* (Enciclopedia Italiana, 1934). Available from www.treccani.it/enciclopedia/marina_Enciclopedia-Italiana/ [Accessed on 28 June 2016].

32   According to Fioravanzo, Italy was in its 'most bright rising phase': G. Fioravanzo, *La guerra sul mare e la guerra integrale, vol. I, Concetti fondamentali* (Turin: Schioppo, 1930), p. 22; Di Giamberardino too argued that the growing Italian population was leading to a growing internal production, both agricultural and industrial, causing the necessity for maritime expansion: O. Di Giamberardino, *Politica marittima* (Bologna: Cappelli, 1932), pp. 133–4.

33   G. Vannutelli, *Il Mediterraneo, Origine e fonte risorgente della civiltà mondiale* (Bologna: Cappelli, 1932), pp. 225, 229–30.

34   F. Bertonelli, *Il nostro mare. Studio della situazione politica militare dell'Italia nel Mediterraneo* (Florence: Bemporard, 1930), p. 147.

35   Bertonelli, *Il nostro mare*, pp. 19, 22; similar statements by Fioravanzo, *Arte militare marittima*, II, p. 1620, and Di Giamberardino, *Politica marittima*, p. 95.

36 Di Giamberardino, *Politica marittima*, p. 13.
37 Bertonelli, *Il nostro mare*, p. 139.
38 N. Arielli, *Fascist Italy and the Middle East, 1933–40* (London: Palgrave MacMillan, 2010), p. 21.
39 G. Schreiber, *Revisionismus und Weltmachtstreben, Marinefürung und Deutsch-Italianische Beziehungen, 1919–1944* (Stuttgart: DVA, 1978), pp. 39–64.
40 Di Giamberardino, *Politica marittima*, p. 135.
41 G. Fioravanzo, *Basi navali del mondo, vol. I* (Milan: ISPI, 1936), p. 113.
42 AUSMM, DG, DG, Studi Politici, b. 2, *Considerazioni del Nostro problema strategico in base alla situazione politica del momento presente*, 26 October 1937, p. 1.
43 Bertonelli, *Il nostro mare*, p. 147.
44 G. Fioravanzo, 'Marine mediterranee e marine oceaniche', *Gerarchia*, November (1929), p. 909. For the importance to enhance the submarine fleet as a sea-denial weapon see V. De Feo, *La Conferenza Navale di Londra*, July–August 1930, p. 15.
45 See Junius (Luigi Einaudi), 'Le prospettive dell'Impero Britannico dopo l'ultima conferenza imperiale', *Nuova Antologia*, September–October 1927, pp. 223–34; S. Gemma, *L'Impero britannico* (Bologna: Zanichelli, 1933), pp. 378–402; V. Morello, *La Germania si sveglia. Dopo Locarno e Thoiry* (Rome: Cremonese, 1931).
46 P. Silva, *Il Mediterraneo da l'unità di Roma all'impero italiano* (Milan: ISPI, 1937), pp. 499, 509–10, 543, see footnotes.
47 E. Squadrilli, *Politica marinara e impero fascista* (Rome: Stabilimento tipografico del genio, 1937), on the relationship with Britain, pp. 44–6; on the Italian ascendancy, pp. 49–53.
48 C. Ipsen, *Demografia totalitaria. Il problema della popolazione nell'Italia fascista* (Bologna: Il Mulino, 1997), pp. 164–82; P. Zunino, *L'ideologia del fascismo: miti, credenze e valori nella stabilizzazione del regime* (Bologna: Il Mulino, 1985), pp. 357–8.
49 M. Knox, 'Fascist Italy Assesses its Enemies, 1935–1940', in E.R. May (ed.), *Knowing One's Enemies* (Princeton, NJ: Princeton University Press, 1986), p. 364; G. Bruce Strang, *On the Fiery March: Mussolini Prepares for War* (Westport: Praeger, 2006), pp. 13–38.
50 Ben-Ghiat, *La cultura fascista*, p. 206.
51 Frascani, *Il mare*, p. 135.
52 A starting point of this tendency was the propaganda book published by the Ministry of the Navy in 1932, on the decennial of the Regime, to celebrate 'the work accomplished with lively sentiment by all the members of the Regia Marina', see Ministero della Marina, *La nostra marina militare* (Novara: De Agostini, 1932).
53 See the semi-official relation of the Navy regarding the Italo-Ethiopian war: A. Ginocchietti, *La R. Marina nella conquista dell'impero, 1935–1936* (Rome: Unione editoriale, 1936), pp. 156–8.
54 R. Bernotti, 'Il nuovo ciclo mediterraneo', in Ministero della Marina (ed.), *Almanacco navale 1938* (Rome: Ministero della Marina, 1938), p. 122.
55 *Opera Omnia, Vol. XXVIII, Per il settantesimo anno di vita della 'Rivista marittima'*, 21 December 1936, p. 96.
56 S. Salza, *Navalismo. Fondamento etico del potere marittimo*, in Ministero della Marina (ed.), *Almanacco navale 1939* (Rome: Ministero della Marina, 1939), p. 12.
57 Ivi, p. 13.
58 E. Cernuschi, *Domenico Cavagnari* (Rome: Rivista marittima, 2000), p. 56.
59 See *La Marina italiana nella Grande guerra, 8 vols.* (Florence: Vallecchi, 1935–1943).
60 F. Leva, *Storia delle campagne oceaniche della Regia Marina* (Rome: Ufficio Storico della Regia Marina, 1936).
61 G. Monina, *La Grande Italia marittima, La propaganda navalista e la Lega navale italiana, 1866–1918* (Soveria Mannelli: Rubettino, 2008).

62   The National Archives, London, Foreign Office 371/15253, C 2814/510/22, Italian Navy League, Naval attaché dispatch No. 5/31 of 21st April 1931 report the activities of the Italian Navy League, 22 April 1931, p. 1.

63   Lega navale italiana, *Italia marinara* (Rome: LNI, 1947), p. 6.

64   See R. Decreto n. 21 December 1884, 1933, and n. 1171, 2 June 1936.

65   'Il cambio di Guardia nella Lega navale', *L'Italia marinara*, January 1940, p. 5.

66   'Vita della Lega navale, Genova', *L'Italia marinara*, June 1934, p. 253.

67   'Vita della Lega navale, Iniziative delle sezioni, Il dominio del mare', *L'Italia marinara*, July 1936, pp. 272–3; 'Vita della Lega navale, Taranto', *L'Italia marinara*, May 1937, p. 153.

68   Atti Parlamentari, Camera, XXIX Legislatura, discussioni, tornata del 15 marzo 1938, pp. 4696–7.

69   Bell, *Seapower and Strategy*, p. 175.

70   A. De Bernardi, *Una dittatura moderna, il fascismo come problema storico* (Milan: Bruno Mondadori, 2006), p. 166.

71   Archivio storico dell'Istituto Luce (ASIL), Giornale Luce, B0543, *Il varo dell'incrociatore 'Maurizio Attendolo'*, September 1934, Trieste.

72   ASIL, Giornale Luce, B0498, *La consegna di combattimento all'incrociatore Gorizia*, 07/1934; ASIL, *La gioventù del littorio consegna la bandiera di combattimento alla R. Torpediniera 'Castore'*, Gela, 28 September 1938.

73   ASIL, Giornale Luce B1060, *La bandiera di combattimento per il sommergibile Corallo*, Torre del Greco, 17 March 1937.

74   Ruger, *The Great Naval Game*, pp. 82–92.

75   J. Wise, *The Role of the Royal Navy in South America, 1920–1970* (London: Bloomsbury, 2014), pp. 17–23; A. Gunnar, *The Rise and the Fall of Soviet Navy in the Baltic, 1921–1941* (London: Frank Cass, 2005), pp. 59, 120–1; D. Stoker, *Britain, France and Naval Arms Trade in the Baltic, 1919–1939: Grand Strategy and Failure* (London: Frank Cass, 2003), pp. 17, 55, 58–63.

76   AUSMM. Rdb, b. 2598, fasc.1, *Crociera nell'Oceano Indiano dei sommergibili Sciesa e Toti. Condizioni di efficienza militari dei due smg 'Sciesa' e 'Toti' durante la crociera*, pp. 3, 21.

77   AUSMM, Rdb, b. 1730, f. 2, Diaz to Maripers, Marina and Maristat, n. 377, 6 February 1935, p. 1.

78   F. Levra, *Storia delle campagne oceaniche della Regia Marina*, vol. III (Rome: Usmm, 1992 reprint), p. 525.

79   See F. De Ninno, 'The Italian Navy and Japan, the Indian Ocean, Failed Cooperation, and Tripartite Relations (1935–1943)', *War in History* (2018), Doi: 10.1177/0968344518777270.

80   For a description see T. Marcon, 'Riviste navali a Napoli negli anni Trenta', *Bollettino d'archivio dell'Ufficio storico della Marina militare*, June 1995; A smaller fourth parade was held in 1939 for the visit of the Yugoslavian King.

81   L. Nonno, 'La manovra navale di Napoli. 5 maggio', *Nazione militare*, May 1938, pp. 401–3.

82   ASIL. Istituto Nazionale Luce, 1938, *Il viaggio del Fuhrer in Italia*.

83   *La Stampa*, Edizione serale, 5 May 1938; *Corriere della Sera*, 6 May 1938.

84   AUSMM, Rdb, b. 2709, Archivio storico, *Visita di S.E. Hitler, Telegrammi trasmessi a S.E. Alfieri sul 'Cavour'*; N. 36194, *Grandi quotidiani di provincia del giorno 5 maggio 1938*; Presidenza del consiglio dei ministri to Cavagnari, *Visita di Hitler in Italia*, b. 15924, 12 November 1938 (on the Japanese naval attachè); Id., Relazione del Capitano di Corvetta Leonardo Gremaglia, 8 May 1938, Gremaglia was ordered to stay in touch with the foreign naval attachés and produce a report of their comments, which he judged positive.

85 G. Giorgerini, *Da Matapan al Golfo Persico: la Marina militare italiana dal fascismo alla Repubblica* (Milan: Mondadori, 1989), p. 372; E. Cernuschi, 'Dietro la rivista, storia e retroscena della rivista navale "H" del 5 maggio 1938', *Rivista marittima*, (June 2010), pp. 79–92.

86 E. Gentile, *Il culto del littorio* (Rome and Bari: Laterza, 1993), pp. 139–74.

87 See F. De Ninno, *I sommergibili del fascismo, Politica, navale strategia e uomini tra le due guerre mondiali* (Milan: Unicopli, 2014), pp. 280–1.

88 At least this was Galeazzo Ciano's opinion: G. Ciano, *Diario 1937–1943* (Milan: Rizzoli, 1990), September 1937, p. 39.

89 P. Corner, 'L'opinione popolare e il tentativo di effettuare la militarizzazione della società italiana sotto il fascismo', in P. Del Negro, A. Staderini and N. Labanca (eds.), *Militarizzazione e nazionalizzazione nella Storia d'Italia* (Milan: Unicopli, 2005), pp. 197–206.

90 A. Kallis, *Fascist Ideology, Territory and Expansionism in Fascist Italy and Nazi Germany* (London: Routledge, 2000), p. 51.

91 G. Rochat, *Le guerre italiane 1935–1943: dall'Impero d'Etiopia alla disfatta* (Turin: Einaudi, 2005), pp. 241–2.

92 Mussolini Memo to the King, 30 March 1940, in R. De Felice (ed.), *Mussolini e il fascismo, Lo stato totalitario, Vol. 2, 1936–1940* (Turin: Einaudi, 1981), p. 774.

93 N. Labanca, *L'istituzione militare in Italia. Politica e società* (Milan: Unicopli, 2002), p. 26.

94 E. Collotti, *Fascismo e politica di potenza* (Florence: La Nuova Italia, 2000), p. 15; also see R.J. Boshworth, *Italy and the Wider World, 1860–1960* (London: Routledge, 1996), p. 42.

10 Revisiting the 'colonial hypothesis'

The policies and language of the Italian Army in Ethiopia and Yugoslavia

Nicolas G. Virtue

Introduction

It has been thirty years since Italian historian Teodoro Sala posited his 'colonial hypothesis.' In a short essay, Sala noted similarities between Italian colonial rule in Africa and military occupation in Yugoslavia. These commonalities included radical schemes of economic exploitation and plunder, legal distinctions between citizens and subjects, the employment of irregular auxiliary bands, the mass internment of non-combatants and brutal reprisal measures justified by racial characterizations of the occupied populations. Moreover, Sala argued, the presence in Yugoslavia of officers with colonial experience and the adoption of colonial phraseology in Italian military reports and directives suggested the existence of causal links between the two cases.[1] The colonial hypothesis suggested that Italian political and military leaders imported ideas and methods from Africa to the Balkans during World War II.

Some historians have accepted Sala's hypothesis wholeheartedly. In his influential examination of Mussolini's Mediterranean new order, Davide Rodogno argues that 'repression in the Balkans [...] was decisively shaped by the colonial experience' gained by the army and regime in Libya and Ethiopia during the 1920s and 1930s.[2] For others, the colonial hypothesis remains an 'open question', especially given the asymmetries between the African and European contexts.[3] Certainly, Mussolini's imperial vision in the Balkans – based on the annexation and incorporation of Slovenia and Dalmatia into the Italian metropole, protectorates over Albania and Montenegro, and informal control over the so-called Independent State of Croatia through an Italian-dominated Imperial Community – was no carbon copy of his colonial projects in Africa. Africans and Slavs occupied different levels within Fascism's racial hierarchy.[4] Militarily and ideologically, the composition of insurgent and counterinsurgent forces in both theatres varied considerably. For example, occupation in Yugoslavia lacked the presence of regular indigenous troops akin to the Eritrean *askari*.[5]

Comparative differences do not in themselves negate knowledge transfers or learning processes between geographic or chronological contexts. At the same time, the dynamics of transfer cannot be fully understood without a thorough comparative analysis that examines both contexts equally.[6] The colonial hypothesis has yet to be tested systematically in this way. It is necessary to examine primary source material from both the African and European cases in order to isolate similarities and linkages in the development of policies and attitudes that fuelled mass violence. Drawing on evidence from Ethiopia and Yugoslavia – the two most important theatres of Fascist empire-building, both contained within the timeframe of Italy's 'decade of war' – this chapter re-examines some of the similarities in policy and language that Sala first highlighted three decades ago.

After re-engaging Sala's hypothesis through the updated historiographical and theoretical framework provided by transfer history, we shall revisit the military aspects of the colonial hypothesis. First, we examine the Italian army's reliance on indigenous irregular forces. Second, we discuss the use of terror by Italian military authorities to reinforce prestige, in particular through their exemplary employment of heavy weapons technologies. Last, we analyse the language and rhetoric adopted by Italian officers to justify their attitudes and policies.

The picture that emerges reinforces the observation that knowledge transfer among imperial and military elites was a complicated and creative process, heavily influenced by structural factors and the pressure of circumstances.[7] Military violence in Ethiopia and Yugoslavia operated according to fundamentally similar dynamics that were typical of imperial wars and colonial occupations. However, there is limited evidence to suggest that a distinctly 'colonial' mentality was the key determining factor behind military decision-making. Rather, military policies and attitudes developed primarily in response to technical conditions imposed by irregular warfare.

Historiographical challenges and opportunities

The colonial hypothesis is worth revisiting in light of recent work concerning the impact of colonial experience on Nazi violence and genocides in World War II. The rediscovery of Hannah Arendt's insights on the connection between imperialism and totalitarianism has ignited new debate over the classification of Nazi rule in the east as a 'colonial endeavour'.[8] Particular attention has been given to the genocidal campaign waged by Wilhelmine military authorities against the Herero and Nama peoples in German Southwest Africa between 1904 and 1907. Jürgen Zimmerer and Benjamin Madley have argued that the experience of a racial war of annihilation in Namibia made genocidal thinking possible for Nazi authorities, who borrowed and expanded upon colonial ideas and methods in their own policies against Slavs and Jews.[9] Critics have argued that 'phenomenological similarities' between Nazi and colonial violence do not necessarily indicate 'direct personal and structural continuities' between men and institutions operating forty years apart.[10] While it can be countered that colonial ideas could persist even without colonies, which Germany lost after World War I, the time gap between the Namibian and European genocides remains a fundamental obstacle to the study of linkages between the two cases.[11]

In this respect, the example of Fascist Italy provides more suitable grounds for an analysis of transfers and learning processes. Not only had Italy maintained a colonial presence in Africa since the 1880s, but the Fascist regime greatly expanded that presence on the eve of World War II by invading Ethiopia in 1935. The invasion was explicitly intended to transfer the experience of colonial conquest, rule and race-thinking to Italy as a means of relaunching the regime's 'anthropological revolution' to create the Fascist 'new man'.[12] The Ethiopian campaign was conducted on a massive scale. Nearly half a million men took part in the invasion, commanded for the most part by senior officers of the regular army. The subsequent occupation and counterinsurgency continued to employ tens of thousands of Italian troops and nearly two hundred thousand *askari* into 1940.[13] Ex-combatants and officers seconded from the Royal Italian Army outnumbered civilian personnel in the colonial administration.[14] Even though most of the army's colonial specialists remained in East and North Africa during World War II, there was no shortage of personal and institutional continuities between the Italian military occupations in Ethiopia and Yugoslavia.[15]

Beyond intra-imperial lesson learning, Fascist empire-building potentially also provided a mechanism for trans-imperial or transnational knowledge transfers. It has been suggested that the Italian invasion of Ethiopia – with its extreme levels of violence and destruction justified by social Darwinist demographic and racist discourse – 'bridged the gap between nineteenth-century European imperialism and the Nazi war for German *Lebensraum*'.[16] As Patrick Bernhard has shown, Nazi planners for eastern resettlement drew lessons and inspiration from the Fascist model established in Italian Africa.[17]

The colonial hypothesis remains significant, then, for what it can reveal about the motivations behind Italian violence in Yugoslavia, about the Royal Army's role in Fascism's programme of national rebirth, and about the singularity or isolation of the German example. The analytical methods and insights provided by the relatively new field of transfer history permit an examination of colonial links that goes beyond cataloguing phenomenological similarities. Here, we use Italian military publications, war logs, correspondence and propaganda to illuminate the dynamics of transfers between Ethiopia and Yugoslavia, and to highlight the relationship between colonial experience and race-thinking, counterinsurgency doctrine and local conditions in Italian military decision-making.

Indigenous irregular forces

The Italian army's use of irregular auxiliary forces best exemplifies how ad hoc responses to circumstances produced similar colonial dynamics in Ethiopia and Yugoslavia. All modern colonial powers relied heavily on indigenous troops to supplement the usually meagre regular forces tasked with preserving colonial rule.[18] In Ethiopia, Italian commanders bolstered their metropolitan and *askari* units with irregular bands [*bande*]. These included permanent garrisons for local defence, temporary bands recruited for specific operations and armed formations loyal to collaborating Ethiopian elites such as *ras* Hailu Tekle Haymanot.[19] In Yugoslavia, the recruitment of Serb and Montenegrin Četniks and of Slovene White Guards into the *Milizia Volontaria Anti-Comunista* (MVAC) became a cornerstone of Italian policy.[20] Eric Gobetti has argued that generals with colonial experience especially leaned towards a pro-Četnik policy in Yugoslavia.[21]

However, while the recruitment of irregular fighters was a typical feature of colonial warfare, in neither case did Italian policies necessarily emanate from colonial lessons. Prior to the invasion of Ethiopia, Italian military theorists and practitioners debated the value of indigenous auxiliaries. Experience in Libya highlighted the effectiveness of regular Eritrean *askari* battalions and of special formations like the horse- and camel-mounted *gruppi sahariani*, but Italian officers expressed doubts over the loyalty and efficiency of other irregular bands.[22] The former military governor of Cyrenaica, Luigi Bongiovanni, concluded that temporary or 'occasional formations' of auxiliaries were best avoided.[23] While he favoured employing indigenous troops over Italian personnel in his mobile operations, General Rodolfo Graziani reduced the number of locally recruited police and garrisons under his command and warned that the leaders of irregular bands were not to be trusted.[24]

In a journal article and war college text, Guglielmo Nasi reiterated the axiom that irregular troops could be relied upon in times of success but were best done without in difficult circumstances. They were unreliable, undisciplined and militarily ineffective, capable only of reconnaissance roles.[25] Nonetheless, following the invasion of Ethiopia, circumstances compelled Nasi, in his role as governor of Harar and later vice-governor of Italian East Africa, to employ irregular auxiliaries in large numbers. After 1936, the return of metropolitan units to Italy and the shortage of Eritrean *askari* led most senior officers to regard irregular forces as an unavoidable and necessary evil.[26] By 1940, the colonial government was spending six million lire each month to maintain its permanent irregular formations in Ethiopia. Nasi wanted to disband them, but he feared that Italian pay was the only thing preventing these warriors from joining the Ethiopian Patriot movement *en masse*.[27]

Poorly trained local defence auxiliaries did not earn a strong reputation among Italian officials in East Africa, either. The recruits were 'not warriors', but 'shepherds, peasants, [and] unemployed beggars who enlist in the bands for the glory of carrying a rifle'.[28] Italian authorities lamented that the residential bands frequently proved incapable of fending off insurgents and that the weapons allotted to them inevitably wound up in enemy hands, either through defeat or desertion.[29] By 1939, the commander of troops in revolt-stricken Amhara, General Quirino Armellini, concluded that bands of armed villages were worthless in combat. While acknowledging the regime's lack of personnel, he recommended that the bands be abolished.[30]

Three years later, Armellini found himself in command of the XVIII Army Corps occupying parts of Croatia, Bosnia and Dalmatia. The environment, he noted, was 'strangely similar' to that encountered in his 'long colonial life'.[31] However, in Yugoslavia, he became a strong advocate of alliances with Serb 'Četnik' bands on the basis that they were 'extremely useful in the struggle against communism'.[32] Armellini's decision to support the expansion of irregular formations in Yugoslavia came in spite of, rather than because of, his experience in East Africa.

The Italian Second Army's reliance on irregular forces to garrison territory and partake in antipartisan operations developed over time for political and military reasons. Politically, the Serbs provided a useful counterweight to the Croatian Ustaše, whom Italian generals blamed for sabotaging Italian expansion in the Adriatic. While the Independent State of Croatia was meant to function as a satellite within Fascism's new Imperial Community, Italian military authorities quickly concluded that the Croatian leadership, resenting Italy's annexation of Dalmatia, had fallen under German influence. Moreover, they considered the chaotic and bloody Ustaša persecution of Serbs counterproductive to the pacification and normalization of the region. Many Italian commanders sympathized with Serb populations and insurgents who sought Italian protection and assistance.[33] Within this context of political resentment, Italian generals in Yugoslavia developed colonial-style martial race theories, which categorized Croats as 'supremely cowardly' compared to the 'chivalrous' Serbs.[34] The resulting policy functioned as a 'divide and conquer' strategy, whereby the Italian army effectively 'aided and abetted' Četnik mass violence against Croats and Muslims as an unsavoury but acceptable cost for Serb support.[35]

By mid-1942, military necessity drove the Second Army to accelerate the development of its irregular units, now formalized under the MVAC label. Italian conscript infantry divisions had proven ill-suited to anti-partisan warfare and were by this point exhausted, with further reinforcement from Italy unlikely. While commanders confined their Italian manpower in large garrisons to rest and refit for eventual grand operations, they relied on MVAC formations and autonomous Četnik bands to fill the void in the territories abandoned by Italian units.[36] The continued growth of the Communist Partisan movement combined with the Second Army's chronic manpower shortage resulted in irregulars shouldering an increasingly heavy portion of the counterinsurgency effort in Yugoslavia through 1942 and into 1943, despite complaints from Italian officers that their MVAC units lacked fighting power, discipline or cohesion.[37]

Although collaboration in the Balkans was driven by ideological, national and irredentist motives that were for the most part lacking in East Africa, the pressures and circumstances that led Italian authorities to lean heavily upon indigenous auxiliaries in both contexts were fundamentally similar.[38] The central role played by irregular forces in Ethiopia and Yugoslavia, while characteristic of imperial wars, was not the automatic result of an imperial-colonial doctrine or mindset. Rather, the recruitment of auxiliaries came in response to growing unrest, a shortage of metropolitan and indigenous regular forces, and the opportunity or convenience of exploiting local ethnic and religious rivalries.

Terror and prestige

The strongest evidence of a shared approach and direct links between the Italian campaigns in Ethiopia and Yugoslavia comes in relation to the military tactics and strategies of repression employed in each theatre. The application of terror and the maintenance of prestige guided Italian strategy in both cases. Italian generals were obsessed with the 'politics of prestige', which – like their civilian Fascist counterparts – they equated primarily with the willingness and ability to use overwhelming force to stupefy and terrorize enemy insurgents and occupied populations alike.[39] This obsession with prestige and lack of distinction between combatant and non-combatant were classic components of colonial warfare in general.[40]

By the 1930s, several colonial powers had targeted non-combatants with deportation and internment. Italian colonial and military authorities likewise resorted to mass internment in Libya and Yugoslavia. Concentration camps played a lesser role in Italian counterinsurgency efforts in Ethiopia; evidence largely is restricted to the Danane camp near Mogadishu, which held former Ethiopian officials, intellectuals, professionals and lesser nobility.[41] To date, the most rigorous effort to test Sala's colonial hypothesis is Costantino Di Sante's examination of Italian practices of internment in Libya and Yugoslavia. His conclusions largely echo our own in relation to the use of irregular forces: Italian authorities in Libya and Yugoslavia developed similar internment policies as the result of an escalation of violence against civilians whom they regarded as hostile enemies. However, Di Sante notes, Italian authorities in Yugoslavia never referred to colonial precedent when justifying or structuring their internment policies. In practice, Libyan internees suffered harsher conditions and much higher death rates than did Yugoslav civilians, partly due to differing Italian racial concepts towards the two groups and partly because Fascist projects of clearing territory for colonization made more headway in Libya.[42]

Italian internment policy in Yugoslavia was developed largely under the leadership of General Mario Roatta, who commanded the Italian Second Army during the pivotal year of 1942. That March, Roatta distributed his now infamous 'Circular 3C', which set the guidelines for the conduct of counterinsurgency in Yugoslavia.[43] Although Roatta's entire career had been spent in Europe, he explicitly referred to colonial models twice within his lengthy circular.[44] The first reference directed commanders of mobile columns to form laager at night, 'as in Africa'. The second reference was more significant:

> The fight that we are waging is not a duel in which we have to compare arms with those of the enemy, nor is it an ordinary form of war in which the means employed are – in the interests of economy – proportionate to the size of the targets. But it is instead comparable to *colonial warfare*, in which it is advisable to give the opponent a clear and immediate sensation of our superiority, and of the inexorability of our reaction.[45]

This same excerpt was repeated as late as March 1943 in a directive issued by Umberto Spigo, who had replaced Armellini as commander of XVIII Corps in Dalmatia. Spigo urged his subordinates to carry out 'colonial style' movements to 'strike fear into the enemy'.[46] By the time that Spigo penned his directive, Partisans in Yugoslavia increasingly were operating as conventional forces. They were far better equipped and organized than Italy's colonial opponents had been.[47] Spigo may have been trying to bolster the flagging morale of his exhausted troops, but his use of this passage indicates his belief that techniques adopted in African colonial wars could be applied to European theatres as well. Indeed, in October 1942, when the Chief of the Army General Staff, former Second Army commander Vittorio Ambrosio, issued a sixty-four-page circular of his own on counterguerrilla warfare, he prefaced it with a reminder that this type of conflict 'does not represent anything new for armies that have been engaged in colonial campaigns and even less for our own, which gained ample experience in Libya and East Africa'.[48]

Specifically, what Roatta and Spigo advocated in their references to colonial warfare was the disproportionate use of force and heavy weaponry against a much more nimble opponent practicing guerrilla warfare. Italian colonial warfare doctrine in fact recognized that, tactically, armoured vehicles and heavy artillery rarely achieved material results in difficult terrain against insurgents who fought in scattered formations and who usually dispersed when faced with overwhelming odds.[49] Nonetheless, authors and practitioners like Nasi, whose treatise on the Libyan war began with the aphorism 'prestige is everything', placed great value on the 'moral effect' that such weapons exerted upon enemy combatants and non-combatants.[50]

Aviation was considered particularly useful in this regard, because aircraft could attack 'groups of rebels [...] and especially the herds, markets, [and] crops of the dissidents (using incendiary bombs)' that slow-moving ground forces could not reach.[51] Alongside their own experiments with air power in Libya, Italian military thinkers followed the use of aerial bombardment in British and French colonies, where authorities likewise touted the 'moral effect' of bombing.[52] These linkages reveal that inter-imperial knowledge transfers also played a role in the development of Italian practices. From these various sources, Italian military theorists understood by 1935 that the real value of heavy weapons technologies in colonial warfare and counterinsurgency lay in their ability to enhance the prestige of the occupying authorities and to terrorize indigenous populations at little risk to Italian military personnel.

Following the same doctrine and rationale, Italian commanders in Ethiopia and Yugoslavia relied heavily on air power and artillery to cow the local populations. Confronted by expanding revolt, the governor of Amhara (and future governor of Montenegro), Alessandro Pirzio Biroli, ordered aircraft to 'bomb and burn [...] without sparing churches or livestock [...] to give a tangible demonstration of our superiority and strength to the populations'.[53] Other aircraft dropped leaflets intended to exploit the awe-inspiring impact of Italian military technology by threatening the populations of Amhara with total destruction:

> People of Gojam, Lasta, and Begemder. You have given heed to irresponsible leaders and are in rebellion. With what hope? Perhaps you believe yourselves able to resist with poorly armed men the might of Italy who can destroy you all if you offend it? The Government asks you to return to

peace and hand in your weapons, returning to your abandoned homes and fields. Obey now and you will be pardoned.[54]

In 1942, the Sassari Division distributed similarly worded leaflets to the populations of western Bosnia, Lika and Dalmatia. Its propaganda exploited a recent scorched earth campaign conducted by Italian forces in the Velebit Mountains, where aircraft again had strafed livestock so to render the region an uninhabitable void.[55]

> The populations that had placed their trust in these enemies of humanity [the Partisans] saw their property destroyed and for the most part were transferred to another part of Lika. The villages of the Velebit – Glogovo – Dabašnica – Bruvno and many other places battered by our cannons, our flamethrowers, our airplanes, were put to the flame or razed to the ground. This is the fate that awaits those who give refuge to communists.[56]

These examples of propaganda highlight the interconnectedness of prestige and terror in Italian military policy in Ethiopia and Yugoslavia.

Colonial rhetoric, dynamics and military culture

As with the use of irregular troops in police operations, the disproportionate application of military force and technology to frighten local populations into submission reflected a typically colonial dynamic. Imperial history is chock-full of colonizers quickly becoming disappointed with 'the refusal of the alleged barbarian to be civilized'.[57] The result tended to be a massively disproportionate response to indigenous resistance.[58] Italian authorities brought with them the rhetoric of a civilizing mission to both campaigns and, in both cases, they turned to race-thinking to explain local conditions of hostility and resistance. Ethiopians were categorized as 'masters of duplicity, [...] cowardly sheep or ravenous hyenas' whose 'way of life is *vendetta* exacerbated by hatred'.[59] Likewise, in Yugoslavia, military propagandists described the Balkans as a land inhabited by 'people that have nothing in common with us, filthy drunks, scoundrels, traitors that neither feel physical pain nor share the refinement of our race'.[60] In both theatres, Italian authorities further delegitimized resistance by labelling insurgents 'rebels', 'brigands', 'bandits', and 'raiders'.

Unique to the case of Yugoslavia was the ideological categorization of the partisan enemy as 'communist'. While some colonial regimes in the Far East faced communist movements during the 1930s, this was not a feature of Italian colonialism in Africa.[61] Anti-communist rhetoric, totally absent in Ethiopia, came to dominate Italian representations of the war in Yugoslavia. A familiar theme to Italians after twenty years of Fascist rule, anti-communism was an effective mobilizing tool. It permitted connections to the so-called 'crusade' being waged against the Soviet Union in defence of European civilization and family values.[62]

In Yugoslavia, anti-communism combined with colonial-style rhetoric to establish and solidify concepts of alterity between Italian occupiers and hostile partisans and populations. Noting similar tendencies during the Spanish Civil War, Sebastian Balfour has argued that nationalist military leaders 'learned' propaganda techniques of 'othering' in Spain's African colonies and then applied those techniques against 'Communists' in the 1930s.[63] In the Italian example, it is difficult to pinpoint such immediate and direct learning processes. World War I had already seen the widespread racialized demonization of enemies within the 'war cultures' of all belligerent nations.[64] Italian trench newspapers of 1915–1918 relied heavily on racial hatred to motivate fighting men at the front.[65]

In fact, rhetoric and policies similar to those employed in Ethiopia and Yugoslavia can be found much earlier in the Italian army's campaign against Southern Italian brigands in the 1860s. When their nation-building project met opposition from guerrilla resistance, Italian military and political leaders came to regard the South 'as a colony' and applied 'colonial-style' methods of repression, two decades before Italy acquired its first African colonial possessions.[66] The Italian view of indigenous resisters as illegitimate outlaws had European as much as colonial roots.[67]

Conclusion

There is little doubt that typically colonial dynamics were at play in the Italian occupations of Ethiopia and Yugoslavia. These dynamics include many of the fundamental patterns identified by Dierk Walter in his magisterial study of five hundred years of imperial warfare: the prioritization of security despite a paucity of military resources; the obsession of military authorities with achieving a decisive outcome; the increasingly political nature of conflict when military decision proved elusive; and, the use of unrestricted violence justified by cultural distance and supposedly brutal local methods of warfare.[68]

There is also little doubt that Italian career officers, one of the few social groups to receive tangible benefits from Italy's empire, shared a colonialist-imperialist ideology steeped in racism, a sense of a civilizing mission and an obsession with order.[69] However, this colonial mentality was not the only, nor the most direct, factor linking Italian military policy and violence in Ethiopia to that in Yugoslavia. There is no evidence that Italian generals in Yugoslavia consulted colonial studies or reports when devising their strategies. Explicit references to colonial experience were relatively scant. When commanders did comment on similarities between the two contexts, it was almost always in relation to the irregular combat methods adopted by their adversaries.

Italian military decision-making in Ethiopia and Yugoslavia was driven primarily by immediate pressures, perceived military necessity, and by institutionally conditioned responses to guerrilla resistance.[70] Like most inter-war armed forces, the Royal Italian Army viewed irregular warfare, in any geographic or political context, as illegitimate and outside the bounds of international law.[71] The army's peculiar inferiority complex, its central role in post-unification nation-building, and the legacy of the Brigands' War exacerbated the contempt for partisan warfare among Italy's military leadership.[72] To be sure, military thinking on how to deal with insurgency was infused with colonial legacies. The colonial operations of Italy and other European empires provided the deepest and most recent bed of experiences, assumptions and attitudes to draw upon when confronting this form of conflict.[73] But these guidelines and assumptions were vague and generic, not context specific.

As Birthe Kundrus has warned, 'to label nearly every form of illegitimate rule, every informal perception of the exotic "colonial"', risks overextending the term and oversimplifying complex historical dynamics.[74] The development of the policies and rhetoric examined in this essay highlight the complex relationships between theoretical doctrine, past experience, and local circumstances that informed Italian decisions. Many Italian generals considered themselves colonial experts, but it was primarily in their role as military technicians that they developed their strategies, methods and justifications for countering guerrilla-type insurgencies.

The concept of military culture provides the greatest explanatory scope for understanding and making sense of Italian violence in Ethiopia and Yugoslavia, and of the linkages between the two cases. Military culture supplied Italian generals with a 'tool kit' of 'unspoken assumptions and tacit codes' to guide their responses to structural conditions and contingent situations.[75] As Isabel Hull has shown in the case of the Imperial German Army's approach to occupation and repression between 1870 and 1918, imperialism and colonial warfare merely served to confirm 'prejudices about the correct way to fight wars'. Elements of colonial ideology, like race-thinking and racism, facilitated military extremism, 'but they did not cause it'.[76] These same conclusions apply to the themes examined here in the context of Italian Fascism's empire.

Moreover, a focus on military culture can help extend the analysis of transfers through the last two years of Fascism's 'decade of war'. After 1943, the typically polarizing dynamics of 'civil war' combined with the trauma of Fascism's collapse to produce an atmosphere of extreme violence in Italy. As Amedeo Osti Guerrazzi points out, the brutal measures employed by military units of the RSI against Italian partisans and their alleged accomplices were consistent with earlier Italian colonial and counterinsurgency operations in foreign territory.[77] Within the anti-Fascist Resistance, the Royal Army's aversion to irregular warfare likely contributed to the mistrust that plagued relations between regular officers and partisans.[78]

While this short chapter cannot claim to provide the systematic examination of evidence necessary for definitive conclusions, it has demonstrated that the analytical methods of transfer history can be applied fruitfully to re-examine Sala's colonial hypothesis. The Italian army's use of indigenous irregular forces, terror, and legitimizing rhetoric in Ethiopia and Yugoslavia were fundamentally similar. However, the linkages between the two cases were complex and indirect, despite the existence of personal continuities. Perhaps more than colonialism, military culture functioned as a primary agent of transfer between Africa and the Balkans. Policies always were shaped in response to military pressures.

The upshot of these preliminary findings is that Italian senior officers did not need to be ideologically committed to Fascist imperialism to employ Fascist or colonial-style violence. Confronted by effective resistance movements in wars for imperial expansion, Italian generals easily found common ground with Fascism.

Notes

1 T. Sala, 'Guerra e amministrazione in Jugoslavia, 1941–1943: Un'ipotesi coloniale', *Annali della Fondazione Micheletti*, 5 (1990–1991), pp. 83–94. The essay is reprinted in T. Sala, *Il fascismo italiano e gli Slavi del sud* (Trieste: Istituto regionale per la storia del movimento di liberazione nel Friuli-Venezia Giulia, 2008), pp. 295–311.

2 D. Rodogno, *Fascism's European Empire: Italian Occupation during the Second World War*, trans. A. Belton (Cambridge: Cambridge University Press, 2006), p. 333.

3 C. Pipitone, 'Dall'Africa all'Europa: Pratiche italiane di occupazione militare', in Istituto romano per la storia d'Italia dal fascismo alla Resistenza (eds.), *Politiche di occupazione dell'Italia fascista: L'Annale Irsifar* (Milan: Franco Angeli, 2008), p. 42; F. Focardi, 'Le politiche di occupazione dell'Italia fascista', *Italia contemporanea*, 252–3 (2008), pp. 544–5.

4 E. Gobetti, *Alleati del nemico. L'occupazione italiana in Jugoslavia (1941–1943)* (Rome and Bari: Laterza, 2013), pp. 92–3.

5 G. Rochat, *Le guerre italiane, 1935–1943: Dall'Impero d'Etiopia alla disfatta* (Turin: Einaudi, 2005), pp. 367–88.

6 J. Kocka and H.-G. Haupt, 'Comparison and Beyond: Traditions, Scope, and Perspectives of Comparative History', in H.-G. Haupt and J. Kocka (eds.), *Comparative and Transnational History: Central European Approaches and New Perspectives* (New York: Berghahn, 2009), p. 20.

7 J. Kreienbaum, 'Deadly Learning? Concentration Camps in Colonial Wars around 1900', in V. Barth and R. Cvetkovski (eds.), *Imperial Co-operation and Transfer, 1870–1930: Empires and Encounters* (London: Bloomsbury, 2015), pp. 228–30.

8 H. Arendt, *The Origins of Totalitarianism* (New York: Harcourt Brace, 1951); W. Lower, *Nazi Empire-Building and the Holocaust in Ukraine* (Chapel Hill: University of North Carolina Press, 2005); B. Kundrus, 'Colonialism, Imperialism, National Socialism: How Imperial Was the Third Reich?', in B. Naranch and G. Eley (eds.), *German Colonialism in a Global Age* (Durham, NC: Duke University Press, 2014), pp. 330–46.

9 J. Zimmerer, *From Windhoek to Auschwitz: On the Relationship Between Colonialism and the Holocaust* (London: Routledge, 2015); B. Madley, 'From Africa to Auschwitz: How German South West Africa Incubated Ideas and Methods Adopted and Developed by the Nazis in Eastern Europe', *European History Quarterly*, 35:3 (2005), pp. 429–64.

10 R. Gerwarth and S. Malinowski, 'Hannah Arendt's Ghosts: Reflections on the Disputable Path from Windhoek to Auschwitz', *Central European History*, 42:2 (2009), pp. 279–300.

11 A. Eckert, 'Germany and Africa in the Late Nineteenth and Twentieth Centuries: An Entangled History?', in H.-G. Haupt and J. Kocka (eds.), *Comparative and Transnational History: Central European Approaches and New Perspectives* (New York: Berghahn, 2009), p. 226.

12 A. De Grand, 'Mussolini's Follies: Fascism in its Imperial and Racist Phase, 1935–1940', *Contemporary European History*, 13:2 (2004), pp. 127–47; E. Gentile, *La Grande Italia: The Myth of the Nation in the Twentieth Century*, trans. S. Dingee and J. Pudney (Madison: University of Wisconsin Press, 2009), pp. 164–8; A. Pes, 'Becoming Imperialist: Italian Colonies in Fascist Textbooks for Primary Schools', *Journal of Modern Italian Studies*, 18:5 (2013), pp. 599–614.

13 G. Brogini Künzi, 'Total Colonial Warfare: Ethiopia', in R. Chickering and
    S. Förster (eds.), *The Shadows of Total War: Europe, East Asia, and the United
    States, 1919–1939* (Cambridge: Cambridge University Press, 2003), p. 316;
    G. Rochat, *Guerre italiane in Libia e in Etiopia: Studi militari 1921–39* (Treviso:
    Pagus, 1991), p. 27.
14 N. Labanca, 'L'amministrazione coloniale fascista: Stato, politica e società', in
    A. Del Boca, M. Legnani, and M.G. Rossi (eds.), *Il regime fascista: Storia
    e storiografia* (Rome and Bari: Laterza, 2005), pp. 378–89.
15 We lack precise statistics on the percentage of Italian officers in European theatres
    with colonial experience; see Pipitone, 'Dall'Africa all'Europa', pp. 32–3.
16 E. Traverso, *The Origins of Nazi Violence*, trans. J. Lloyd (New York: New Press,
    2003), p. 67.
17 P. Bernhard, 'Hitler's Africa in the East: Italian Colonialism as a Model for
    German Planning in Eastern Europe', *Journal of Contemporary History*, 51:1
    (2016), pp. 61–90.
18 J. Osterhammel, *Colonialism: A Theoretical Overview*, 2nd ed., trans. S.L. Frisch
    (Princeton, NJ: Markus Wiener, 2005), p. 43; C. Tripodi, 'Power and Patronage:
    A Comparison of Tribal Service in Waziristan and South-West Arabia, 1919–1945',
    War and Society, 33:3 (2014), pp. 172–3.
19 M. Dominioni, *Lo sfascio dell'Impero: Gli italiani in Etiopia, 1936–1941* (Rome
    and Bari: Laterza, 2008), pp. 229, 274.
20 M.J. Milazzo, *The Chetnik Movement and the Yugoslav Resistance* (Baltimore, MD:
    Johns Hopkins University Press, 1975); J. Tomasevich, *War and Revolution in Yugo-
    slavia, 1941–1945: Occupation and Collaboration* (Stanford, CA: Stanford Univer-
    sity Press, 2001).
21 E. Gobetti, *L'occupazione allegra: Gli italiani in Jugoslavia (1941–1943)* (Rome:
    Carocci, 2007), pp. 184–5.
22 N. Arielli, 'Colonial Soldiers in Italian Counter-Insurgency Operations in Libya,
    1922–1932', *British Journal for Military History*, 1:2 (2015), pp. 61–2.
23 L. Bongiovanni, 'Questioni militari coloniali', *Rivista delle colonie italiane*,
    March 1930. The article was reviewed favourably in the Italian army's official jour-
    nal, the *Rivista militare italiana*, 4: 7 (1930), pp. 1186–7.
24 R. Graziani, *Pace romana in Libia* (Milan: Mondadori, 1937), pp. 82, 250–1. The
    book is a republication of Graziani's two previous volumes on the Libyan campaign:
    Verso il Fezzan (1930) and *Cirenaica pacificata* (1932).
25 G. Nasi, 'Operazioni coloniali', n.d., pp. 71–5, in Archivio dell'Ufficio Storico dello
    Stato Maggiore dell'Esercito, Rome (AUSSME), L-3, b. 79, fasc. 5. G. Nasi, 'La
    guerra in Libia', *Rivista militare italiana*, 1:1 (1927), pp. 85–6.
26 Nasi to Marghinotti, 2 November 1936, AUSSME, D-6, vol. 169. E. Formento, *Kai
    Bandera: Etiopia, 1936–1941. Una banda irregolare* (Milan: Mursia, 2000), p. 163.
27 Dominioni, *Lo sfascio dell'Impero*, p. 229.
28 C. Poggiali, *Diario AOI: 15 giugno 1936–4 ottobre 1937* (Milan: Longanesi, 1971),
    p. 278.
29 Hazon memorandum, October 1937, Archivio Centrale dello Stato, Roma (ACS),
    Fondo Graziani (FG), b. 47, fasc. 42, sf. 1c. See also Governor Mezzetti's political
    reports for July and November 1938, in Archivio Storico del Ministero degli Affari
    Esteri, Rome (ASMAE), Ministero dell'Africa Italiana (MAI), pos. 181/53, fasc. 248.
30 'Relazione sul fatto d'arme di Debra Uork', 29 September 1939, AUSSME, L-14,
    fasc. 4.
31 'Organizzazioni militari in Dalmazia', 2 July 1942, AUSSME, N1-11, b. 782, Diario
    Storico (DS) XVIII Corps, July 1942, allegati.
32 'Situazione', 25 May 1942, National Archives and Records Administration, College
    Park, MD (NARA), T-821/65/0976-79.

33   'Situazione politica in Croazia', 23 July 1941, in A. Biagini and F. Frattolillo (eds.), *Diario storico del Comando Supremo: Raccolta di documenti della seconda guerra mondiale* (DSCS) (Rome: USSME, 1992), vol. 4, tome II, pp. 180–9; 'Politica croata nei territori della 2ª e 3ª zona', 23 January 1942, DSCS, vol. 6, tome II, pp. 36–41. M. Bucarelli, 'Disgregazione jugoslava e questione serba nella politica italiana', in F. Caccamo and L. Monzali (eds.), *L'occupazione italiana della Iugoslavia* (Florence: Le Lettere, 2008), pp. 11–59; E. Gobetti, 'The Royal Army's Betrayal? Two Different Italian Policies in Yugoslavia (1941–1943)', in G. Albanese, R. Pergher (eds.), *In the Society of Fascists: Acclamation, Acquiescence, and Agency in Mussolini's Italy* (New York: Palgrave Macmillan, 2012), pp. 189–209.

34   'Premessa al Diario storico militare, bimestre: giugno–luglio', AUSSME, N1-11, b. 523, DS 12th 'Sassari' Division, June–July 1941; 'Relazione periodica', 3 May 1942, AUSSME, N1-11, b. 772, DS XVIII Corps, May 1942, allegati; 'Montenegro', 12 August 1941, DSCS, vol. 4, tome II, pp. 243–5.

35   D. Conti, *L'occupazione italiana dei Balcani: Tra crimini di guerra e mito della brava gente* (Rome: Odradek, 2008), pp. 71–2; M.A. Hoare, *Genocide and Resistance in Hitler's Bosnia: The Partisans and the Chetniks, 1941–1943* (Oxford: Oxford University Press, 2006), p. 154.

36   'Situazione dopo operazione del Velebit e attività futura', 25 July 1942, NARA, T-821/63/0854–56; 'M.V.A.C.', 13 September 1942, AUSSME, N1-11, b. 1004, DS 12th 'Sassari' Division, September–October 1942, allegati.

37   'Armamento e munizionamento formazioni M.V.A.C.', 23 September 1942, AUSSME, N1-11, b. 769, DS 12th 'Sassari' Division, February–March 1942, allegati; 'Azioni della M.V.A.C.', 16 November 1942, Berardi to Piazzoni, 24 December 1942, and Berardi to Piazzoni, 26 December 1942, AUSSME, N1-11, b. 1004, DS 12th 'Sassari' Division, November–December 1942, allegati; 'Precisazioni varie', 1 January 1943, AUSSME, N1-11, b. 1189, DS 22nd 'Cacciatori delle Alpi' Division, January–February 1943, allegati.

38   On the differences between 'Eurasian' and 'colonial' collaboration, see M. Cuzzi, '"Traditori patriottici". Le collaborazioni durante la seconda guerra mondiale', *Italia contemporanea*, 252–253 (2008), p. 578.

39   E. Ryan, 'Violence and the Politics of Prestige: The Fascist Turn in Colonial Libya', *Modern Italy*, 20:2 (2015), pp. 124–5.

40   D. French, 'The Dardanelles, Mecca and Kut: Prestige as a Factor in British Eastern Strategy, 1914–1916', *War and Society*, 5:1 (1987), pp. 45–61; A.D. Moses, 'Empire, Colony, Genocide: Keywords and the Philosophy of History', in A.D. Moses (ed.), *Empire, Colony, Genocide: Conquest, Occupation, and Subaltern Resistance in World History* (New York: Berghahn, 2008), pp. 26–8.

41   N. Labanca, 'Italian Colonial Internment', in R. Ben-Ghiat and M. Fuller (eds.), *Italian Colonialism* (New York: Palgrave Macmillan, 2005), p. 33; G. Ottolenghi, *Gli italiani e il colonialismo: I campi di detenzione italiani in Africa* (Milan: Sugarco, 1997), pp. 164–6; A. Sbacchi, 'Italy and the Treatment of the Ethiopian Aristocracy', *International Journal of African Historical Studies*, 10:2 (1977), pp. 216–8.

42   C. Di Sante, 'Deportazione e campi di concentramento in Cirenaica e in Jugoslavia', *Italia contemporanea*, 252–253 (2008), pp. 547–66.

43   H.J. Burgwyn, 'General Roatta's War against the Partisans in Yugoslavia: 1942', *Journal of Modern Italian Studies*, 9:3 (2004), pp. 314–29.

44   'Roatta, Mario', by F. Focardi, in *Dizionario biografico degli italiani*. Available from www.treccani.it/enciclopedia/mario-roatta_%28Dizionario-Biografico%29/ [Accessed on 2 February 2020]. Gobetti notes that, as head of Italian military intelligence (SIM), Roatta kept himself well informed on developments in East Africa, see Gobetti, *L'occupazione allegra*, p. 184.

45 M. Legnani, 'Il "ginger" del generale Roatta. Le direttive della 2a armata sulla repressione antipartigiana in Slovenia e Croazia', *Italia contemporanea*, 209–210 (1997–1998), p. 170. Italics added.

46 'Potenza di reazione e sicurezza', 9 March 1943, AUSSME, N1-11, b. 1188, DS XVIII Corps, March–April 1943, allegati.

47 Rochat, *Le guerre italiane*, pp. 367–8.

48 *Circolare n. 36.000: Combattimenti episodici ed azioni di guerriglia*, Roma, SMRE, Ufficio Addestramento, 1942. Available from www.icsm.it/articoli/documenti/docit storici.html [Accessed on 2 February 2020].

49 See, for example, M. Ferrabino, 'Questioni di artiglieria relative alla guerra nelle nostre colonie libiche', *Rivista militare italiana*, 5:1 (1931), pp. 85–104; U. Businelli, 'La guerra coloniale 1914–18 nell'Africa Orientale tedesca', *Rivista militare italiana*, 5:2 (1931), pp. 209–36; and, Nasi, *Operazioni coloniali*, pp. 85–8.

50 Nasi, *La guerra in Libia*, pp. 67, 86–7.

51 Ivi, p. 90.

52 A. Calderara, 'L'aviazione nell'Africa Settentrionale', *Rivista militare italiana*, 1:4 (1927), pp. 545–62; E. Frattini, review of 'Forze aeree e terrestri in spedizioni punitive', by J.B. Glubb, *Rivista militare italiana*, 1:4 (1927), pp. 636–8; Ten. col. Ortona, review of *Quelques enseignements des campagnes du Riff, en matière d'aviation (1925–1926)*, by Gen. Armengaud, in *Rivista militare italiana*, 4:6 (1930), pp. 978–85; Y. Tanaka, 'British "Humane Bombing" in Iraq during the Interwar Era', in Y. Tanaka and M.B. Young (eds.), *Bombing Civilians: A Twentieth-Century History* (New York: New Press, 2009), pp. 9–29.

53 Pirzio Biroli to Graziani, 15 November 1937, ACS, FG, b. 27, fasc. 29, sf. 33a.

54 Graziani to Lessona, 9 September 1937, ACS, FG, b. 27, fasc. 29, sf. 33a.

55 'Relazione sulla operazione del Velebit', 2 August 1942, AUSSME, N1-11, b. 782, DS XVIII Corps, July 1942, allegati.

56 'Popolo della Bosnia, Lika e Dalmazia', August 1942, AUSSME, N1-11, b. 999, DS 12th 'Sassari' Division, July–August 1942, allegati.

57 J. Osterhammel, *Europe, the 'West' and the Civilizing Mission* (London: German Historical Institute, 2006), pp. 30–1.

58 M. Levene, 'Empires, Native Peoples, and Genocide', in A.D. Moses (ed.), *Empire, Colony, Genocide: Conquest, Occupation, and Subaltern Resistance in World History* (New York: Berghahn, 2008), pp. 190–4.

59 'Psicologia indigena e contegno imperiale', 12 March 1937, AUSSME, D-6, vol. 172.

60 'Al partigiano comunista addosso sempre!', *La Tradotta del Fronte Giulio*, 23 May 1943, p. 5.

61 On British, Dutch, and French security concerns regarding communist movements in Malaya, Indonesia, and Vietnam, see M. Thomas, *Violence and Colonial Order: Police, Workers, and Protest in the European Colonial Empires, 1918–1940* (Cambridge: Cambridge University Press, 2012).

62 M. Stone, 'The Changing Face of the Enemy in Fascist Italy', *Constellations*, 15:3 (2008), pp. 332–50; A. Osti Guerrazzi, *L'Esercito italiano in Slovenia 1941–1943: Strategie di repressione antipartigiana* (Rome: Viella, 2011), p. 34. See, for example, 'Per chi combattono!', *La Tradotta del Fronte Giulio*, 10 January 1943, p. 1.

63 S. Balfour, *Deadly Embrace: Morocco and the Road to the Spanish Civil War* (Oxford: Oxford University Press, 2002), 283–6.

64 'War culture' refers to 'how belligerents represented conflict and violence to themselves and others', its main function being 'to polarize collective identities'. J. McMillan, *War*, in D. Bloxham, R. Gerwarth (eds.), *Political Violence in Twentieth-Century Europe* (Cambridge: Cambridge University Press, 2011), pp. 41, 50–62.

See also A. Kramer, *Dynamic of Destruction: Culture and Mass Killing in the First World War* (Oxford: Oxford University Press, 2007).

65 M. Isnenghi, *Giornali di trincea, 1915–1918* (Turin: Einaudi, 1977), pp. 144–75.

66 A.S. Wong, *Race and the Nation in Liberal Italy, 1861–1911: Meridionalism, Empire, and Diaspora* (New York: Palgrave Macmillan, 2006), pp. 16–22; C. Petraccone, *Le due civiltà: Settentrionali e meridionali nella storia d'Italia dal 1860 al 1914* (Rome and Bari: Laterza, 2000), pp. 62–4; A. Del Boca, *Italiani brava gente? Un mito duro a morire* (Vicenza: Neri Pozza, 2005), p. 57.

67 D. Forgacs, *Italy's Margins: Social Exclusion and Nation Formation since 1861* (Cambridge: Cambridge University Press, 2014), p. 125. See also J. Dickie, 'A Word at War: The Italian Army and Brigandage, 1860–1870', *History Workshop Journal*, 33:1 (1992), pp. 1–24.

68 D. Walter, *Colonial Violence: European Empires and the Use of Force*, trans. P. Lewis (Oxford: Oxford University Press, 2017), pp. 265–6.

69 L. Ricci, *La lingua dell'impero: Comunicazione, letteratura e propaganda nell'età del colonialismo italiano* (Rome: Carocci, 2005), p. 10; Labanca, *L'amministrazione coloniale fascista*, pp. 352–95; Osterhammel, *Colonialism*, pp. 105–12.

70 For a similar argument, but regarding the role of Fascist ideology rather than colonial transfers in the Second Army's decision-making, see H.J. Burgwyn, *Empire on the Adriatic: Mussolini's Conquest of Yugoslavia, 1941–1943* (New York: Enigma, 2005), p. 48.

71 P. Lagrou, 'Irregular Warfare and the Norms of Legitimate Violence in Twentieth Century Europe', in J. Dülffer and R. Frank (eds.), *War, Peace and Gender from Antiquity to the Present* (Essen: Klartext, 2009), p. 170; Pipitone, *Dall'Africa all'Europa*, pp. 34–5.

72 T. Hof, '"Legionaries of Civilization": The Italian Military, Fascism and Extreme Violence, 1922–1943', in T. Hof (ed.), *Empire, Ideology, Mass Violence: The Long 20th Century in Comparative Perspective* (Munich: Herbert Utz, 2016), pp. 113–21; J. Whittam, *The Politics of the Italian Army, 1861–1918* (London: Croom Helm, 1977), pp. 12, 77–80.

73 D. Porch, *Counterinsurgency: Exposing the Myths of the New Way of War* (New York: Cambridge University Press, 2013), pp. 75–6.

74 B. Kundrus, 'From the Periphery to the Center: On the Significance of Colonialism for the German Empire', in S.O. Müller and C. Torp (eds.), *Imperial Germany Revisited: Continuing Debates and New Perspectives* (New York: Berghahn, 2011), p. 261.

75 M. Knox, 'The First World War and Military Culture: Continuity and Change in Germany and Italy' in S.O. Müller and C. Torp (eds.), *Imperial Germany Revisited: Continuing Debates and New Perspectives* (New York: Berghahn, 2011), p. 214.

76 I.V. Hull, *Absolute Destruction: Military Culture and the Practices of War in Imperial Germany* (Ithaca, NY: Cornell University Press, 2005), pp. 330–3.

77 A. Osti Guerrazzi, 'Italians at War: War and Experience in Fascist Italy', *Journal of Modern Italian Studies*, 22:5 (2017), p. 595. On the long-held notion of civil war as a particularly brutal form of warfare, see D. Armitage, *Civil Wars: A History in Ideas* (New York: Alfred A. Knopf, 2017), and B. Kissane, *Nations Torn Asunder: The Challenge of Civil War* (Oxford, Oxford University Press, 2016).

78 C. Pavone, *A Civil War: A History of the Italian Resistance*, trans. P. Levy and D. Broder (London: Verso, 2013), pp. 122–9.

11 What 'new order'?

Fascist expansionism and the Jews: the case of south-eastern France, 1942–1943

Luca Fenoglio

Introduction

This chapter explores the relationship between Fascist Italy's expansionist aims and anti-Semitic policy. It focuses on Jewish policy that Fascist Italy carried out in south-eastern France during the eight-month period between the Italian Army's invasion of that region and Corsica on 11 November 1942 and the collapse of the Fascist regime following the arrest of Benito Mussolini on 25 July 1943.

The invasion of south-eastern France and Corsica in November 1942 marked the last act of Fascist Italy's expansionist campaign begun seven years earlier with the attack on Ethiopia in October 1935. However, six years after Mussolini's proclamation of Italy's African Empire in May 1936 the international scenario, and Fascist Italy's standing within it, had drastically changed. After the end of Mussolini's 'parallel war' – launched with the stab in the back to an already Nazi-defeated France in June 1940 – Fascist Italy was relegated to a militarily subordinate position within the Axis alliance. From early 1941 onwards, Fascist Italy's ambition of making the Mediterranean its exclusive domain was entirely dependent on German military success. The landing of an Allied expedition force in French North Africa on 8 November 1942 further undermined Fascist Italy's expansionist dreams, instead paving the way to the definitive expulsion of the Axis forces from Africa in May 1943 and the eventual collapse of the Fascist regime only two weeks after the Allies' landings in Sicily on July 10.[1]

However, in the short term, the Allied landings in Morocco and Algeria helped Fascist Italy to partly fulfil territorial claims by seizing Nice and Corsica.[2] Following the Allied landings in North Africa, Nazi Führer Adolf Hitler ordered the swift occupation of the French metropolitan territory's southern part, the so-called free France or Unoccupied Zone, which following the Franco-German armistice of June 1940 was under the authority of a French collaborationist government based in Vichy. As part of the Axis forces' takeover of the French Mediterranean shores to defend against the threat of an Allied landing in southern Europe, the Italian Fourth Army was entrusted with securing the coastline from east of German-occupied Marseille to the French-Italian border. From the coast, the Italian occupation zone extended inland up to the Savoie region in the north, comprising a total of ten completely or partially occupied French departments east of the Rhône.

It was against this backdrop that, similarly to what happened in Croatia and Greece, Rome and Berlin collided over the treatment of Jews living in the territories under the Forth Army's rule. In south-eastern France, the Fascist government prevented the Vichy government from handing over to the Nazis Jews who lived in the Italian zone, irrespective of their nationality, with the result that these were shielded from the Nazi policy of extermination. Data collected by French authorities between the end of 1942 and the beginning of 1943 offered the highly approximate figure of 140,000 Jews living in the former Unoccupied Zone. Exact figures for the ten departments occupied by the Fourth Army are not available, but Jews certainly numbered some tens of thousands. The Nice region alone hosted some 15,000 Jews primarily concentrated on the Côte d'Azur.[3]

The overlapping of Fascist Italy's expansionist aims with the opposition to the handover of Jews in the Italian zone to the Nazis therefore makes the Italian occupation of south-eastern France an interesting case study to investigate the Italian top military and diplomatic officials' 'vision' of the Fascist sphere of interests in the Mediterranean.

The history of a paradox?

Scholars have investigated the rationale for Fascist Italy's protection of Jews in Croatia, Greece and France since the very early post-war years. Generally, the debate has been explicitly or implicitly engrossed with solving what Léon Poliakov, as early as 1946, termed the Italian 'paradox'. This paradox centred on the notion that as an anti-Semitic country between 1938 and 1943 Fascist Italy persecuted Jews but, unlike its Nazi ally, did not pursue their annihilation.[4] Taking Nazi policies against the Jews as a paradigm, Poliakov's Italian paradox was predicated upon the assumption that there exists a necessary progression from anti-Semitism to persecution, and from persecution to outright extermination. Interestingly, the existing solutions to the paradox are conceptually symmetrical. They all involved 'dropping' one of the two extremes of the afore-mentioned progression from anti-Semitism to extermination. Initially, and for a long time, historians maintained that the Italians were immune from anti-Semitism, or at least from the rabid biological anti-Semitism of the Nazi kind, and thereby construed the refusal to hand over the Jews as a rescue policy rooted, *inter alia*, in Italian humaneness.[5] More recent interpretations upend that approach. Emphasising the presence of anti-Semitism among the highest echelons of the Italian Army and diplomacy, these interpretations jettison any ideas of an Italian rescue or even protection of the Jews and thereby explain the refusals to surrender them as 'pragmatic' decisions purely dictated by political and opportunistic considerations.[6]

These two explanations not only reflected a different understanding of the rationale behind the Italian authorities' decisions concerning the surrender of Jews to the Nazis, but they also involved an opposing understanding of Fascist Italy in relation to Nazi Germany. The rescue thesis was consistent with an analysis of the two regimes that placed greater emphasis on their differences,[7] epitomised by the Nazi policy of extermination of the Jews and the concurrent protection offered to them by the Italians in the occupied territories until 8 September 1943. By contrast, albeit acknowledging the critical difference between the ultimate consequences of the Jewish policies pursued by the Axis partners in their respective spheres of interests before September 1943, the more recent sceptical explanations reflect an approach that foregrounds the points of convergence between Nazi Germany and Fascist Italy in the context of their common aspirations to redraw the geopolitical map of Europe. Davide Rodogno's influential book on 'Fascism's European Empire' embodies the latter approach. Rodogno argues that the Italian authorities' refusals to surrender Jews were devoid of any humanitarian motive and should instead 'be interpreted as an attempt to respond pointedly and assertively to Nazi interference in Fascism's imaginary *domaine reservé*' across the Mediterranean.[8] Rodogno's analysis fits within a broader interpretation of Fascist Italy's expansionism as driven by the ultimate goal to conquer *spazio vitale*, the equivalent of *Lebensraum* pursued by the Nazis in eastern Europe, and thereby establish a Fascist 'New Mediterranean Order', adjacent to, but in competition with, the Nazi New Order.[9]

Interpretations like the one put forward by Rodogno have the merit of situating Italian refusals to hand over Jews more firmly within their surrounding geopolitical, military and diplomatic contexts – the relevance of which, however, was never underestimated by the proponents of the rescue thesis. Moreover, they refocus scholarly attention on aspects such as the anti-Semitism and racism of the Italian Army that diverge from the established image of *Italiani brava gente*, namely an image of Italians as humane, sympathetic and unable to commit the atrocities perpetrated by the Nazis. At the same time, however, the effort to rectify the post-war political narrative of the *brava gente*[10] has led to an often mechanical overturning of that problematic image, without engaging with the assumptions underpinning its widespread receipt in the scholarly historical writing.[11]

In order to disentangle the discussion from its 'political and moralistic undertone',[12] and thereby gain fresh insight into the relationship between Fascism's aggressive expansionism and anti-Semitic policies, it is useful to closely investigate Fascist Italy's actual treatment of Jews in the context of wartime occupations. This will allow testing the core assumption that underpins existing explanations of the Italian refusal to hand over Jews and thereby verify if in fact Fascist Italy's approach to the 'Jewish problem' in the occupied territories between 1941 and 1943 was paradoxical.

Fascist Italy's Jewish policy in south-eastern France

In Italian-occupied south-eastern France, Jewish policy initially developed within the larger framework of the security policy that Italian military and police services launched simultaneously with the beginning of the Fourth Army's advance into French territory on 11 November 1942.[13] This security policy originated from the military necessities connected to the defensive nature of the Axis powers' invasion of the Unoccupied Zone in response to the Allied landings in Morocco and Algeria on 8 November. Besides the arrests of generically 'hostile' civilians, two other operations were initially launched. The *Centro CS*, or Counterespionage Unit, in Nice targeted enemy intelligence agents and their informers. Meanwhile, the political police unit headed by the *commissario di pubblica sicurezza* (police commissioner) Rosario Barranco targeted Italian antifascists, most notably communists.[14]

It was not until the beginning of December 1942 that Jews *qua* Jews came to the attention of the Italian authorities. On 3 December, the Supreme Command of the Italian Armed Forces notified the Oberkommando der Wehrmacht of the Italian decision to arrest all citizens of countries at war with the Axis and to intern Jews residing in the Italian zone.[15] The Supreme Command confirmed this decision to the Italian Foreign and Interior Ministries on 12 December: 'following concerns raised by the Germans, it has been decided up on high [Mussolini] that all subjects of enemy states deemed dangerous must be arrested immediately, and Jews resident in metropolitan French territory must be interned'.[16] The operations against enemy aliens and Jews were entrusted to a newly formed police unit led by *commissario* Barranco,[17] who also retained the political police duties for which he had been originally deployed in southeastern France in 1939.[18] Barranco's unit would operate under the jurisdiction of the Fourth Army Command with the support of the *Centro CS* and the Foreign Ministry's representatives in France.[19]

The operations against enemy aliens deemed dangerous began on 29 December 1942.[20] Once arrested, these were confined in the concentration camp that the Fourth Army established in Sospel, a French village north-east of Nice. However, on 27 December the Fascist police chief Carmine Senise informed the Supreme Command that, due to the low capacity of the camp and the concurrent urgency to purge the Italian zone of 'foreigners', it had been decided that the 'arrest and internment' in Sospel would affect the 'most dangerous' elements only and that their apprehension would take priority. All other 'less dangerous' enemy aliens would instead be confined to compulsory residence (*residenza forzata*) 'away from the coast and militarily sensitive centres'.[21] By 11 February 1943, some two hundred enemy aliens, including French citizens, citizens of countries under German and Italian occupation and people deemed politically hostile to the Axis powers, in addition to British and American nationals, were arrested and confined in Sospel.[22] Among them were also a group of enemy aliens of Jewish origins and another group of 'eleven foreign Jews'.[23] In both cases their nationality and possibly their political leanings and/or activities rather than their 'race' led to their arrest, as in the case of Carol Bitter, a Polish Jew whom Barranco described as 'hostile to the Axis'.[24]

Preparations for the internment of foreign (other than Italian and French) Jews began around early January 1943. Barranco devised a plan to place them in compulsory residence in the interior of French territory under the surveillance of the Carabinieri (military police).[25] Barranco's plan, which was eventually approved by the Fourth Army Command, meant that almost all for-eign Jews fell *de facto* in the category of 'less dangerous' (but still dangerous) elements – a categorization consistent with the Supreme Command's message of 12 December. It should be stressed here that the Italian military authorities esti-mated the number of foreign Jews and enemy aliens living at that point in the Alpes-Maritimes department at 'around 7,000'. Initially, compulsory residence was to be forced upon some 1,200, although it is unclear in what proportion. The beginning of the operations was set for 20 February 1943.[26]

It was against this backdrop that the Fascist government and the Vichy gov-ernment clashed over the surrender to the Nazis of Jews living in the Italian zone at the end of 1942 and the beginning of 1943. The Vichy government had been carrying out its own anti-Jewish persecution since October 1940. Subse-quently, during the summer of 1942, the Vichy government became a collaborator and accomplice in the arrest and deportation of tens of thousands of Jews to Auschwitz.[27]

The clash between Rome and Vichy over Jews was indirectly caused by the Nazi authorities. Fascist security policy was coordinated with the German mili-tary authorities.[28] However, in those same weeks of early December 1942 the SS, namely the driving force behind Nazi extermination policy in France,[29] pressured the Vichy government into concentrating those non-French Jews who had established their domicile within thirty kilometres of the Mediterranean coast and the Franco-Spanish border after 1 January 1938 to the French interior. This measure was intended to facilitate the new phase of deportations to Ausch-witz that the SS launched in early 1943.[30]

In the Italian-occupied Alpes-Maritimes department, the evacuation order was issued around 20 December 1942. It concerned 1,400 Jews who were commanded to relocate to the Drôme department, which despite being in the Italian zone also contained German troops, and to the German-controlled Ardèche department.[31] On 29 December the Italian Foreign Ministry cabled its liaison office with the Fourth Army Command that 'it cannot be accepted that in the zones occupied by the Italian troops the French Authorities force foreign Jews, including Italian Jews, to transfer to localities occupied by German troops'. The cable added that 'the precautionary measures towards foreign and Italian Jews may be taken exclu-sively by our organs to which the criteria to follow [in the matter] have already been communicated'.[32] The Supreme Command also issued instructions to oppose the French evacuation order to the Fourth Army Command.[33]

On 30 December 1942, the Italian authorities notified their French counter-parts that all the prefects of the Italian zone were prohibited from interning Jews, whatever their nationality.[34] A few days later, Foreign Minister Galeazzo Ciano confirmed the Italian opposition to the expulsion of Jews and the claim to exclusive responsibility in Jewish matters inside the Italian occupation zone, including matters concerning French Jews.[35] As a result, the French authorities in the Alpes-Maritimes department were forced to end the implementation of two other anti-Jewish measures ordered by Vichy also in December 1942. These measures prescribed the stamping of the letter 'J' of *Juif* (Jew) onto

Jews' identity papers and the drafting of certain categories of foreign and state-less Jews into labour battalions.[36]

The Foreign Ministry and the Supreme Command's reactions to the attempted French handover of non-French Jews to the Nazi authorities were consistent with Mussolini's order to intern Jews in the Italian zone. These reactions were meant to assert the primacy of Fascist Italy's military and political interests over French sovereignty in the territories under the Fourth Army's control.[37] But the Foreign Ministry's cable included more. The reference to the instructions that the Italian authorities on the ground had already received on how to carry out the operations against enemy aliens and Jews did not serve only as a reminder. The Foreign Ministry had issued those instructions only a week before, on 22 December. They stated that 'the criteria' for the internment of Jews 'should not be different from those adopted' in Italy 'towards some foreign Jews' and that 'therefore some consideration will have to be used towards the elderly, children, women and sick people'.[38] This reference presumably took into consideration the reports submitted to the Foreign Ministry about the French public's disapproval of the French-Nazi joint operations to deport Jews in the second half of 1942.[39] Most importantly, that reference was made at a time that the murderous reality of Nazi Jewish policy had become known in Rome.[40] Its function was, therefore, also to explicitly differentiate between the French and Nazi, on the one hand, and the Fascist, on the other hand, approaches to the 'question' of Jews. More specifically, that reference under-scored that Fascist Italy did not consider internment and deportation to the east as equivalent measures to solve that 'question'. In this respect, equally import-ant to define the Italian approach to the 'Jewish problem' in southern France was the Foreign Ministry's strong recommendation to the Italian military and civilian authorities on the ground that it was not in Italy's 'best interest to foster the flow of undesirable elements [non-Italian Jews] into the territories occupied by the Italian troops'. By contrast, Italian Jews were allowed to transfer from the German into the Italian zone. However, the Foreign Ministry clarified that Italian Jews deemed 'dangerous' were also subjected to Italian security measures.[41]

From the standpoint of the SS and the Nazi diplomatic services in France, the Italian opposition to the French measures to concentrate Jews in the interior pending their deportation was the one that mattered. After the Nazi policy of extermination of the Jews reached a truly European gamut in 1942,[42] the SS and the Nazi diplomatic personnel in Paris came to view all measures against the Jews, including their internment, as nothing but intermediate steps towards the final goal of a *judenrein* (cleansed of Jews) France. Consequently, unlike their Italian allies, the Nazi authorities perceived the Italian opposition to the French evacuation order to be in complete contradiction to the earlier message from the Supreme Command announcing, *inter alia*, the internment of Jews in the Italian occupation zone. From January 1943 onwards, reports about the per-ceived Italian Army's volte-face began therefore to seethe from Paris towards Berlin.[43] The renewed obstacles that the Fourth Army put to the French attempt to expel Jews, as well as British and American nationals, from the Italian to the

German zone in February 1943 exposed the fundamental divergence that existed between the Axis partners' approaches to security policy and the 'Jewish problem' in their respective zones.[44] As a result, between late-February and mid-March 1943, the Italian Army's 'inexplicable' – from the Nazi point of view – stand on the matter became the subject of discussions between Mussolini and the Reich Foreign Minister Joachim von Ribbentrop.[45]

Pressed by Ribbentrop to bring his Generals into line, Mussolini made two decisions. First, on 13 March the Undersecretary of State for Foreign Affairs Giuseppe Bastianini forwarded instructions 'approved high up', that is, by Mussolini himself, to the Supreme Command and the police to turn back non-Italian Jews who sought to escape the Nazi and Vichy police by fleeing into the Italian zone, thus hardening the Foreign Ministry's earlier recommendation of late December 1942.[46] On 26 March 1943, the Fourth Army Commander, General Mario Vercellino, forwarded Bastianini's instructions down to the subordinate commands. In the meantime, Jews who starting that day entered the Italian zone must be surrendered to the German authorities (if the German authorities requested them and after having ascertained the date of Jews' arrival).[47] Second, a few days later, Mussolini excluded the Italian Army from managing Jewish policy in southern France and put the Italian civilian police in charge of the matter.[48] Hence, from 19 March 1943, scant weeks after the internment operations of foreign Jews and 'less dangerous' enemy aliens in compulsory residences had begun, the internment of non-Italian Jews, now including French Jews, in the Italian zone became the responsibility of a Royal Inspectorate for Racial Police based in Nice and headed by the police inspector-general Guido Lospinoso (while Barranco and the Fourth Army retained responsibility for apprehending enemy aliens and other hostile individuals).[49] Internment operations under the supervision of the Inspectorate began in early April 1943. Jews were now primarily directed to compulsory residences in the Haute-Savoie department.[50] By the second half of August 1943, more than 4,000 Jews lived in generally difficult but tolerable conditions in villages scattered across the Italian zone.[51] All this concerned the operational level, for even after Lospinoso's appointment decisions regarding Jewish matters in southern France ultimately remained in Mussolini's hands in his capacity of Minister of Interior.

It was precisely one of Mussolini's direct subordinates, the recently appointed new police chief Renzo Chierici, who issued the order for Lospinoso on 15 July 1943 to grant the request of the SS *Einsatzkommando* in Marseille to surrender German Jews in the Italian zone. In the following weeks, Lospinoso travelled twice to Marseille and, according to the surviving German documentation, handed over 'some lists' of Jews residing in the Italian zone to his Nazi colleagues.[52] However, no Jews were handed over, as following Mussolini's arrest and the ensuing creation of a new government in Rome led by Marshal Pietro Badoglio, Lospinoso did not carry Chierici's order through to completion.[53] Meanwhile, the internment of Jews in compulsory residences was suspended following the Supreme Command's decision to withdraw the Fourth Army from southern France.[54] Against this backdrop, the announcement of the armistice between Italy and the Allies on 8 September 1943 caught the Fourth Army off guard, thereby facilitating the swift occupation of south-eastern France by the Wehrmacht.

Beyond the paradox: Fascist Italy's protection of Jews and its limits

The intra-Axis dispute over the internment and handover of Jews in the Italian zone in February to March 1943 typifies the different understandings of the 'Jewish problem' of the Axis partners in their common effort to win the war. Peter Longerich explains that 'at the heart of National Socialist political thinking was the idea that all the most pressing problems besetting Germany could be solved with the introduction of a fully comprehensive "new racial order"'.[55] The major obstacle to the creation of the New Order were the Jews, whom the Nazis perceived as 'the ultimate enemy, supposedly exploiting all others'.[56] In the context of total war, this ideological vision coupled with ever-growing security concerns, eventually offering the Nazi leadership a political, military and ethical warrant to pursue the most radical of 'solutions' to the 'Jewish problem', namely outright extermination.[57]

The Italian military and police authorities in southern France operated under a different set of priorities dictated by the political affiliation and military dangerousness of their enemies and only in the second instance by their 'race'.[58] This does not diminish in any way the anti-Semitic nature of Mussolini's order to intern Jews. That order and the policy that it generated were predicated upon a vision of 'the Jew' as intrinsically dangerous and, indeed, they reproduced *mutatis mutandis* the internment of certain categories of foreign and Italian Jews that Fascism carried out domestically from the summer of 1940 onwards.[59] The Italian military and civilian authorities treated Jews as a real danger; yet, crucially, they did not perceive Jews as a mortal threat. In addition to the milder approach to the internment of Jews in early 1943, this divide between the Nazi and Italian Fascist approaches emerged at the local level in the wake of three attacks, one of them deadly, that the French Resistance carried out against the Italian military authorities in Nice and Grenoble in April–May 1943.[60] On two occasions, the Italian military commands responded to the attacks by imposing a curfew and fining the cities of Grenoble and Nice.[61] Moreover, in Nice, the Fourth Army Command carried out a vast round-up operation of 'communists' on 6–7 May.[62] On the third occasion, the attacker was a French resistant of Jewish origins who was immediately apprehended and interned in the infamous Italian prison at the Lynwood Villa in Nice.[63] After the war, former inmates of the Lynwood Villa reported the systematic use of torture by the Italian authorities.[64] Yet, none of those attacks sparked retaliation aimed at all Jews, as instead it repeatedly happened in the German-occupied areas in France at the hand of the Nazi authorities after the invasion of the Soviet Union in June 1941.[65] In fact, when reporting to their superiors in Paris about the attack in Grenoble, the SS *Einsatzkommando* in Lyon stressed that the Italian military authorities had barred the

French authorities from arresting Jews, despite the fact that ten of them lived close to the Gambetta hotel where the attack took place.[66]

German sources on this highly sensitive – from the Nazi viewpoint – issue must be approached with great caution.[67] This said, the afore-mentioned three episodes reflect a pattern that can be explained neither in terms of humanitarianism nor with purely political and military considerations. Instead, the Italian military authorities' decision to not to retaliate against all Jews point to the different significance that the 'Jewish question' had acquired by spring 1943 in the Nazi and Fascist camps, and consequently how vigorously that 'question' should be addressed and 'solved' in the pursuit of military success. This analysis does not ignore the importance that the defence of Italy's geopolitical interests, reasons of honour and prestige, as well as national and personal interests in view of a post-war reckoning had in the Italian authorities' refusal to hand over Jews to the Nazis.[68] Yet, none of these rationales can alone explain the decisions to intern Jews and prevent others from entering the Italian zone, and this is because Fascist Italy's Jewish policy in south-eastern France cannot be explained only in relation to the geopolitical and military contexts of the occupation.[69] Equally important is another context that proponents of the rescue and the sceptical theses alike have generally overlooked or underestimated, namely that of the distinct Italian-Fascist understanding and resulting approach to the 'Jewish question'.[70] Within this analytical framework, the afore-mentioned rationales should be understood as a series of variables that combined in different ways at different times against the background of a worldview that did not perceive the 'solution' of the 'Jewish problem', that is, the killing of Jews *qua* Jews, as crucial for Fascist Italy's final victory.

Anti-Semitism and persecution do not necessarily lead to extermination.[71] It follows that there was no such thing as the Italian paradox. Consequently, also the discussion over the 'protection' of non-Italian Jews in south-eastern France is misconceived. The moment the Foreign Ministry and the Supreme Command refused to surrender Jews or prevented the French authorities from doing so they were protecting them irrespective of the fact that foreign Jews, unlike Italian Jews, did not enjoy 'diplomatic protection'.[72] It is also clear that the Foreign Ministry and the Supreme Command were doing so deliberately. This is not tantamount to arguing that the Italian diplomats and military leaders were plotting against Mussolini to sabotage the Holocaust.[73] Rather, it means that the awareness of the fate of death that awaited Jews once in German hands was *one* of the elements at stake in their opposition to the surrender of those Jews (this argument, however, cannot be extended to Mussolini). This conclusion is supported by the way in which the Supreme Command understood the rationale underpinning Mussolini's decision to hand over Jewish matters to the Italian police in March 1943. A senior Supreme Command officer explained that rationale to the Fourth Army Command as 'to save the Jews' in the Italian occupation zone 'whatever their nationality'.[74]

The interpretative problems with Fascist Jewish policy in southern France do not lie in the existence of the Italian protection, but rather in its limits. These limits materialized in the Fascist government's decision to prevent the deportation of those Jews who lived within the Italian zone, while simultaneously taking steps to prevent others from seeking refuge in the territories under the Fourth Army's control (and thereby knowingly leaving non-Italian Jews in the German zone to their deadly destiny).[75] Yet, limits to the Italian protection existed also for those non-Italian Jews who lived within the Italian zone, in that they were prohibited from entering Italy or crossing into Switzerland (in addition to being subjected to internment).[76] Moreover, Italian protection could be revoked at any time, as proven by Chierici's order to hand over German Jews to the Nazis in July 1943.

The Italian limited protection of Jews in south-eastern France was consistent with a worldview that deemed Jews as potential but minor threats to Italian military security. It asserted Fascist Italy's primacy in its occupation zone, and thereby its superiority over the Vichy enemy and parity vis-à-vis the Nazi ally, while simultaneously respecting the latter's status and its right to pursue its own Jewish policy in the German sphere of interests.

Conclusion

In south-eastern France, the opposition to the deportation of Jews was one portion of a larger anti-Semitic policy that the Fascist government implemented between November 1942 and July 1943. As far as the top Italian military and diplomatic officials were concerned, this policy reflected a vision that, unlike the Nazi vision for a New Order, did not revolve around the 'solution of the Jewish problem'.[77]

This conclusion does not in any way overlook the Axis powers' common drive for war and conquest.[78] Nor does it deny the role that racism and anti-Semitism played in the Fascist dictatorship.[79] On the contrary, if placed in the framework of the Fascist 'decade of war' that began with the invasion of Ethiopia in 1935, the afore-mentioned conclusion suggests – as a working hypothesis – that the policy towards Jews in the occupied territories in 1941–1943 should be understood not only in terms of a response of the 'junior partner' to the powerful Nazi ally,[80] but also as the outcome of an expansionist drive in which the interaction of violence, racism, anti-Semitism and political enmity played out in fundamentally different – albeit no less criminal – ways than it did in the Nazi *Lebensraum*. This is not tantamount to establishing a direct connection between what happened in south-eastern France and other theatres of war from 1935 onwards – and among the latter.[81] Instead, it points to the insights that we can gain in the analysis of the ideological roots of that interaction through reframing the discussion beyond Fascist Italy's poor military performance in World War II.[82]

Consequently, to acknowledge that Fascist Italy offered a limited protection to non-Italian Jews in south-eastern France does not mean to ignore the dire consequences that the persecution systematically enforced since 1938 had on Jews in Italy.[83] Nor ought that limited protection conceal Fascist Italy's violence against Jews in other contexts[84] and against other 'enemies' in southern France and elsewhere prior to and during World War II.[85] Yet, to assume that the latter was more representative of Italian Fascism's 'true' nature than the former is analytically fallacious.[86] Both similarities and differences between Nazi and Fascist Italy's policies in their respective spheres of interests between 1940 and 1943 were relevant and therefore require careful explanation.[87] Against this backdrop, the task for historians is to shed light on the concrete meanings that *spazio vitale* and *nuovo ordine* had for Mussolini and the Fascist leaders as these meanings were reflected, *inter alia*, in Italian violence (and its varying degrees of intensity) against different ethnic, religious, political and social groups in Africa and Europe.

Acknowledgement

I want to thank Stephan Malinowski who invited me to think more carefully about the connections between Fascist Italy's anti-Semitism and expansionism. I am also grateful to Giorgio Fabre, Dan Michman, Michał Palacz, Chelsea Sambells, Michele Sarfatti and Karine Varley for their comments on earlier versions of this essay. Part of this chapter was presented as a seminar paper at the Columbia Seminar in Modern Italian Studies. My gratitude to Ernest Ialongo, Natalia Indrimi and Alessandro Cassin for inviting me to New York and to Susan Zuccotti for her insightful comments on my paper. Susanne Class helped me with the translation of German documents. Research for this study was funded by a Doctoral scholarship in Modern History from the University of Edinburgh's College of Humanities and Social Science, a Claims Conference Saul Kagan Fellowship in Shoah Studies, a European Holocaust Research Infrastructure Fellowship, a Holocaust Educational Foundation's Sharon Abramson Research Grant for the Study of the Holocaust, a Scouloudi Historical Award from the London Institute of Historical Research, and a Postgraduate Research Support Grant from the Royal Historical Society.

Notes

1 M. Knox, *Hitler's Italian Allies: Royal Armed Forces, Fascist Regime and the War of 1940–1943* (Cambridge: Cambridge University Press, 2000), pp. 10–21.
2 E. Costa Bona, *Dalla guerra alla pace. Italia-Francia 1940–1947* (Milan: Franco Angeli, 1995), pp. 12, 21.
3 R. Poznanski, *Jews in France during World War II* (Hanover and London: University Press of New England, 2001), pp. 356–7.
4 L. Poliakov, *La condition des Juifs en France sous l'occupation italienne* (Paris: Éditions du Centre, 1946), pp. 17–8.
5 Ibid.; R. De Felice, *Storia degli ebrei italiani sotto il fascismo* (Turin: Einaudi, 1993 [1961]), pp. 402–16; J. Steinberg, *All or Nothing: The Axis and the Holocaust, 1941–1943* (London and New York: Routledge, 2002 [1990]).
6 D. Rodogno, *Fascism's European Empire: Italian Occupation during the Second World War* (Cambridge: Cambridge University Press, 2006 [2003]); D. Rodogno, 'La politique des occupants italiens à l'égard des Juifs en France métropolitaine: Humanisme ou pragmatisme?', *Vingtième Siècle*, 93 (2007), pp. 63–77; T. Schlemmer and H. Woller, 'Der italienische Faschismus und die Juden 1922 bis 1945', *Vierteljahrshefte für*

Zeitgeschichte, 53:2 (2005), pp. 165–201, see pp. 190–2; M. Knox, 'Das faschistische Italien und die 'Endlösung', 1942/43', *Vierteljahrshefte für Zeitgeschichte*, 55:1 (2007), pp. 53–92.

7　Most prominently by De Felice, *Storia degli ebrei italiani*, pp. xxviii–xxx.

8　Rodogno, *Fascism's European Empire*, p. 363.

9　Ibid., ch. 2.

10　F. Focardi, *Il cattivo tedesco e il bravo italiano. La rimozione delle colpe della seconda guerra mondiale* (Rome and Bari: Laterza, 2013).

11　D. Roberts, 'Italian Fascism: New Light on the Dark Side', *Journal of Contemporary History*, 44:3 (2009), pp. 523–33, see pp. 530–1; L. Fenoglio, *Angelo Donati e la «questione ebraica» nella Francia occupata dall'esercito italiano* (Turin: Silvio Zamorani, 2013), pp. 165–7.

12　P. Fonzi, 'Beyond the Myth of the "Good Italian": Recent Trends in the Study of the Italian Occupation of Southeastern Europe during the Second World War', *Südosteuropa*, 65:2 (2017), pp. 239–59, see p. 247.

13　Archives Nationales (AN), AJ41/439, dossier (d.)A-II; Archivio dell'Ufficio storico dello Stato Maggiore dell'Esercito (AUSSME), N1-11, b. 1099, Fourth Army Command's military log (October–December 1942), entry 20 November 1942 and allegato 39.

14　Archivio Centrale dello Stato (ACS), Ministero dell'Interno (MI), Gabinetto, Ufficio Cifra (UC) Arrivo, raccolte 1942(34, 35, 36), Barranco to police chief and to head of political police, various dates.

15　Centre de Documentation Juive Contemporaine (CDJC), I-33, XLVIIIa-10, German Embassy in Paris to various recipients, 16 December 1942; A. Biagini and F. Frattolillo (eds.), *Diario storico del Comando Supremo*, vol. VIII, tomo 1 (Rome: USSME, 1999), p. 951.

16　Quoted in Rodogno, *Fascism's European Empire*, p. 394. Also see M. Sarfatti, 'Le disposizioni di carattere generale dell'Italia fascista sugli ebrei nella Francia occupata, novembre 1942 – luglio 1943', *Documenti e commenti*, 9. Available from www.michelesarfatti.it/documenti-e-commenti/le-disposizioni-di-carattere-generale-dellitalia-fascista-sugli-ebrei-nella-francia-occupata-novembre-1942-luglio-1943 [Accessed on 24 May 2018].

17　ACS, MI, Gabinetto, UC Partenza, raccolta 1942(91), Senise to Barranco, 8 December 1942.

18　ACS, MI, Direzione Generale della Pubblica Sicurezza (DGPS), Divisione del Personale di Pubblica Sicurezza (DPPS), versamento 1973, b. 119bis, fascicolo (f.) Rosario Barranco; M. Canali, *Le spie del regime* (Bologna: il Mulino, 2004), pp. 137–8, 473–4.

19　Archivio storico-diplomatico del Ministero degli Affari Esteri (ASMAE), Affari Politici (AP) 1931–1945, Francia, b. 54, f. 11, Foreign Ministry to Minister Bonarelli, head of the Foreign Ministry's liaison office with the Fourth Army Command, et al., 22 December 1942; D. Schipsi, *L'occupazione italiana dei territori metropolitani francesi (1940–1943)* (Rome: USSME, 2007), pp. 730–1.

20　ACS, MI, Gabinetto, UC Arrivo, raccolta 1942(39), Barranco to police chief, 29 December 1942; ASMAE, Telegrammi 1935–1944, Piccola Registrazione Arrivo 1943, 1–600, Bonarelli to Foreign Ministry, 4 January 1943.

21　ACS, MI, DGPS, Divisione Affari Generali e Riservati (DAGR), Massime, b. 110, f. 16.1.46, Senise to Supreme Command, 27 December 1942; ASMAE, AP 1931–1945, Francia, b. 80, f. 7, Barranco to Alberto Calisse, Consul General in Nice, 6 January 1943.

22　ACS, MI, Gabinetto, UC Arrivo, raccolte 1942–1943, Barranco to police chief, various dates.

23　ACS, MI, Gabinetto, UC Arrivo, raccolte 1943(1, 3), Barranco to police chief, 14 and 27 January 1943.

24 ACS, MI, DGPS, DAGR, Massime, b. 110, f. 16.1.46, Political Police to DAGR, 17 January 1943.

25 ASMAE, AP 1931–1945, Francia, b. 80, f. 7, Barranco to Calisse, 6 January 1943; ASMAE, AP 1931–1945, Francia, b. 69, f. 6, Bonarelli to Calisse et al., 17 February 1943.

26 AUSSME, N1-11, b. 1100, First Army Corps Command's military log (January-February 1943), Allegato 39, First Army Corps Command to 'Divisione Celere EFTF' Command et al., 14 February 1943; ASMAE, AP 1931–1945, Francia, b. 80, f. 7, Bonarelli to Calisse et al., 26 February 1943; ACS, MI, DGPS, DAGR, Massime b.110, f.16.1.46, Army General Staff to Umberto Albini, undersecretary of State at the Interior Ministry, 24 February 1943.

27 M. Marrus and R. Paxton, *Vichy France and the Jews* (New York: Basic Books, 1981).

28 G. Conti, *Una guerra segreta. Il Sim nel secondo conflitto mondiale* (Bologna: il Mulino, 2009), p. 348.

29 Marrus, Paxton, *Vichy.*

30 Ibid, p. 304 ff.; Archives Départementales des Alpes-Maritimes (ADAM), 616W242, d. 17, Rhône regional prefect to Nice regional prefect, 7 December 1942; Schleier to Reich Foreign Minister, 23 January 1943 in *Akten zur Deutschen Auswärtigen Politik 1918–1945* (ADAP), Serie E, band V, Göttingen, Vandenhoeck & Ruprecht, 1978, pp. 132–3.

31 ADAM, 616W242, d. 17, Rhône regional prefect to Nice regional prefect, 7 December 1942, and Alpes-Maritimes prefect to Rhône regional prefect, 18 December 1942.

32 ASMAE, AP 1931–1945, Francia, b. 64, f. 8, Foreign Ministry to Bonarelli et al., 29 December 1942.

33 AUSSME, M3, b. 69, f. 1627, General Alessandro Trabucchi, Fourth Army Chief of Staff, to unknown recipients, [30] December 1942.

34 ADAM, 616W242, d. 17, Italian Armistice Commission with France to French liaison officer Colonel Emile Bonnet, 30 December 1942.

35 ASMAE, AP 1931–1945, Francia, b. 80, f. 7, Ciano to Bonarelli et al., 2 January 1943.

36 ADAM, 616W242, d. 17.

37 D. Carpi, *Between Mussolini and Hitler: The Jews and the Italian authorities in France and Tunisia* (Hanover and London: University Press of New England for Brandeis University Press, 1994), p. 92; Rodogno, *Fascism's European Empire*, p. 394.

38 ASMAE, AP 1931–1945, Francia, b. 54, f. 11, Foreign Ministry to Bonarelli et al., 22 December 1942; ACS, MI, DGPS, DAGR, Massime, b. 110, f. 16.1.46.

39 ASMAE, AP 1931–1945, Francia, b. 64, f. 8.

40 M. Sarfatti, *The Jews in Mussolini's Italy: From Equality to Persecution* (Madison: University of Wisconsin Press, 2006), pp. 159–60; Knox, *Das faschistische Italien*, pp. 53–66.

41 ASMAE, AP 1931–1945, Francia, b. 64, f. 8, Foreign Ministry to Bonarelli et al., 29 December 1942.

42 P. Longerich, *Holocaust: The Nazi Persecution and Murder of the Jews* (Oxford: Oxford University Press, 2010), p. 311 ff.

43 Schleier to Reich Foreign Minister, 23 January 1943 in ADAP, Serie E, band V, pp. 132–3; CDJC, XXVa-257a, Reich Foreign Office [to German Embassy in Paris], 31 January 1943; S. Klarsfeld, *Vichy-Auschwitz: Le rôle de Vichy dans la solution finale de la question juive en France. 1943–1944* (Paris: Fayard, 1985), pp. 203–6, 214.

44 AN, F-1cIII-1152, Monthly report from prefect of Drôme department, 1 March 1943; AN, F-1cIII-1186, Monthly report from prefect of Savoie department to Vichy Interior Ministry et al., 24 April 1943; AN, F-1cIII-1187, Monthly report from prefect of

Haute-Savoie department to Vichy Interior Ministry et al., 4 March 1943; AN, F-1cIII-1200, Lyon regional prefect to head of government, 7 March 1943; AN, AJ41, 1182, General Carlo Avarna di Gualtieri, Supreme Command's representative in Vichy, to Vichy government, 2, 17, 29 March and 27 April 1943; ASMAE, AP 1931–1945, Francia, b. 80, f. 7, Supreme Command to Avarna et al., 1 March 1943.

45 Klarsfeld, *Vichy-Auschwitz*, pp. 228, 235–40, 243–6.

46 ASMAE, AP 1931–1945, Francia, b. 80, f. 7, Bastianini to Supreme Command et al., 13 March 1943.

47 AUSSME, M3, b. 476, ff. 3126 (3121) and 3127, Vercellino to subordinate commands, 26 March 1943.

48 ASMAE, Telegrammi 1935–1944, Piccola Registrazione Partenza 1943, 9001–10000, Foreign Minister Mussolini to Fourth Army Command and Italian Armistice Commission with France, 19 March 1943.

49 On Lospinoso's controversial actions in southern France, see L. Fenoglio, 'Between Protection and Complicity: Guido Lospinoso, Fascist Italy and the Holocaust in occupied Southeastern France', *Holocaust and Genocide Studies*, 33:1 (2019), pp. 90–111.

50 Archives départementales de Haute-Savoie (ADHS), 22W19, d. Juifs et étrangers, Head of Renseignement Généraux of Haute-Savoie to Haute-Savoie prefect, 9 April 1943.

51 AN, AJ41, 1179, Report from Colonel Bonnet, 4 June 1943; ADAM, 166W10, d. Troupes italiennes d'occupation, Intercepted letter from an internee in Saint-Martin-Vésubie, April 1943; CDJC, CCXIV-18, Report on conditions in Saint-Gervais-les-Bains, 3 July 1943; K. Voigt, *Il rifugio precario. Gli esuli in Italia dal 1933 al 1945*, vol. 2 (Scandicci: La Nuova Italia, 1996), p. 319.

52 ACS, MI, DGPS, DPPS, versamento 1959, b. 168, f. Guido Lospinoso, Mission abroad expenses claim forms 1–31 July and 1–31 August 1943.

53 Klarsfeld, *Vichy-Auschwitz*, pp. 330, 339–41; M. Sarfatti, 'Fascist Italy and German Jews in south-eastern France in July 1943', *Journal of Modern Italian Studies*, 3:3 (1998), pp. 318–28.

54 AUSSME, L3, b. 59, Memorandum concerning decisions taken during a meeting held on 28 August 1943 with representatives of Foreign Ministry, Interior Ministry and General Staff; ACS, MI, DGPS, DAGR, Massime, b. 248, f. 39; Schipsi, *L'occupazione italiana*, pp. 465, 735.

55 Longerich, *Holocaust*, p. 30.

56 D. Bloxham, *The Final Solution: A Genocide* (Oxford: Oxford University Press, 2009), p. 18.

57 Ibid., part II; Longerich, *Holocaust*; W. Bialas, 'Nazi Ethics: Perpetrators with a Clear Conscience', *Dapim: Studies on the Holocaust*, 27:1 (2013), pp. 3–25.

58 AUSSME, N1-11, b. 1100, First Army Corps Command's military log (January–February 1943), Allegato 39, First Army Corps Command to 'Divisione Celere EFTF' Command et al., 14 February 1943.

59 Voigt, *Rifugio precario*, pp. 4–22; Sarfatti, *Jews in Mussolini's Italy*, pp. 141–2, 146–7.

60 ASMAE, Telegrammi 1935–1944, Piccola Registrazione Arrivo 1943, 15401–16000, Bonarelli to Foreign Ministry, 25 May 1943; ACS, MI, Gabinetto, UC Arrivo, raccolte 1943–1913, 14, Barranco to police chief, 2, 24 May 1943.

61 Archives départementales de l'Isère, 52M434; AUSSME, N1-11, b. 1218, Fourth Army Command's military log (March–April 1943), entries 27, 28, 29 April 1943 and allegati 72, 73.

62 AUSSME, N1-11, b. 1326, Fourth Army Command's military log (May–June 1943), entry 8 May 1943 and allegati 9a-b-c; AN, AJ41, 1180, d. XXXV.

63 ACS, MI, Gabinetto, UC Arrivo, raccolta 1943–1944, Barranco to police chief, 24 May 1943; CDJC, CCXVIII-90, Testimony of Maurice Blanchard, 6 May 1945.

64 CDJC, CCXVIII-90, Testimony of Maurice Blanchard, 6 May 1945; ACS, Presidenza del Consiglio dei Ministri, Alto Commissariato per le sanzioni contro il fascismo, Titolo XVI, f. 11–111; J.-L. Panicacci, *L'Occupation italienne. Sud-Est de la France, Juin 1940–Septembre 1943* (Rennes: Presses Universitaires de Rennes, 2010), pp. 231–3.
65 Marrus, Paxton, *Vichy*, pp. 223–7, 306–8.
66 CDJC, XXVa-295, *Einsatzkommando* Lyon to commander of Nazi security services in France (Helmut Knochen), 27 May 1943.
67 Fenoglio, *Angelo Donati*, pp. 120–25; L. Fenoglio, 'On the use of Nazi sources for the study of Fascist Jewish policy in the Italian-occupied territories: The case of south-eastern France, November 1942–July 1943', *Journal of Modern Italian Studies*, 24:1 (2019), pp. 63–78.
68 Rodogno, *Fascism's European Empire*, ch. 11; Knox, *Das faschistische Italien*, pp. 72–5, 83–90.
69 As done by Rodogno, *Fascism's European Empire*, ch. 11.
70 Ibid., p. 406; Knox, *Das faschistische Italien*, p. 92.
71 As implicitly acknowledged by Rodogno (*Fascism's European Empire*, pp. 406–7). On the broader point, see Bloxham, *Final Solution*, pp. 39–40.
72 Rodogno, *Fascism's European Empire*, p. 363.
73 Steinberg, *All or Nothing*.
74 A. Biagini and F. Frattolillo (eds.), *Diario storico del Comando Supremo*, vol. IX, tomo 2 (Rome: USSME, 2002), p. 307.
75 AUSSME, N1-11, b. 1218, Fourth Army Command's military log (March–April 1943), Allegato 31, Fourth Army Monthly report for the period 21 February-20 March 1943, 8 April 1943.
76 ADHS, 22W19, d. A-1; ACS, MI, DGPS, DAGR, A16, b. 47, f. 11.
77 P. Fonzi, 'Il Nuovo Ordine Europeo nazionalsocialista. Storia e storiografia', in M. Fioravanzo and C. Fumian (eds.), *1943. Strategie militari, collaborazionismi, Resistenze* (Rome: Viella, 2015), pp. 101–19, see pp. 110–9; Longerich, *Holocaust*, pp. 313, 422–35; see also note 70.
78 Rodogno, *Fascism's European Empire*; A. Kallis, *Fascist ideology: Territory and expansionism in Italy and Germany, 1922–1945* (London and New York: Routledge, 2000); M. Knox, *Common Destiny: Dictatorship, Foreign Policy, and War in Fascist Italy and Nazi Germany* (Cambridge: Cambridge University Press, 2000), part I.
79 R. Gordon, 'Race', in R. Bosworth (ed.), *The Oxford Handbook of Fascism* (Oxford: Oxford University Press, 2009), pp. 296–316; N. Labanca, 'Il razzismo istituzionale coloniale: genesi e relazioni con l'antisemitismo fascista', in M. Flores, S. Levis Sullam, M.-A. Matard-Bonucci and E. Traverso (eds.), *Storia della Shoah in Italia. Vicende, memorie, rappresentazioni*, vol. 1 (Turin: UTET, 2010), pp. 193–218.
80 Rodogno, *Fascism's European Empire*, ch. 11; Schlemmer and Woller, *Der Italienische Faschismus*, pp. 190–1; E. Collotti, *Il fascismo e gli ebrei. Le leggi razziali in Italia* (Rome and Bari: Laterza, 2003), p. 120.
81 On the complex and roundabout connections between the African and Balkan theatres of war, see the excellent chapter by Nicolas G. Virtue in this volume.
82 P. Bernhard, 'Renarrating Italian Fascism: New Directions in the Historiography of a European Dictatorship', *Contemporary European History*, 23:1 (2014), pp. 151–63, see p. 163.
83 Sarfatti, *Jews in Mussolini's Italy*, ch. 4.
84 P. Bernhard, 'Behind the Battle Lines: Italian Atrocities and the Persecution of Arabs, Berbers, and Jews in North Africa during World War II', *Holocaust and Genocide Studies*, 26:3 (2012), pp. 425–46.

85 Rodogno, *Fascism's European Empire*, ch. 10; E. Sica, *Mussolini's Army in the French Riviera: Italy's occupation of France* (Urbana: University of Illinois Press, 2016), pp. 127–34, 139–44; A. Stramaccioni, *Crimini di guerra. Storia e memoria del caso italiano* (Rome and Bari: Laterza, 2016).
86 Here I follow Bloxham, *Final Solution*, pp. 330–1.
87 An example of the tension between comparative approach and identifying Italian Fascism's 'true face' in Schlemmer and Woller, *Der Italienische Faschismus*, pp. 196–201, quotation p. 199.

12 Radio propaganda during the war

The Mediterranean scenario in Radio Bari's broadcasts (1940–1943)[1]

Arturo Marzano

This chapter will analyse representations of the Mediterranean war theatre in Radio Bari's broadcasts during World War II (1940–1943). In those years, Radio Bari's programme schedule relied primarily on news bulletins which, on the one hand, covered the events in the main theatres of war and the Mediterranean in particular and, on the other, attacked the key players (namely, Great Britain, the USSR and the USA). In the next pages, I will focus on Radio Bari news' content as well as on its representations of the Allies between 1940 and 1943, taking into account that these broadcasts have to be analysed within the wider framework of the role that Radio Bari played during the 'Fascist decade of war'. At the same time, I will attempt to assess Arab audiences' responses to Radio Bari's broadcasts during the war. Did Radio Bari play any part in influencing Arab public opinion and building support for Rome? Were the Arab 'hearts and minds' conquered by Italian Fascist propaganda, or were other radio broadcasts more appealing?

Radio Bari: an overview

Owned and operated by EIAR (Ente Italiano Audizioni Radiofoniche, the Italian Radio Broadcasting Authority), Radio Bari went on air from its studios at 247 Via Putigliani on 6 September 1932, during the third Fiera del Levante (Levant Fair). Arabic broadcasts began on 24 May 1934, at the behest of Galeazzo Ciano (then Undersecretary for the Press and Propaganda Office of the Prime Minister, which in May 1937 became the Ministry of Popular Culture). This was made possible by the installation of Bari I, a twenty-kilowatt medium wave transmitter second only to the EIAR stations in Rome and Milan located in Ceglie, a hamlet on the city's outskirts.[2] A second one-kilowatt transmitter (Bari II) was installed in 1935 near the fairgrounds in the port area. Radio Bari broadcasted on medium wave from Bari and on short wave from Rome, more specifically from the Centro Radio Imperiale (Imperial Radio Centre), which opened on the city's outskirts on 31 October 1938.[3] According to the military attaché at the American embassy in Rome, the latter could 'be considered the most powerful and modern short-wave station of the world'.[4]

When Radio Bari started its Arabic broadcasts in 1934, news bulletins were aired three times a week, but then became a daily service in December 1937. Programme duration progressively increased: from fifteen minutes in 1934 to forty minutes in December 1937, to fifty minutes in February 1938.[5] Starting in August of the same year, two news bulletins were aired daily, one in the morning and one in the evening. From December 1938 onwards, the evening bulletin was rescheduled from 6.10 p.m. to 6.30 p.m. to draw listeners from competing Arabic radio broadcasts and from Radio Daventry[6] in particular (the BBC's Arabic service established in January 1938, also known as Radio London).[7] In December 1940, Arabic broadcasts grew to four and were aired daily at 11.30 a.m., 1.30 p.m., 7.00 p.m. and 9.50 p.m., for an overall duration of two hours.[8] *Radyo Bari–Radio Araba di Bari*, a monthly sixteen-page magazine, began publication in January 1938. In addition to radio programme listings in Italian, English, French and Arabic, it also featured a digest of articles on the Mediterranean and the Middle East from the Italian press.

Programmes were generally divided into three sections: Arab music, country-specific news bulletins and talk shows. In 1938 and 1939, Radio Bari offered two main formats: 'politics' and 'arts and culture'.[9] The first consisted of news bulletins and talk shows focusing on the political situation of the Arab countries. Most of the time, if not always, these gave Radio Bari a chance to lambaste France and Britain for their colonial policies in North Africa and the Middle East, as if Libya were not an Italian colony, a contradiction that was not lost on contemporary authors, the Arabic press and rival radio stations.[10] Arts and culture programmes featured Arab and European music as well as talks on literature, arts and theatre, again both Arab and European. Italian and Islamic law and theology also figured among the topics discussed. Commenting on a talk on the topic of Islamic and Roman law, which was aired on 4 January 1939, Mr Nagib, a BBC employee in charge of monitoring and evaluating Radio Bari's Arabic broadcasts, provides clues as to the quality of the programme: 'the best talk I have heard on this subject'.[11]

The language used for the news bulletins was literary Arabic. Despite what some historians have stated, spoken Arabic was very rarely used.[12] The Italian consul in Tangier, Mario Badoglio, advised against the use of spoken Arabic in radio broadcasts, citing an earlier, unsuccessful attempt by Radio Daventry.[13] Nonetheless, spoken Arabic was actually employed on rare occasions, such as on 16 May 1941, at least according to the French authorities.[14]

Radio Bari and the 'Fascist decade of war'

As stated, Radio Bari started its Arabic transmissions in May 1934. Even though it was shut down on 8 September 1943, it basically broadcasted during the entire 'Fascist decade of war'. It was certainly a main character of Fascist policy during those years, as it aimed at increasing Rome's political role in North Africa and the Middle East by courting Arab nationalism and challenging the French and British presence in those areas.

The beginning of Radio Bari's Arabic transmissions in May 1934 was not a coincidence. As Davide Rodogno recalls, Mussolini had stated on 19 March 1934: 'Italy's historical aims have two names: Asia and Africa [...]; it's not about conquest [...] but rather about territorial expansion'.[15] Actually, since the early 1930s, several educational institutions had been created with the aim of attracting Arab university students to Italy, the general idea being that these and other activities would enhance political and economic relationships with Arab countries. Radio Bari was part of this strategy, and it slowly became the most important soft power tool of Fascist foreign policy in North Africa and the Middle East.[16] In fact, medium- and short-waves made it possible for its Arabic broadcasts to be received in several countries, from Morocco to Egypt, Lebanon, Yemen and Iraq, thus allowing Fascist propaganda to reach all Arab audiences.

Radio Bari went along the entire Fascist policy between 1934 and 1943, strongly supporting all wars that Rome fought in those years and being Fascist Italy's mouthpiece in the Arab countries. The Ethiopian war was presented by Radio Bari as a war that Italy was fighting to protect the Muslim population living in Ethiopia and discriminated by the Negus. In 1935–1936, Italy carried out an intense propaganda activity in the Arab countries with the main aim of justifying its invasion of Ethiopia and gaining the Arab population support. Several brochures and leaflets were published in Arabic in order to highlight the anti-Islamic position of the Negus, while at the same time displaying the Fascist pro-Islamic position. Just to make an example, in 1936 a photographic brochure titled *'ataf Italia 'ala al-Islam fi Afriqa* [What Italy has done in Africa for Islam] was printed and distributed through the Italian delegations in North Africa and the Middle East.[17] Radio Bari employed the same type of message, presenting Italy as a power that was supporting Islam and the Muslim population. In December 1935, during the Muslim holy month of *Ramadan*, this message was delivered in addition to 'readings of several pages of the Koran' and 'wishing happiness and prosperity to Muslims all over the world' on *'id al-fitr* [Feast of breaking of the fast].[18]

The same argument was employed by Radio Bari in April 1939: the occupation of Albania was depicted as a means to protect the Albanian Muslim population 'from the tyranny and misrule of King Zog I', since Italy was 'a great protector of Muslims'.[19] During the 'Fascist Decade of War', Radio Bari was therefore on the front line to support Fascist foreign policy. Even though between 1935 and 1939 there were ups and downs in the Fascist attacks against France and Great Britain,[20] Radio Bari Arabic transmissions strongly supported the Imperial dream of replacing London and Paris as major powers in the Mediterranean and the Arab world thus achieving hegemony in those regions.

Radio Bari could behave as Fascism's mouthpiece in the Arab countries since it was fully under the control of the Ministry of Popular Culture. Radio Bari news bulletins and talk shows focusing on the political situation of the Arab countries were run by the so-called *Reparto arabo* [Arab Department]. This one was under the supervision of the *Ispettorato per la radiodiffusione e la televisione*

[Inspectorate for radio and television], which was in charge of preparing the draft of the news broadcasted by the Italian radio.[21] It was the Cabinet of the Ministry of Popular Culture that was monitoring the *Ispettorato* and therefore controlling that the *Reparto arabo* would set up Radio Bari Arabic transmissions in line with Fascist policies.[22]

The beginning of the war: Italian non-belligerence (1939–1940)

Between 1 September 1939 and 10 June 1940, Radio Bari acted as the perfect mouthpiece for Fascist Italy's non-belligerence. In line with what had happened in 1938–1939, namely a sort of 'war of the waves' between rival radio stations, France and Britain used Arabic broadcasts to attack the Axis powers.[23] For example, Arabs were warned that, should Germany win the war, they would suffer the same fate that had befallen Europe's conquered nations, such as Czechoslovakia and Poland. By contrast, anti-British and anti-French attacks were not a priority for Radio Bari. Of course, its news bulletins were often critical of British and French policies towards the Arabs, such as on 27 October 1939, when the radio reported: 'cotton crisis more acute [...]; Britain buys Turkish tobacco but not Egyptian cotton and hopes to profit from Egypt's difficulties'.[24] On 18 January 1940, it was France's turn to be attacked for 'the conditions of Arab workers in Tunisia'.[25]

Yet, Italy's willingness to maintain peace and security in Europe and the Mediterranean, thanks to Mussolini's efforts, was the central message in Radio Bari's broadcasts. Its understated approach was very different from that of Radio Berlin,[26] which in the same period was launching an aggressive propaganda campaign against London and Paris.[27] For instance, on 4 November 1939, following an 'exchange of notes between Italy and Greece', Radio Bari reported: '[Arabic] newspapers comment on the time-honoured spiritual relations between the two countries and Greece's admiration for Italy'.[28] And on 13 January 1940, a news bulletin highlighted that, according to 'the Egyptian press [...], Italy's influence in the Balkans and Mediterranean [...] is a key factor in preserving peace in both spheres'.[29] Finally, in February, Radio Bari quoted a Palestinian newspaper that had 'paid a high tribute to the personality and the policies of the Duce as a statesman', reporting that 'the Duce is doing his utmost to keep his country out of the war'.[30] In the first six months of the war, Radio Bari's intent was therefore to spread a reassuring message about Italy's commitment to a policy aimed at maintaining peace.

Nevertheless, Italian non-belligerence did not prevent Rome from concentrating its efforts on military preparedness, nor Radio Bari from covering the topic in its Arabic broadcasts. Good examples of this are the news that 'with great effort and determination, the Duce is providing the Italian army with modern equipment' (24 November 1939),[31] or the fact that a meeting between the Duce and General Rodolfo Graziani on 21 March 1940, was heralded as proof of 'the continual activity of Italy to strengthen her armies [...] to safeguard Italy's vital interests'.[32]

During the spring of 1940, Radio Bari's broadcasts became more aggressive in terms of both content and form. On 25 April, a news bulletin railed against France for sentencing to death a number of Syrian nationalists, thus drawing attention to the terrible conditions facing Syrians under French rule.[33] On 13 May, similar news was broadcast concerning Palestine: following 'the death sentences passed on the seven Palestine leaders a week ago, [...] the Military Court in Palestine has passed a death sentence on an innocent *sheikh*'. On the same day, France also came under attack by Radio Bari for the 'ill-treatment' of Tunisian locals.[34]

Those were the harshest attacks against London and Paris since 1 September 1939. After that, on 10 May the Battle of France had begun, Rome was considering the possibility of entering the war, and for this reason the Ministry of Popular Culture was devising a media campaign that could serve the war effort.

Radio Bari's broadcasts during the war (1940–1943)

On 11 June, both the morning and afternoon news reported on Italy's entry into the war. On the one hand, Radio Bari reported that 'the Duce's speech was received with great enthusiasm all over Italy and the Italian Empire', thus implying that the Fascist regime was enjoying support throughout Italy and its colonies. On the other hand, in keeping with the message delivered in the previous months, that is to say Italy's efforts to maintain peace in the Mediterranean,[35] it stressed the fact that Mussolini had been very clear in asserting that 'Italy does not wish to involve [...] Switzerland, Greece, Turkey, and Egypt [...] in the war'.[36]

However, significant changes soon began to affect Radio Bari's Arabic broadcasts. First, from the summer of 1940 onwards, all news bulletins opened with a focus on the military operations that were taking place along the various war fronts. Radio Bari was not different from other Italian radios, whose news bulletins were dominated by war dispatches.[37] In this regard, Philip Cannistraro has argued that 'the war radically changed Italian radio programmes, crucially increasing their politicisation and giving huge prominence to the war effort to the detriment of cultural programmes'.[38] Second, while criticism of France and Great Britain gradually subsided, the attacks against the two major powers, namely the United States and the Soviet Union, increased. In fact, the Fascist regime was progressively identifying the USA and the USSR as the most dangerous enemy powers: as a consequence, the Arabic transmissions started targeting Moscow and Washington more than London and Paris. Radio Bari's news bulletins kept condemning the British and French colonial attitude and presence in the Arab countries but starting from June and December 1941 respectively, they focused on discrediting Moscow and Washington. More specifically, anti-Semitic discourses and stereotypes were purposely employed to depict Americans and Soviets as mere instruments in the hands of the international Jewry, whose alleged aim was to destroy the Axis powers.[39] Attacks against Moscow, for example for the way Communists were treating Muslims under the Soviet regime, would routinely turn into attacks against Washington. In fact, a major theme at the core of Radio Bari's propaganda was that Communists and capitalists were none other than Jews. Accordingly, 'both Stalin and Roosevelt are of Jewish descent',[40] and the USA, the USSR and the British Empire, allegedly under the control of Jewish lobbies, were presented as united in their attempt to conquer first the Middle East, starting with Palestine, and then the entire world. A case in point is the following report broadcast in August 1942:

> Roosevelt has stated that one of his reasons for entering the war was to support and strengthen Judaism. There is nothing strange about it, since the highest American officials are puppets of the Jews. They have reached their high places of office thanks to Jewish money, and thus the Jews are able to dominate public opinion through them. [...] The Jews work secretly in other countries, but in our country they work in the open without any fear, because they know the Anglo-Saxons are supporting them.[41]

Radio Bari was no less anti-Semitic than Radio Berlin. On the contrary, as stated by Benedict Magnes in a March 1942 dispatch to the U.S. government, it was 'the most anti-Semitic among the radio stations transmitting in Arabic'.[42]

As for Radio Bari's representation of the war, its strategy was twofold. News bulletins only reported Axis victories, be they real or imagined. And even when acknowledging defeat was inevitable, they invariably ascribed it to the enemy's technical superiority rather than to the Italian Army's faults. Italian soldiers were depicted by Radio Bari as brave and fearless, fighting as best as they could. On 31 March 1941, the Italian defeat at Keren, in the territory of present-day Eritrea, was described with the following words: 'the British were superior in number and equipment. They also had the advantage of transport facilities, and reinforcements were sent from Egypt and Sudan. The Italian forces were fighting day and night without relief'.[43]

However, not differently from any other belligerent state's radio broadcasts, Radio Bari rarely provided unbiased accounts of war events and was quick to dismiss conflicting news as enemy propaganda. Italian and German defeats simply disappeared from the broadcasts, and the loss of Ethiopia in May 1941 was never mentioned. Between 1940 and 1943, Radio Bari maintained a triumphalist stance, as if the Axis powers were winning everywhere from the Mediterranean to the Pacific to the Russian front. Radio Bari's reports on the El Alamein battle provide interesting insights. The battle was first mentioned on 2 July 1942, when a news bulletin announced that 'the great battle at El Alamein preludes the final expulsion of the British from Egypt and the liberation of the Egyptian people from British tyranny'.[44] Such triumphalism did not subside in the months that followed. On 27 July, Radio Bari reported that according to 'some Australians captured near El Alamein, [...] whenever the word *bersaglieri* is mentioned, it causes panic among the British'.[45] On 10 September, Radio Bari announced that 'the Axis powers have gained the mastery of the air over all fronts, in Russia, the Atlantic, North Africa, the Channel and elsewhere'.[46] And on 10 October, it boasted that

> there was a time when the British fleet was supreme in the Mediterranean, but those days are gone and will never return; [...] Britain has lost her command of the sea. [...] After twenty-eight months of fighting, the Italian fleet has gained supremacy over the Mediterranean.[47]

When military events took a turn for the worse, they started disappearing from the news. After 23 October, when the El Alamein battle began, Radio Bari refrained from mentioning the North African front, save for a passing reference on 28 October:

> The enemy continues to attack on the Alamein front without regard to losses. The Italian and German resistance is superior to the bravery shown by the enemy, who is bitterly punished. [...] The enemy is throwing fresh troops into action. He has been obliged to use tank support. He is met with heavy artillery of every calibre. Thus, after a heavy battle the enemy has been forced to stop fighting without reaching his objective. The British have made no advance, and the battlefield is full of British corpses.[48]

No mention of the North African front was made in the following days. In a partial admission of defeat on 6 November, Radio Bari conceded that 'Axis forces have put up a very stubborn resistance against a numerically superior enemy. Following fierce battles, the Axis forces had to withdraw slightly'.[49]

During the first months of 1943, Radio Bari's coverage of the situation on the war fronts was quite optimistic. What appeared to be an almost sure defeat in North Africa was presented instead as still unpredictable, and the Axis forces as having a chance at victory: 'the battle for Tunis [...] clearly reveals Italy's and Germany's military capabilities in the face of the enemy's overwhelming superiority. The strong defence of the Axis forces and the heavy losses they have inflicted on the enemy were acknowledged by London and Washington'.[50] The reality, of course, was completely different. And when the Axis forces surrendered on 13 May, Radio Bari neglected to mention the event, focusing instead on the 'bloody battles [that] have taken place between the followers of De Gaulle and those of Giraud in North African towns'.[51] News of the defeat of the Axis forces was met with silence, and the North African front simply disappeared from the news.

On 14 June, Radio Bari mentioned the Italian front for the first time with a passing reference to the Allied landing at Pantelleria and Lampedusa. Unable to ignore the events, the radio station tried to play down their relevance: 'the two islands are [...] very far from Sicily [...]. Pantelleria is half-African and half-European and it is closer to Africa than to Europe. The Allies lost 1,000 aircraft and a huge naval fleet during occupation'.[52] And on 11 July, a still triumphant announcer declared that:

All enemy parachutists who attempted to land in Sicily have been annihilated. They intended to spread confusion among the Italian population and facilitate landing operations. Many of those who landed were rounded up, and many others were trapped and then captured. Those who dropped over landed estates were caught by peasants, who handed them over to the military authorities after teaching them a severe lesson. [...] Italian and German forces are concentrated in Sicily and have hastened to put a resolute resistance to the enemy, forcing him to change his plans. The Italian and German troops are fighting with daring and gallantry, supported by the whole Italian nation.[53]

On 26 July, the day after Mussolini's defeat at the famous meeting of the Grand Council of Fascism, Radio Bari broadcasted a music programme: 'after announcing in Italian that the broadcast was intended for Arab audiences, excerpts from Italian operas were played. No Arabic bulletins or music were broadcast'.[54] The previous night had been too hectic to have a normal broadcasting service.[55] On 27 July, the radio briefly announced 'Mussolini's resignation and Marshal Badoglio's proclamation'.[56] The following day, the news bulletin reported that 'order has been restored in all Italian cities and calm now prevails everywhere in Italy after the enthusiastic, patriotic demonstrations that took place when the Italian people heard the orders of the King-Emperor'.[57]

In the following weeks, Radio Bari's news bulletins gave more information about the military front in Sicily. On 22 August, the radio once again emphasized 'the heroic resistance of the Italian forces in Sicily',[58] but no word was given on a defeat that the Italian government knew would soon come. Between the end of August and the beginning of September, the radio station did not cover the events on the Sicilian front line. On 5 September, even though the armistice had already been signed two days earlier,[59] Radio Bari proclaimed that 'the Italian nation finds itself today more united than ever. [...] Italian railwaymen and workers are fighting in the same spirit as their comrades, the Italian soldiers, for their nation's honour'.[60] On 8 September, the afternoon news bulletin went so far as to assert that 'the Italians are determined to fight to the bitter end. Contrary to enemy propaganda claims, Italian morale is high. Everywhere abroad people must not believe enemy propaganda but rather respect Italy's honour at a time of fighting'.[61] The bulletin then moved on to other news items related to the Middle East, as if nothing had happened. But everything had indeed changed and at 9 p.m., Radio Bari broadcast in Arabic what Italian radios had announced one hour earlier: an armistice with the Allies had been signed.[62] It was Radio Bari's last broadcast in Arabic.

The impact of radio Bari's broadcasts during the war

Given the lack of reliable data, listener figures for Radio Bari's programmes are not easy to measure. However, some sources may help to assess audience size, the most important of which is the number of radio sets that were distributed in the Arab countries.[63] What is much more difficult to determine is audience reaction to Radio Bari's programmes and whether it was perceived as a credible news provider. A lack of appropriate sources, since at that time no surveys were distributed to its audience, hinders attempts to evaluate Radio Bari's impact. Moreover, surveys may not be very useful, and several scholars have argued that the impact of radio propaganda is basically 'impossible' to gauge.[64]

Nevertheless, a brief report on the impact of radio propaganda, drafted by the American diplomatic delegation in Iraq in April 1942, is the only available source that may be likened to a survey. According to the report, British propaganda had some impact on the better-educated population, while it had almost no impact on the poorer classes. The report's author, William S. Farrell, explained that the questionnaire was distributed to a group of people; the first question read: 'at what time does BBC Arabic broadcast?' Key findings were as follows:

> Generally speaking, the results are positive, even though – as it was expected – less educated categories such as peasants and *ghari* drivers have demonstrated an almost total ignorance of the BBC programs timetable. Almost 50% of the sheiks and the hotels' domestic personnel have replied correctly; almost 75% of the merchants and Iraqi soldiers, and almost all newspapers owners, coffee shops owners and functionaries of the Iraqi government have replied correctly. Clearly it has emerged that evening transmissions are much more popular than morning transmissions.[65]

The report was obviously methodologically problematic, as the sample selection lacked scientific rigour. At the same time, it does not really help to understand whether, and if so to what extent. BBC Arabic was appreciated by the Iraqi population. Indeed, knowledge of the programme schedule does not automatically equate to audience appreciation.

Given the lack of surveys, other sources can be used to evaluate the impact of Radio Bari's broadcasts. Three sources may be suitable for this purpose: the reports drafted by Italian, British, French and American diplomatic personnel in charge of listening to and monitoring Radio Bari broadcasts; listeners' feedback from the pages of the monthly magazine *Radyo Bari-Radio Araba di Bari*; newspaper articles from Arab-speaking countries.

Among these sources, diplomatic dispatches appear to be most useful for evaluating Radio Bari's wartime broadcasts. This is not an easy source. First of all, the reports differ widely according to the country or city in which the diplomats were based. Good radio reception was a significant factor: the same broadcast would be more (or less) appreciated depending on signal strength, which differed from country to country or from city to city. At the same time, diplomatic personnel may have been far from neutral in their opinion, under or overestimating the impact of Radio Bari's broadcasts depending on their own or their government's position.

Yet, from the analysis of the diplomatic dispatches that I was able to locate in several archives, a general conclusion can be reached. According to those dispatches, between 1940 and 1943, there was a falling off of interest in Radio Bari's programmes among Arab audiences, while Radio Daventry, that is to say Radio London, and Radio Berlin developed a large following.

Three main reasons may explain what happened. The first one is related to Radio Bari's programme schedule. Before the war, and in particular in 1938–1939, the radio station was appreciated more for its arts and culture programmes than for the political ones. At the onset of World War II, however, culture programmes were progressively marginalized, thereby diminishing Radio Bari's appeal among Arab listeners. Second, Radio Bari was less successful than its two rivals due to a combination of factors including content and style. Radio London seemed more impartial: those who sought unbiased news and information turned to BBC Arabic. Those who were not fond of Radio London for political reasons tuned in to Radio Berlin, where the news was delivered with unrivalled passion. In June 1941, the Italian delegation in Jeddah sent off a detailed report on Arabic radio broadcasts:

> Radio Bari does have a following in this country, thanks to the universal thirst for news and the Arabs' passion for politics. Yet, we have to admit that those who have a preference for news delivered with passion will tune in to Yunus Bahri at Radio Berlin;[66] on the contrary, those wishing to take advantage of perfect language (a prized feature among Arabs) and culture programmes, will tune in to Radio London.[67]

Finally, there may have been a correlation between audience numbers and military success. At least this is what Thomas M. Wilson, the American ambassador to Baghdad, believed. During the battle of El Alamein, he sent a telegram to Washington, in which he stated that there was a strict relationship between radio's impact and military success:

> The ineffectiveness of Axis broadcasts continues. The number of listeners increases with Allied failures but wanes with Allied successes. The growing currency inflation and supply crisis in Iraq and the surrounding area would enormously increase the effectiveness of Axis broadcasts, if the Allies were to suffer serious military setbacks.[68]

Going by what Wilson argued, we might conclude that Italian military failures negatively affected Radio Bari's impact during the war. The more the Italian Forces were defeated on the ground, the less Radio Bari's broadcasts were considered appealing by Arab public opinion.

Conclusion

Between 1940 and 1943, Radio Bari made significant changes to its schedule, cutting back on arts and culture content so as to accommodate a stronger emphasis on news bulletins. As for the news content, the war and its evolution were Radio Bari's primary focus: in those years, the Arabic transmissions were serving the war effort and totally supporting Fascist imperial policy. Furthermore, whether directly attacking Great Britain, the USA and the USSR, or providing updates on the political situation of the Arab countries, its broadcasts invariably contained harsh criticism of the Allies. It is worth noting that it was very difficult if not impossible for Radio Bari to provide fresh news on those countries' internal situation. On the one hand, Italy had severed diplomatic relations with all independent Arab states as well as with the French and British mandates and colonies, and all diplomatic representatives had been recalled from their posts. This meant that, unlike Radio London, Radio Bari could not count on receiving the latest news and updates from consular and diplomatic missions. On the other hand, Italy could not afford to invest as much as Nazi Germany in radio propaganda. As remarked by Malte König, 'Germany's expenditure on radio propaganda abroad was five times higher than Italy's'.[69]

The main consequence was that Radio Bari's appeal among Arab audiences, which owed so much to its arts and culture programmes, waned during the war. Paradoxically, at a time when Italy most needed to wield its soft power, Radio Bari failed to meet the Fascist government's expectations and did not conquer the 'hearts and minds' of the Arab population.

Notes

1 Unless otherwise noted, all translations are my own.
2 For a list of transmitting stations operating in the early 1930s, see Archivio Centrale dello Stato (ACS), Presidenza del Consiglio dei Ministri, (PCM), *La radiofonia italiana nel 1932* [Italian radios in 1932], (1934–1936), b. 13.1/2057.
3 R. Chiodelli, 'L'EIAR per l'Impero', *Africa Italiana*, 2, December 1938, pp. 19–20.
4 *New Italian Short-Wave Broadcasting Service*, Report of the Military Attaché at the American Embassy in Rome to the Department of State, 6 December 1939, in National Archives at College Park, MD (NACP), Record Group (RG) 59, Central Decimal Files (CDF) 1930–1939, Entry M 1423, film 27, document 865.76/31.
5 *Propagande italienne dans les milieux musulmans* [Italian propaganda towards Muslim countries], Tunis, 7 December 1937, in Archives Diplomatiques de Nantes (ADN), Protectorat Tunisie (PT), PV, Service de presse et d'information (1923–1955) (SPI), b. 119, f. 5.
6 Note, 7 December 1938, in ADN, PT, PV, Fonds ESTEVA et guerre (1939–1945) (FEG), b. 2327, f. 1.
7 See A. Briggs, *The History of Broadcasting in the United Kingdom*, vol. 2, *The Golden Age of Wireless* (London: Oxford University Press, 1965); S.J. Potter, *Broadcasting Empire: The BBC and the British World, 1922–1970* (Oxford: Oxford University Press, 2012).
8 Telex, Italian Embassy in Ankara to Ministry of Foreign Affairs, 10 December 1940, in Archivio Storico del Ministero Affari Esteri, Rome, (ASMAE), Affari Politici (AP) (1931–1945), Italia, b. 73, f. 4.
9 A. Marzano, *Onde fasciste. La propaganda araba di Radio Bari (1934–43)* (Rome: Carocci, 2015), pp. 144–98.
10 E. Monroe, *The Mediterranean in Politics* (London: Oxford University Press, 1938).

11 *Report on Bari's Talks by Mr. Nagib*, BBC Internal Circulating Memo, 6 January 1939, in BBC Written Archives Centre, Caversham Park, Reading (BBCWAC), E2/288 'Foreign Languages: Arabic', b. 2.

12 M. Williams, *Mussolini's Propaganda Abroad: Subversion in the Mediterranean and the Middle East, 1935–1940* (London: Routledge, 2006), p. 200.

13 Telegram, Italian Consulate in Tangier to Ministero della Cultura Popolare (Ministry of Popular Culture, MINCULPOP), 16 December 1940, in ACS, MINCULPOP, Reports, b. 6, f. 51.

14 *Emission en arabe parle du Poste de Radio Bari, le 16 Mai 1941*, in *Bulletin Mensuel de Renseignements sur les Pays Musulmans*, in Archives Nationales d'Outre-Mer, Aix-en-Provence (ANOM), Affaires politiques (AP), C 917.

15 D. Rodogno, *Il nuovo ordine mediterraneo. Le politiche di occupazione dell'Italia fascista in Europa (1940–43)* (Turin: Bollati Boringhieri, 2003), p. 73.

16 See N. Arielli, *Fascist Italy and the Middle East, 1933–40* (New York: Palgrave Macmillan, 2010).

17 A copy is located in ADN, Mandat Syrie-Liban (MSL), Fond Beyrouth (FB), Premier Versement-Cabinet Politique (PV-CP), b. 1062, f. 1.

18 The Interior Minister to the Minister for Foreign Affairs, 31 December 1935, in ADN, MSL, FB, PV-CP, b. 623, f. 3.

19 *Bari. Emission en langue arabe, 8 avril 1939* [Bari, Arabic transmissions, 8 April 1939], in ANOM, Affaires Militaires (AM), Fond du Cabinet Militaire du Gouverneur général de l'Algérie (FCMGGA), b. 3R16.

20 A. Marzano, 'La "guerra delle onde." La risposta inglese e francese alla propaganda di Radio Bari nel mondo arabo (1938–39)', *Contemporanea. Rivista di Storia dell'800 e del '900*, 15:1 (2012), pp. 3–24.

21 P. Ferrara, ''Introduzione', in Il Ministero della cultura popolare. Il Ministero delle poste e telegrafi', in P. Ferrara and M. Giannetto (eds.), vol. IV, *L'amministrazione centrale. Dall'Unità alla Repubblica. Le strutture e i dirigenti*, edited by G. Melis (Bologna: il Mulino, 1992), p. 27.

22 Marzano, *Onde fasciste*, pp. 61–2.

23 Marzano, *La 'guerra delle onde'*.

24 'Bari Short Wave: In Arabic for Middle East and Near East, 18:30 BST', 27 October 1939, in Bibliothèque de documentation international contemporaine, Nanterre (BDIC), Summary of World Broadcasts (SWB), Microfilm (MFM), 163/3.

25 Unsigned message, French Embassy in Rome, 18 January 1940, in ASMAE, AP (1931–45), Italia, b. 73, f. 4 'Propaganda araba da Radio Bari'.

26 Nazi Germany began broadcasting in Arabic on 25 April 1939, from a short-wave transmitter at Zeesen, south of Berlin. See J. Herf, *Nazi Propaganda for the Arab World* (New Haven, CT: Yale University Press, 2009), p. 37.

27 Ibid.

28 'Rome Short Wave: In Arabic for the Middle East and Near East, 18:30 BST', 4 November 1939, in BDIC, SWB, MFM 163/3.

29 'Rome Short Wave: in Arabic for the Middle and the Near East, 17:08 GMT', 13 January 1940, in BDIC, SWB, MFM 163/6.

30 'Bari Short Wave: In Arabic for the Near and Middle East, 17:08 GMT', 13 February 1940, in BDIC, SWB, MFM 163/8.

31 'Rome Short Wave: In Arabic for the Middle East, 17:30 GMT', 24 November 1939, in BDIC, SWB, MFM 163/4.

32 'Bari Short Wave: In Arabic for the Near and Middle East, 18:15 BST', 21 March 1940, in BDIC, SWB, MFM 163/10.

33 'Bari Short Wave: In Arabic for the Near and Middle, 18:15 BST', 25 April 1940, in BDIC, SWB, MFM 163/12.

34 'Bari Short Wave: In Arabic for the Middle and Near East, 18:15 BST', 13 May 1940, in BDIC, SWB, MFM 163/13.

35 'Rome Short Wave: In Arabic for the Near and Middle East, 10:30 BST', 11 June 1940, in BDIC, SWB, MFM 163/15.

36 'Rome Short Wave: In Arabic for the Near and Middle East, 10:30 BST', 11 June 1940, in BDIC, SWB, MFM 163/15.

37 See A. Monticone, *Il fascismo al microfono. Radio e politica in Italia (1924–1945)* (Rome: Studium, 1978), p. 183.

38 See P.V. Cannistraro, *La fabbrica del consenso. Fascismo e mass media* (Bari: Laterza, 1975), p. 259.

39 Marzano, *Onde fasciste*, pp. 209–32.

40 *Bari in Arabic*, 8:00 p.m., 21 June 1942, NACP, RG 84, Egypt, Cairo, Entry 2410, b. 77.

41 Talk 'American Intentions', by Sheikh Abdel Kader el Kasmy, in *Bari in Arabic*, 8:00 p.m., August 21, 1942, in NACP, RG 84, Egypt, Cairo, Entry 2410, b. 77.

42 *Arabic shortwave broadcasts: The Axis, the British and our own*, Report by Benedict Magnes, 31 March 1942, in NACP, RG 208, Records of the Office of War Information (ROWI), Overseas Branch Bureau of Overseas Intelligence (OBBOI), Central Files (CF), Information File on the Near East (IFNE) (1941–46), Entry 373, b. 418.

43 'Rome 25,51 m: In Arabic for Arab World, 18:00 BST', 31 March 1941, in BDIC, SWB, MFM 163/40.

44 'Rome 31,15 m: In Arabic for the Arab World, 19:00', 2 July 1942, in BDIC, SWB, MFM 163/75.

45 'Rome 31,15 m: In Arabic for the Arab World, 19:00', 27 July 1942, in BDIC, SWB, MFM 163/78.

46 *Bari in Arabic*, 10 September 1942, 8:00 p.m., TAK, in 84, Egypt, Cairo, Entry 2410, b. 77.

47 *Bari in Arabic*, 10 October 1942, 8:00 p.m., in NACP, RG 84, Egypt, Cairo, Entry 2410, b. 77.

48 *Bari in Arabic*, 28 October 1942, 10:30 p.m., in NACP, RG 84, Egypt, Cairo, Entry 2410, b. 77.

49 *Bari in Arabic*, 6 November 1942, 8:00 p.m., in NACP, RG 84, Egypt, Cairo, Entry 2410, b. 77.

50 'Rome 31,15 m: In Arabic for the Arab World, 19:00', 28 April 1943, in BDIC, SWB, MFM 163/102.

51 'Rome 31,15 m: In Arabic for the Arab World, 19:00', 13 May 1943, in BDIC, SWB, MFM 163/103.

52 'Rome 31,15 m: In Arabic for the Arab World, 19:00', 14 June 1943, in BDIC, SWB, MFM 163/106.

53 In *Bari in Arabic*, 11 July 1943, 8:00 p.m., TAK, in NACP, RG 84, Egypt, Cairo, Entry 2410, b. 93.

54 In *Bari in Arabic*, 25 July 1943, 8:00 p.m.; 11,00 p.m., TAK, in NACP, RG 84, Egypt, Cairo, Entry 2410, b. 93.

55 For an account of the days that followed, see M. Franzinelli, 'Il 25 luglio', in M. Isnenghi (ed.), *I luoghi della memoria. Personaggi e date dell'Italia unita* (Rome and Bari: Laterza, 1997), pp. 219–40.

56 'Rome 31,15 m: In Arabic for the Arab World, 19:00', 27 July 1943, in BDIC, SWB, MFM 163/109.

57 'Rome 31,15 m: In Arabic for the Arab World, 19:00', 28 July 1943, in BDIC, SWB, MFM 163/109.

58 'Rome 31,15 m: In Arabic for the Arab World, 18:00', 22 August 1943, in BDIC, SWB, MFM 163/111.

59 See E. Aga-Rossi, *Una nazione allo sbando. L'armistizio italiano del settembre 1943 e le sue conseguenze* (Bologna: il Mulino, 1993).

60 'Rome 31,15 m: In Arabic for the Arab World, 18:00', 5 September 1943, in BDIC, SWB, MFM 163/112.

61 'Rome 31,15 m: In Arabic for the Arab World, 18:00', 8 September 1943, in BDIC, SWB, MFM 163/113.

62 'Rome 263 m: In Arabic for the Arab World, 21:40', 8 September 1943, in BDIC, SWB, MFM 163/113.

63 Marzano, *Onde fasciste*, pp. 385–91.

64 N.J. O'Shaughnessy, *Politics and Propaganda: Weapons of Mass Seduction* (Manchester: Manchester University Press, 2004), p. 37; P. Ortoleva, *Il secolo dei media: riti, abitudini, mitologie* (Milan: Il saggiatore, 2009), p. 41.

65 *Mass observation of Public Opinion in Iraq*, American delegation in Iraq to the Department of State, Baghdad, 15 April 1942, in NACP, RG 59, European War (EW) (1939–45), Entry M 982, reel 116.

66 An Iraqi journalist and the most popular announcer at Radio Berlin.

67 Telex, Italian Legation in Jeddah to Minculpop, 23 August 1941, in ACS, MINCULPOP, Reports, b. 6, f. 55.

68 Telegram, American Legation in Baghdad to the Department of State, 27 October 1942, in NACP, R47 84, Baghdad, GR, 1942, Entry 2751, b. 68.

69 M. König, 'Censura, controllo e notizie a valanga. La collaborazione tra Italia e Germania nella stampa e nella radio 1940–1941', *Italia Contemporanea*, 271:2 (2013), pp. 233–55, see p. 242.

Part IV
A decade of war?

13 Fascist Italy chooses endless war, 1935–1936

Continuity and break

MacGregor Knox

If after Ethiopia he'd only stopped…

Italian popular saying

The unprovoked attack on Ethiopia in the early hours of 3 October 1935 by the Italian State, armed forces, and people-in-arms inaugurated a decade of almost ceaseless slaughter. War was no novelty for united Italy: its trajectory since 1861 included aggression against the Papacy (1870), Ethiopia (1895–1996), the Ottoman Empire and Libyan Arabs (1911), and on two occasions almost fifty years apart (1866, 1915) against the 'unchanging enemy, Austria'.[1] The wars initiated by the *Regio Esercito Italiano*'s second crossing of the River Mareb into Ethiopia and ended by the German and Allied conquest of Italy in 1943–1945 were nevertheless qualitatively far different from what had gone before. Yet many of those differences emerged directly from, and only partially masked, continuities that stretched back to the foundation of the Italian State.

Premises

The principal sources of continuity were the objectives, both foreign and domestic, of united Italy's literate elites, and the striking disjunction between those aims and the Italian State's cultural, organizational, technological, industrial, and economic capabilities and resources. Vincenzo Gioberti had imprudently claimed a global moral and civilizational *primato* for a peninsula fragmented into mutually antagonistic agrarian societies in which fewer than 10% of the population spoke the eventual national language. Giuseppe Mazzini had erected a national faith – a *fede* – based upon collective victimhood and individual martyrdom, had demanded a nation '*una, indivisibile*' bound by blood, and had damned as 'traitors' all who embodied Italy's many divisions.[2] Worse still, he had piled upon the heavy burden of Gioberti's spiritual mythology an earthly Roman imperial mission to bring 'a new and more powerful Unity to the nations of Europe'. And in the end the apostle of liberty had claimed the Mediterranean as '*mare nostro*' and had foreseen an Italian civilizing mission in North Africa – where as France had bloodily demonstrated in Algeria since 1830, only violence far beyond Mazzini's limited imagination could impose and maintain European domination.[3]

Yet territorial unification in 1859–1870 had brought neither the great-power status implicit in the myths of the *Risorgimento* nor the society '*una, indivisibile*' that Mazzini demanded. The obvious route to both aims – in refutation of the stinging diatribes of impassioned *literati* against the pedestrian mediocrity of Liberal Italy – was war. But the new Italy's first major colonial wars, launched with equal precipitation by a ferocious former Mazzinian, Francesco Crispi, and by the embodiment of cool, calculating Liberal statesmanship, Giovanni Giolitti, failed to conquer Ethiopia and seized bloodily a meagre toehold in Libya. Only a truly great war could 'cement internally, through the anguish of mortal perils, the unity of the national spirit' while giving Italy 'its natural boundaries'.[4] Those words of Alfredo Oriani, the peculiar recluse later celebrated as foremost prophet of fin-de-siècle Italian nationalism and – like Crispi – as an indispensable 'precursor' of Fascism, summed up the ambitions of the most adventurous of Liberal Italy's elites. That *fede* drove the interventionist mobs that coerced parliament and people into war in the violent spring of 1915, and opened a civil war that endured until 1945, fought to impose the national mission and seamless national integration upon the Italian people. Benito Mussolini saw the destination clearly as early as November 1917: '*The entire nation must be militarized*'.[5]

Liberal Italy's greatest war and 'supreme triumph' in 1918 destroyed the Liberals.[6] The ungrateful allies rejected the more far-fetched of Italy's long list of war aims; at home, peasantry and industrial workers rose in revolt against the national mission and the postwar order. Mussolini's 1919 political invention – the *fasci di combattimento* – could thus claim and conquer a monopoly of the national cause and the heritage of interventionism. It resumed the civil war of 1915 on a far wider scale, with infinitely greater ferocity, and with all the expertise in organized violence that the Great War had bestowed.

Implementation

The resulting dictatorship sought from its beginnings to 'fascistize the nation' and to conduct the 'supreme experiment in making Italians in our [national] history' – the mission inherited from the Risorgimento at which Liberal Italy had – in Fascist eyes – so miserably failed.[7] The break of October 1922 reaffirmed the continuity of the internal and external aims imposed by Mazzini, whose 'genuine radicalism and totalitarianism' at last came into its own.[8] The regime explicitly claimed that heritage, joyously affirmed the abject enslavement of the individual by the national – Fascist – *fede*, and proclaimed Italy's imperial mission. The Great War, Mussolini believed, had been 'profoundly educational'; but evidently not sufficiently so, for Fascism sought from 1922 onward to further 'grasp, chisel [*sagomare*], and mould' the 'Italian race' and 'scrape off and obliterate the sediments deposited, in the character and mentality of the Italians, by those disgraceful centuries of political, military, and moral decadence that run from 1600 to the advent of Napoleon'. In private Mussolini frequently railed at 'these pathetic cowardly Italians', this 'race of sheep'. His remedy was foreordained since 1917: to 'keep them in ranks and in uniform from morning to night'.[9] Publicly he preached a brutish xenophobia, contempt for Italy's 'disgusting craven bourgeoisie', and race-war against Africans, Jews, and the Western 'demo-plutocracies'. The 1938 race-laws were no sudden inspiration. They derived from anti-Semitic hatreds traceable far back into Mussolini's socialist past, and were a calculated effort to imbue Fascism with the totalitarian racist radicalism that Mussolini admired in his German allies.[10] The wars of 1935–1945 were the intended culmination of that effort: 'When Spain is done, I'll invent something else; the character of the Italians must be created through combat'.[11] Endless war both implemented and justified the regime's increasingly ferocious pursuit of its totalitarian vocation.

The seizure of power in 1922, as Mussolini freely admitted to the faithful in August 1924, had remained radically incomplete: 'a victorious insurrection, not a revolution; the revolution comes later'.[12] At home, the monarchy stood squarely in the way; slow encroachment on its prerogatives proved the only way forward. Abroad, the overwhelming naval preponderance of Britain and France, Italy's geostrategic 'imprisonment' in the Mediterranean, and the economy's galling dependence on seaborne imports and foreign loans imposed extreme caution.[13] Covert patronage of Macedonian and Croat terrorists appeared to offer a path, which Mussolini pursued assiduously if vainly, to undermining the post-1918 European order and dismembering Italy's despised and hated eastern neighbour, Yugoslavia.[14] Mussolini also followed the last Liberal governments in attacking the Arab tribal and religious confederations that controlled virtually all of Libya except a few coastal cities. Colonial 'pacification' faced neither domestic nor external constraints, and by 1931–1932 Mussolini and the *Regio Esercito* had crushed all resistance with genocidal vigour.[15] By then the Great Depression had so shaken the international order that Japan, first of the future Axis powers, could seize Manchuria – to Mussolini's private glee.[16]

The tutelage of London, Washington, and Wall Street fell away, and Mussolini began to imagine that the vengeful revival of German nationalism had so immobilized Belgrade's French protector and ally that he could at last strike. The threat of a Franco-Italian-Yugoslav two-front war that would crush Italy nevertheless moved King Victor Emmanuel III to quash the 'Croat plan' in January 1933. Even the assassination of King Alexander of Yugoslavia by Mussolini's terrorist clients in October 1934 failed to provoke the uprising that would justify Italian invasion and the creation of a Croat vassal state.[17]

By that point Mussolini's warlike enthusiasm had found easier prey: the Ethiopia that Crispi had failed to conquer. France had long signalled its blessing for Italian ambitions in East Africa in exchange for Italian backing against Germany. Military planning began in spring 1932.[18] And the accidental assassination alongside King Alexander of France's foreign minister, Georges Barthou, led to his replacement by the fawning Pierre Laval, who eagerly opened the door to an Italian campaign.

As early as March 1935 Mussolini saw far beyond Ethiopia, to a triumphant breakout from Mediterranean imprisonment: 'and afterward we shall conquer Egypt and the Sudan!'[19] His war directive left the armed forces and king in no doubt about the immediate objective: 'the destruction of the Ethiopian armed forces and the total conquest of Ethiopia; the *impero* cannot be made in any other way'. The imperial way demanded the massive deployment of motor transport, aircraft, and Italy's diminutive tanks, 'absolute superiority in artillery and gas [warfare]', 'munitions in abundance', and overwhelming numbers of metropolitan troops alongside the Eritrean and Libyan levies that customarily fought Italy's colonial wars. Swift victory would forestall threats in Europe while Italy was engaged on the Horn of Africa.[20] But behind that strategic rationale lay the overriding domestic aim that determined the immense scale and consummate brutality of the East African campaign of 1935–1936: a nation '*una, indivisible*' and an Italian 'race' hardened and 'fascistized' through ceaseless war.

Consequences

Transmuting dogma into warfare radically altered Italy's place in the international order, its domestic balance of forces, the character of the Fascist regime, and its prospects for survival. London twice sought to fob Mussolini off with scraps of Ethiopia, attempted diffidently to deter him with its naval might, and organized League of Nations sanctions too feeble to serve as more than a welcome theme for the xenophobic diatribes of the regime's swiftly expanding propaganda apparatus. Mussolini replied with public defiance, a rain of mustard gas upon Ethiopian troops and villagers, and covert rapprochement with National Socialist Germany. The mighty ally bent upon the overthrow of the global balance of power, anticipated and sought since the 1920s, was at last at hand. Italy's Austrian client, whom Mussolini had noisily defended against the Reich in 1934, was now expendable.[21]

The *Duce* encouraged Hitler to remilitarise the Rhineland in March 1936. He followed up his East African triumph with war against the Spanish Republic alongside Germany that summer and autumn. He invented the Rome–Berlin 'Axis' in November 1936, and in November–December 1937 joined the German–Japanese Anti-Comintern Pact and contemptuously departed the League of Nations. He supinely accepted the Reich's absorption of Austria in March 1938; stood at Hitler's side in the dismemberment of Czechoslovakia that autumn; seized Albania in April 1939; and bound Italy irrevocably to National Socialist Germany in the 'Pact of Steel' war-alliance in May.[22]

War, as Mussolini had intended since the 1920s, tilted the domestic balance decisively against the monarchy. Ethiopia was not yet the long-awaited Mediterranean hegemonic war in which victory would allow him to 'push aside the unwarlike king'.[23] But East African triumph and increasingly cordial relations with Hitler nevertheless inspired Mussolini in March–April 1938 to promote himself – and concurrently demote Victor Emmanuel III – to the newly invented rank of 'First Marshal of the Empire'. The king was furious, abidingly resentful, and impotent.[24] And when Hitler's 1940 victories at last opened the road to the long-coveted hegemonic *'guerra fascista'* and demanded the establishment of an Italian high command, Victor Emmanuel III surrendered his most fundamental constitutional prerogative, and sullenly delegated to the dictator 'command of the forces operating on all fronts'. A prescient general sought disingenuously to console the king with the happy thought that evading direct responsibility might in due course free the crown to 'save the Nation should the Regime become shaky or actually threaten to crumble'.[25]

Three years of defeat on all fronts, Anglo-American conquest of Sicily, massive American air bombardment of Rome itself, and the defection of Mussolini's inner circle in July 1943 at last forced the hesitant king to act. Removing the discredited dictator proved surprisingly easy, but king and high command inevitably bungled Italy's ensuing defection to the Western Allies, delivering the peninsula from Naples northward to Wehrmacht and Waffen-SS, and the Italian people to twenty months of war and civil war. Fascism survived fitfully north of the Anglo-American front, while twenty years of complicity with Mussolini and the pusillanimous disorderly flight from Rome on 9 September 1943 of king, crown prince, and high command ultimately destroyed the monarchy by delayed action.[26]

Fascism's collapse and afterlife under German patronage completed the process Mussolini had inaugurated in 1935, stripping the regime of twenty years of monarchist and establishment accretions. Only hatred and the resolve to exact revenge remained. Warriors of the 1943–1945 'Italian Social Republic' shared with their National Socialist allies the conviction that 'the Italians' were a 'traitor *Volk*'.[27] The Germans had tactfully repressed that article of faith, born of Italy's 1914 repudiation of its alliance with Germany and Austria-Hungary, until Italy's 1943 defection seemingly reconfirmed it to the fullest. The Fascists derived it both from the immediate royal and military 'betrayal' of July–September 1943, and from over twenty years of Mussolinian disquisitions on 'the Italy of the past, the Italy of embezzlers, swindlers, and poltroons' and on 'the congenital deformities of the Italian character, [...] shallowness, fecklessness', and 'habitual sloppiness [*pressapochismo*]'.[28]

Before July 1943 circumstances had nevertheless inhibited close cooperation with Germany's global programme of racial extermination, despite Mussolini's private 1938 promise to visit upon Italy's 'repulsive Jews' a 'massacre as the Turks did [to the Armenians]', and his personal assurances to Heinrich Himmler in 1942 that mass murder was 'the only possible solution'.[29] But after his political resurrection at Hitler's hands in September–October 1943, all restraint fell away. The 'Italian Social Republic' collaborated whole-heartedly with its German masters in robbing all Jews within range of their remaining assets and in deporting almost 8,000 to their deaths.[30] The regime, even as it went down in ruin, realized to the limit of its meagre abilities its leader's genocidal ambitions.

And ruin was long foreordained. Mussolini had challenged the 'demo-plutocracies' at the side of his German ally to a contest Italy could only lose. National Socialist Germany itself had committed the supreme imprudence of launching a global war, fought with machines, with less than 3% of world oil production within its grasp. Fascist Italy however possessed neither oil nor appreciable supplies of coal, produced less steel annually than a single Soviet city in the Urals, and was almost wholly dependent on seaborne imports at the mercy of the British Royal Navy. Unlike its ally it also lacked military institutions capable of comprehending, much less effectively conducting, modern warfare.[31] Italy's reputedly 'most intelligent general', Mario Roatta, proposed only half-jestingly in mid-war a remedy for the army's conspicuous incompetence: 'leasing it out to a great industrialist' who would immediately fire its entire leadership, since no business leader 'would dream of trying to run a firm with people like that in charge'.[32]

Yet Mussolini had remained megalomaniacally undeterred, although even at the outset victory in the Mediterranean and Africa over Britain alone was far beyond Italy's strength. In summer-autumn 1940 he escalated enthusiastically into a series of catastrophic defeats, until Hitler resentfully committed air units, U-boats, and ground forces to rescue his ally in the Mediterranean, North Africa, and the Balkans. In 1941–1942 Mussolini nevertheless imposed a further massive dispersion of Italy's failing war effort, the dispatch of 230,000 men to join Hitler's failed war of enslavement and extermination in Russia; over 85,000 perished.[33] A few elite Italian units fought with distinction, particularly in mid-war. And after September 1943 both Mussolini's savage, embittered militias and the *partigiani* who fought Fascists and Germans with valour and skill rarely gave or sought quarter. But Italy's failure in war, the human activity its twenty-year dictatorship had celebrated above all others, nevertheless remained ungraceful, indecorous, and total.[34] The national catastrophe of 1943–1945 broke forever the grip of the founding myths of the Italian State that Fascism had inherited, radicalized, and sought to implement through ceaseless violence.

Notes

1 A. Oriani, *La lotta politica in Italia*, 3 vols. (Florence: La Voce, 1921), vol. 3, p. 354, gleefully quoted by Mussolini, 14 March 1915: *Opera omnia di Benito Mussolini*, 44 vols. (Florence and Rome: La Fenice and Giovanni Volpe, 1951–80), vol. 7, p. 254.
2 Background: M. Knox, *To the Threshold of Power: Origins and Dynamics of the Fascist and National Socialist Dictatorships*, vol. I (Cambridge: Cambridge University Press, 2007), pp. 52–4, 110–2; A.M. Banti, *La nazione del Risorgimento. Parentela, santità e onore alle origini dell'Italia unita* (Turin: Einaudi, 2000), pp. 80, 97, 129–30, 163, 177.
3 G. Mazzini, *Scritti: politica ed economia. Pensiero e azione* (Milan: Sonzogno, n.d.), p. 19 ('Note autobiografiche', 1861) and p. 553 ('Politica internazionale', 1871). Available from www.liberliber.it/online/autori/autori-m/giuseppe-mazzini/scritti/ (accessed 6 February 2020).
4 A. Oriani, *Fino a Dogali* (Milan: Libreria Editrice Galli, 1889), p. 184; Knox, *Threshold*, 111–2; further background: F. Chabod, *Storia della politica estera italiana dal 1870 al 1896*, vol. I, *Le Premesse* (Bari: Laterza, 1971), pp. 215–373; and for Oriani's posthumous prominence in the regime's 'liturgy', G. Alessandri, *Il caso Oriani: analisi di una appropriazione*, PhD thesis (University of Trento, 2011), ch. 4. Available from http://eprints-phd.biblio.unitn.it/1034/ (accessed 6 February 2020).

5 Mussolini, *Opera omnia*, vol. 10, p. 38 (italics in original); P. O'Brien, *Mussolini in the First World War: The Journalist, the Soldier, the Fascist* (Oxford: Berg, 2005), pp. 170–82.

6 Quotation: R. Romeo, *Dal Piemonte sabaudo all'Italia liberale* (Rome: Laterza, 1974), p. 311.

7 Mussolini, *Opera omnia*, vol. 21, p. 362; vol. 20, p. 284. Fascist *dictatorship* dates from 1922: E. Gentile, *E fu subito regime. Il fascismo e la marcia su Roma* (Rome: Laterza, 2012).

8 Quotation: L. Salvatorelli (a democratic liberal), *Il pensiero politico italiano dal 1700 al 1870* (Turin: Einaudi, 1942), p. 251 (1949 edition, p. 276). Mazzini was obviously no more a 'premature Fascist' than the Jean-Jacques Rousseau of '*quiconque refusera d'obéir à la volonté générale y sera contraint par tout le corps*'. But Mazzini's fanatical insistence upon seamless unity and the death of 'traitors' nevertheless places him squarely at the root of Fascism's ancestral tree.

9 Mussolini, *Opera omnia*, vol. 24, pp. 283–4; vol. 19, p. 266; vol. 22, p. 100; C. Petacci, *Mussolini segreto. Diari 1932–1938* (Milan: Rizzoli, 2009), p. 424 (11 October 1938); G. Ciano, *Diario 1939–1943* (Milan: Rizzoli, 1971), pp. 247, 249 (29 January, 7 February 1940).

10 For Mussolini's decisive role in initiating the persecution of Italy's Jews, see M. Sarfatti, *Mussolini contro gli ebrei* (Turin: Silvio Zamorani, 1994); for his longstanding anti-Semitism, G. Fabre, *Mussolini razzista* (Milan: Garzanti, 2005); and for the broader context, M. Sarfatti, *Gli ebrei nell'Italia fascista* (Turin: Einaudi, 2000), and T. Schlemmer and H. Woller, 'Der italienische Faschismus und die Juden 1922 bis 1945', *Vierteljahrshefte für Zeitgeschichte*, 53 (2005), pp. 164–201.

11 G. Ciano, *Diario 1937–1938* (Rocca San Casciano: F. Cappelli, 1948), p. 50 (13 November 1937).

12 Mussolini, *Opera omnia*, vol. 44, p. 10.

13 'Prisoner of the Mediterranean': M. Knox, *Mussolini Unleashed, 1939–1941* (Cambridge: Cambridge University Press, 1982), pp. 39–40; Id., *Common Destiny: Dictatorship, Foreign Policy, and War in Fascist Italy and Nazi Germany* (Cambridge: Cambridge University Press, 2000), pp. 75, 113, 118–20.

14 M. Knox, 'Fascist Italy and Strategic Terrorism, 1922–1941: The Quest for Success', in T. Schlemmer, H. Woller (eds.), *The Fascist Challenge* (Munich: Institut für Zeitgeschichte, forthcoming.

15 See G. Rochat, *Le guerre italiane in Libia e in Etiopia dal 1896 al 1939* (Udine: Gaspari, 2009), pp. 64–136.

16 P. Aloisi, *Journal (25 Juillet 1932–14 Juin 1936)*, M. Toscano (ed.) (Paris: Plon, 1957), p. 7.

17 Ibid, pp. 225–6; Knox, 'Strategic terrorism', pp. 34–42; Knox, *Common Destiny*, pp. 134–6, 139.

18 Brilliant analysis: G. Rochat, *Militari e politici nella preparazione della campagna d'Etiopia* (Milan: Franco Angeli, 1971), chs. 1–4.

19 Knox, *Common Destiny*, p. 140.

20 All from Italy, Ministero degli Affari Esteri, *I documenti diplomatici italiani*, Series 7, vol. 16, Roma, Libreria dello Stato, 1990, doc. 358 (30 December 1934); for Italy's lavish use of mustard gas and other chemical agents during and after the campaign, Rochat, *Guerre italiane*, pp. 163–93.

21 Knox, *Common Destiny*, pp. 124–6, 132–3, 136–42.

22 See particularly G.B. Strang, *On the Fiery March: Mussolini Prepares for War* (Westport, CT: Praeger, 2003).

23 Knox, *Common Destiny*, p. 69.

24 R. De Felice, 'Mussolini e Vittorio Emanuele III Primi Marescialli dell'Impero', in Università degli Studi di Messina, *Scritti in onore di Vittorio De Caprariis* (Rome: P. Tombolini, 1970), pp. 347–68.

25 P. Puntoni, *Parla Vittorio Emanuele III* (Milan: Aldo Palazzi, 1958), p. 12; Mussolini, *Opera omnia*, vol. 34, pp. 426–7.

26 Masterful analysis: E. Aga Rossi, *A Nation Collapses: The Italian Surrender of August 1943* (Cambridge: Cambridge University Press, 2000).

27 A. Osti Guerrazzi, *Storia della Repubblica sociale italiana* (Rome: Carocci, 2012), pp. 25–6, 41, 63–4, 72, 81, 112–4, 178–88; C. Pavone, *Una guerra civile* (Turin: Einaudi, 2006), pp. 225–32. German attitudes, theory, and practice: M. Geyer, '"Es muß daher mit schnellen und drakonischen Maßnahmen durchgegriffen werden." Civitella in Val di Chiana am 29. Juni 1944', in H. Heer, K. Naumann (eds.), *Vernichtungskrieg. Verbrechen der Wehrmacht 1941–1944* (Hamburg: Hamburger Edition, 1995), especially pp. 227–8; and C. Gentile, *Wehrmacht und Waffen-SS im Partisanenkrieg. Italien, 1943–1945* (Paderborn: Ferdinand Schöningh, 2012).

28 Mussolini, *Opera omnia*, vol. 19, pp. 277–8; vol. 22, pp. 23–4, 86, 100; and vol. 31, p. 16; see also vol. 43, p. 52.

29 Petacci, *Mussolini segreto*, pp. 422–4 (9–11 October 1938); M. Knox, 'Das faschistische Italien und die "Endlösung" 1942/43', *Vierteljahrshefte für Zeitgeschichte* 55 (2007), p. 59.

30 Sarfatti, *Ebrei nell'Italia fascista*, pp. 245–71.

31 M. Knox, *Hitler's Italian Allies* (Cambridge: Cambridge University Press, 2000), and M. Knox, 'Fascismo, forze armate e il carattere della disfatta del 1940–1943', in P. Bianchi and N. Labanca (eds.), *L'Italia e il 'militare'* (Rome: Edizioni Storia e Letteratura, 2014), pp. 237–59.

32 Ciano, *Diario 1939–1943*, p. 502; G. Zanussi, *Guerra e catastrofe d'Italia*, vol. 1 (Rome: Libreria Corso, 1946), p. 148.

33 Strategy: Knox, *Allies*, pp. 77–84, and L. Ceva, *La condotta italiana della guerra* (Milan: Feltrinelli, 1975), pp. 84–118. Outcome: T. Schlemmer, *Die italiener an der Ostfront 1942/43* (Munich: Oldenbourg, 2005), pp. 70–5.

34 Knox, 'Carattere della disfatta'; E. Galli della Loggia, *La morte della Patria* (Rome: Laterza, 1996), pp. 3–18.

14 Changing perspectives

Italian studies on Italy in World War II

Nicola Labanca

Introduction

Why should World War II scholars be interested in the history of Italy, this European country, not too large or small, currently living through a difficult moment, in full de-industrialization, and with little political sway in major world issues? Why abandon many entertaining, comfortable old stereotypes about Italy, such as 'Italians as good people' and the 'land of sun'? Why try to overcome such strong language barriers, which have often led World War II studies to ignore Italian historical dynamics (except to simply resort to such stereotypes)?[1]

Everyone can choose the reason they prefer. Maybe it is because Italy came out of World War I as the fifth largest European power in population, military, economic and political terms. Or because it was in Italy that a totalitarian form of a political regime – whose fullest application would be later found in Germany, with many more nuanced versions in Europe – was created. Or it could be because having attacked an independent Ethiopia in the Autumn of 1935, then Spain and then Albania, Italy was a 'junior partner' in helping destroy peace in Europe and the world. Also, it could be because Italian history during World War II had the traits of the war in general, even if tangled with complex national events.[2] Or it could be because (though perhaps this is of interest only to military historians, and not all historians), contrary to stereotypes, Italians generally tried to gain as much as they could from the military means available to them (few and often inadequate), and fought their war. This was often not a war of conquest, but one of occupation, consolidation and counterinsurgency. And they did not always act like 'brava gente' (good people).[3]

What actually happened almost completely inverted the stereotypes about Italians who did not fight, changed alliance mid-war and were unfit for battle (ignoring the effect of military institutions at the level of each platoon, in training, learning curves and so forth). You will have understood by now that, in my opinion, Italy – this European country neither large nor small – should matter to World War II scholars because the war would be simply impossible to understand without it. Depending on interests and language skills, those who want to study Italy in World War II, or, conversely, the effect of World War II on Italy, will have different points of focus.

In either case, while the historiography of 1939– (or 1937–) 1945 – which Evan Mawdsley called 'the most complex event of the twentieth century'[4] – is today increasingly global in scale, it seems rather odd that general histories of World War II almost completely ignore Italy. Such a broad topic has already been studied by great historians in turn, and moving quickly through it will, in one respect or another, inevitably upset many. The difficulty is heightened by the fact that involvement in a war was once limited to its military aspects. A total war, however, affects all realms of politics, economy, social, culture and both the public and private spheres.[5]

International historiography on Italy

For a long time Italy has almost been absent from international military historiography about World War II. In recent general histories, such as those by Keegan,[6] Weinberg,[7] and Mawdsley's impressive three-volume *Cambridge History of the Second World War*,[8] there are only scant mentions of Italy: quite often incorrect, and almost never considering Italian academic literature. Few signs of greater interest bring to mind the Italian proverb that one swallow does not necessarily make a summer: they do not mean and guarantee that Italian history has been fully integrated in international history.[9]

Of course, there has been a long tradition of attention – especially British – to the history of Italian Fascism. At times it has also given attention to Italian wars, with Denis Mack Smith, John Gooch and MacGregor Knox at the forefront. Mack Smith's work was filled with criticism of Fascism's incompetence, in both peace and war.[10] Gooch closely analysed the relationships between civilians and the military, poorly professionalized.[11] Knox, instead, started a major comparison of Italian and German histories, focusing both on aspects of military history and economic-social and political-ideological history.[12] These authors' contributions, however, have often been little considered by general World War II histories.

Despite these scholars' work, a great number of interesting topics have yet to be studied. This fact vastly expands room for (young) international scholars who want to investigate the history of Italy or the transnational history of which Italy is part. Unfortunately, quite a few scholars seem less interested in the history of Italy and more interested in the history of World War II in Italy – in other words applying to the Italian case standards and rules developed for other national cases or general contexts. The specificity of Italy's history is measured by its deviations and differences. Furthermore, times are changing. A few years ago, Andrew Bacevich hoped that the time for revisionism had arrived, and not only for studies on World War II.[13] He, even if not alone, did not consider many of the available historical reconstructions as offering a 'usable past', and he maintained that it was necessary to consider new research topics and a new overall meaning of reconstruction.

From this perspective as well, there is no lack of reasons to study the history of Italy in World War II. A few ingredients of a history with current implications could perhaps be found in the fate of a country ruled by an anti-democratic political regime, full of many ambitions, with the eventual outcome of the failure of its war and its necessary 're-education' to democracy. How to approach the remnants of undemocratic regimes that still have mass support is not a relevant question only for the 1943–1945 timeframe. It could seem to foreshadow quite recent events as forces of democracy had to make their way with military and political tools. However, the past does not always foreshadow the present, and a 'usable past' runs the risk of engulfing the past and deceiving the present. That said, we could indeed learn a few lessons for the present from this Italian past.

Whether we are interested in Italy's history in World War II in itself or in how the history of World War II reflected on Italy's history as a case study, the fact is that we first need to know and understand the Italian studies that have already been published.

Three phases, three generations of historians

Both Jay Winter, in his introduction to the *Cambridge History of the First World War*,[14] and then John Ferris and Evan Mawdsley, in their introduction to the first volume of the *Cambridge History of the Second World War*,[15] wrote that – after hundred or seventy years since the wars in their fields of studies – we have seen three generations in action, and a fourth getting started.

Though the timelines of each field are quite different as well as their features, they do align to a considerable degree. In both cases, the first generation is made up of official publications and of those who were personally involved; the second generation is that of scholars; and the third of critical scholars, who are further from the myths and controversies of the now-passed Cold War. It is too soon to judge how much and if the fourth generation – still more a hope than a fully formed reality – would be that of young scholars, transnational in their training and interests. In Italian studies as well – though with a few particular national features – we can see the succession of three generations, differently subject to internationalization, who often bring different topics, approaches and judgements.

These are, of course, broad generalizations which need to be further broken down. Within a single generation, historical judgements and interests may diverge; and each generation emerges because a few scholars from the previous one served as critics and dug into its foundations. Bearing this in mind, this rough division into three generations still stands.

I. In approximately the first 20 or 25 years after the war, the Italian history of World War II was considered to coincide with the 1940–1943 period. This is not to say that there was no discussion on 1943–1945 and the war of liberation, especially on the Resistance and its role in the foundation of the Republic. However, excluding the very early years of 1945–1947 and the governments of national unity, the official Italy of the 'centrismo' (up to the Centre-Left governments) saw the partisan war as an inconvenient episode, defended by protagonists and studied by a group of scholars, but in some ways compartmentalized. The Italian war was still the Fascist war.[16]

Diplomats and members of the military were the first to publish about it, followed by the historical offices of the armed forces. After twenty years of Fascism, there were plenty of controversies between democrats and those nostalgic for the regime. These controversies, however, had ultimately little impact on the population, who had already distanced themselves from the official version during the closing years of the regime.

Excluding the openly nostalgic, fascist-supporting publications, in this first period the judgement on the war was positive – a war fought with honour by traditional armed forces, as long as possible, in the face of overpowering opponents.[17] Only at a lower level an appreciation for the just war of Liberation emerged.[18] It brought Italy to the 'right' side, with the same new Allies who had won the Italian campaign and then wanted to include Italy in NATO.

II. In the second twenty-five years, under the Centre-Left democratic governments, there was a considerable shift in types of scholars, objects of study and judgements – from 1968, at the latest, until the end of the Cold War.

This period was scholarly highly productive and full of different perspectives. The shift in perspective was dramatic. There was a comparative delay to be overcome; universities were on the rise; history was of interest both in and of itself and for political reasons. Several top historians focused on the topic. A generational shift was underway, and military history offices were relatively open and full of resources.

Publications about World War II were now (not exclusively, but primarily) the realm of scholars, mostly from universities. The availability of archival sources had been established and was expanding. The subject of study had been correctly and firmly identified in its parts: the Fascist war of 1940–1943 was now complemented by the war of Liberation (or civil war) in 1943–1945, with the Resistance now solidly the focus of the scholars' academic interest.[19] Though many aspects of diplomatic history were still being studied (such as the intervention in the war, relationships between Fascist Italy and Nazi Germany, and the armistice of September 8 among others), the interest of scholars had shifted considerably. The political history and the history of society were now the focus of study.[20] Even the military history of involvement in the war/wars was taking a completely new approach – less about the decisions of leaders than about the composition of the armies, life in the units, the experience of imprisonment and the differences between the theatres of war. The war was now seen as more than a traditional conflict between military units and was fully considered a total war. The engagement of the country's entire resources, first in the Fascist war, and then in the war of Liberation and the campaign of Italy, became the focus of all studies and interpretations. Even the Resistance was seen, in essence, as one aspect of it.

Historical judgement on the war had changed dramatically since the previous twenty-five years. The 1940–1945 war was now perceived as a tragedy for the Italian people, who were led to defeat in the first phase and split in two factions by a civil war in the second phase;[21] this tragedy, thanks to the Resistance, regained the features of a just war. The sufferings of the war were deemed, in this framework, necessary to establish the Republican democracy.

General works were finally published on the themes that had been roughly outlined in the previous period. New directions in the historiography also outlined themes that would be widely explored in the following two decades. Because the war had a foundational value for the Italian Republic, with the offspring of the Resistance, World War II was seen, during this entire second period, as a just, necessary war that produced democracy (putting aside Taylor's goads, however useful).[22]

Except for a minority of nostalgic writers, Renzo De Felice launched the only true attack on this interpretation. Though his biography of Mussolini did not actually pay close attention to the regime's military policy or wars (from the colonial wars to the preparation of the world war, with the exception of the last volume), his interpretation had a clear effect on how to approach the history of Italians at war. Volume after volume, always from different perspectives, he maintained that Fascism had enjoyed genuine popular support ('consenso', 1974), that it was not a warmongering regime (1981), and that Mussolini would have gladly reached a peace agreement (1990). Only De Felice's death prevented him from explaining whether the Italian Social Republic was a bump on the road or a logical continuation of Mussolini's ideas and regime (1997).[23]

Not surprisingly, the reaction of the majority of historians – especially those tied to the institutes for the history of the Resistance – was inevitably quite harsh and often rigid. The Fascist regime was first and foremost a warmongering regime, far more than it was a modernizing one; the Fascist war – even more than the World War in general – had forced Italians into a total war. Though historians no longer believed in the slogan of the war of Resistance as the 'people's war', in their opinion the war itself had led Italians to a quite broad reaction of parting from the regime, sinking into a perspective of victims – it was 'la guerra di tutti' (everyone's war).[24] The war had dug deep into the social realm and it was there that research went. Notwithstanding a scarce familiarity with Marwick[25] and *Alltagsgeschichte*,[26] Italian historians in the 1970s and 1980s investigated society in depth, with an exceptional broadening of perspective on the war compared to the solely diplomatic and military-operational perspective of the previous decades. Both in society and among scholars, the Resistance always kept its political, or at least its moral, advantage even though its image was not immaculate and some rejection of old rhetoric was present.[27]

III. Much has changed again in the last twenty-five years, following the end of the Cold War. The fall of many of the ideologies that had been instrumental in building the Republican democracy, and the rise of ideologies in the government of the country which did not feel bound to Italian constitutional and anti-fascist values had an impact on Italian historiographical developments.

In this period Italy, not unlike other countries, underwent major changes both in terms of common historical understanding and historiography: such as the end of the ideological contrast that defined the Cold War, the awareness of the paradigmatic nature for the entire twentieth century of the Holocaust racial extermination (paradoxically concurrent with the death of the generation affected by it), the emergence of a victim-based paradigm, the importance of topics tied to memory of the past and the start of memorial legislation. A new generation of studies and interests had emerged, which broadly expanded the range of documentary sources to fully include oral, iconographic and folk writing ('scrittura popolare') sources.

In addition to these more general trends, shared with other countries on an international scale, Italy also presented some specific, national features. While historical studies on World War II seem to have taken steps forward in some ways, in other ways they have moved backwards. We can no longer take a view that historiography has evolved in a straight, essentially progressive line.

One of the steps forward was the growing realization that Italians had been at war not only in 1940–1943, or only in 1940–1945, but in 1935–1945.[28] The specific character of the Fascist regime, its warmongering and expansionism, required giving greater attention to the military campaigns of the war in Ethiopia (the third largest mass conflict, in terms of numbers, fought by Italians in the twentieth century), the war in Spain, as well as the one in Albania and so forth. Another step forward is that more and more Italian history is now being considered within the framework of a global history, no longer just a European or national one.

In other ways, however, numerous steps backwards were taken. Historians had to engage in public controversies concerning the historical meaning of events that had seemed already settled: 8 September 1943 (no longer seen as the moment of non-fascist Italy's resurrection, but now as the 'morte della patria', death of the fatherland),[29] and the Resistance (flattened under the weight of the illegal killings during the turbulent final days of the war, now defined as 'sangue dei vinti', the blood of the vanquished).[30] Also important were the 'foibe massacres', the crimes committed in the border areas between Italian people and Yugoslav resisters,[31] with its impact on the judgement of the Peace Treaty of 10 February 1947, which in 2004 was transformed into a victim-oriented 'day of memory' by Centre-Right governments. Though these controversies ended up actually helping to clarify important, sensitive aspects that had not yet been investigated thoroughly, there is no question that those who ignited these controversies were motivated by a great desire to have the historiography and common understanding of those historical events move backwards.

Regardless, what matters most is that in the end, sixteen years before the publication of the present volume, the history of Italians between Fascism and World War II had to be reconsidered in a longer perspective. It was no longer limited to the regular war of 1940–1943, nor to the complexity of the total war of 1940–1945, but in some sense it expanded to cover the entire span of 1935–1945. In 2005 Giorgio Rochat first named this perspective in his *Le guerre italiane 1935–1943* (Italian Wars: 1935–1943),[32] though he excluded the war of Liberation and Resistance from its pages, a topic on which he already had extensive knowledge and had written about in several contributions.

Rochat's book was a general work, though with many open questions. *Le guerre italiane* was accepted as the completion of a long era of study, though it was little discussed precisely because it was a broad summary of the major happenings of the second decade of Fascism and mostly focused on military aspects of those years, while being aware of the most important political and social aspects as well.

In contrast, in this same period, a new approach to the historical study of the Fascist regime (in peace, if not war) gained ground. This approach showed less interest in the larger general dynamics of the war – what could be called its macrophysics – with the population often seen as passive to the regime, and paid instead closer attention to the small-scale dynamics – the microphysics of its power.[33] It has been the period of studies on popular public opinion, local (not central) interactions between the country and Fascism, *Alltagsgeschichte* and the Italians' agency from below during the Fascist regime. Many of these studies might risk returning to a split between the peacetime and wartime regime, already seen in previous studies on Fascism; yet, this risk was somehow reduced by new attention on issues such as the mobilisation from the bottom up, the war in Ethiopia and the society during the world war.

One of the most important results of all these complex aspects of the last twenty-five years of study may be the overall reconsideration of the historical judgement on the Italians' involvement in World War II, or more precisely, in the cycle of wars culminated in that war. In recent years, many have given less emphasis to the final positive outcome – democracy building – and more to the barbaric, disturbing aspects of the wars – barbarization – and the endurance and penetration of Fascist ideology in Italian society. The attention of scholars was drawn less to the traditional 'physiology' of combat and more to the 'pathology' of certain previously neglected aspects, such as the war of occupation, including war crimes in France, Russia and the Balkans, both committed and suffered, and the violence inherent in the colonial war, whose legacy is also sought in regular wars. The war of Resistance – though its morality had been reclaimed – has now also been studied in its controversial aspects, read without the ideological indulgences of the past including issues such as partisan military justice, partisan violence and battles between its bands.

What many studies along these 25 years have ended up revealing in all three phases of this 'long war' of 1935–1945 (1935–1940, 1940–1943 and 1943–1945) seems to be the violence of war – or we might say the 'culture of war', even if we should immediately qualify the term, as Jay Winter and Antoine Prost did,[34] with all possible precautions, and as Michael Geyer and Adam Tooze wrote,[35] taking into account that it needs to be completely reconsidered in the context of World War II and particularly the Fascist war. It could now be called a 'horror war', unlike the 'traditional war' of the first-generation war and the 'total war' of the second. Or perhaps a centreless war, where military operations once were – a war broken into its countless aspects, with no centre; a war from the perspective of cultural relativism.

What has changed?

Italian historiography on World War II did not evolve in a vacuum. We have focused so far mainly on internal dynamics because those of international historiography are already very well known.

Outside of Italy as well, the historiographical perception of the war profoundly changed as it moved between phases. The operations-war of the generals and their critics like Liddell Hart[36] were joined or replaced by the society-war of Michael Howard[37] and the experience-war, in Paul Fussell's literary version[38] and John Keegan's military version.[39] In addition to these, a 'combat history' emerged,[40] a new line of study that was more attentive to the technological and technical aspects of the war, and to the military combat effectiveness, with Allan R. Millett, Williamson Murray,[41] and Martin Van Creveld[42] leading the way. A war-culture perspective had been barely sketched and would take on more importance in the following years, bringing diverse authors to the forefront, such as Victor Davis Hanson,[43] John Lynn,[44] Azar Gat[45] and, in France, Stéphane Audoin-Rouzeau[46] and Annette Becker.[47]

Italian historians were actually quite removed from the debate, though the best of them were at least aware of it. Some looked as far as France, which was also quite resistant to historiographical influences from abroad. But Italian studies still had too much ground to make up for. Further, the historiographical renewal in Italy seemed to prefer studies on World War I rather than World War II. When the Cold War, and coincidentally the era of Liddell Hart, ended to be replaced by that of Gerhard L. Weinberg,[48] Christopher R. Browning,[49] Richard Overy[50] and the Militärgeschichtliches Forschungsamt series[51] – whose seminal general works and monographs were all available in the early 1990s – Italian studies on World War II had just entered a full new phase.

That said, what led Italian historiography to progressively expand its scope throughout the succession of its three phases? Why was there a change in perceiving Fascist/Italian wars along the gradual shift from 1940–1943 to 1940–1945, and now 1935–1945 that we have previously mentioned? Was it merely an academic game among historians, or does this shift really help us to better understand the place of Fascist Italy in World War II? And where did all of this lead?

At least four points need to be stressed – one in terms of method and three in content. In terms of method, the trajectory of Italian historiography seems not to differ much from those of other historiographies in other countries, even though the latter often have devoted more time and vast amounts of studies and resources, have better functioning archives and more readily available sources. The Italian trajectory was particular, but not exceptional or different. This is another reason why young, international scholars should know about it in its entirety. We have the impression that the historiographical framework of too many recent studies rely heavily only on two or three of the latest books. The lack of deep familiarity with Italian historiography leads some of the recent studies to retrace past paths and judgements, in order to re-assess them.[52]

In terms of content, Italian participation in one or several different wars will always be judged based on the performance in the field of soldiers, officer corps and armed forces. Unfortunately, especially in international historiography, there has been a great deal of falling back on stereotypes on this topic. Of course, we can no longer accept the triumphalism of Fascist regime's rhetoric, which considered its soldiers always victorious heroes. Equally useless, however, are worn-out stereotypes that appear frequently in international studies, all relying on the old '*Les Italiens ne se battent pas*'. On the contrary, Italians fought in quite varied ways. They won and lost wars; soldiers fought differently to sailors and airmen; career officers received a different training than reserve officers. The military showed different attitudes in Ethiopia and in Spain, they behaved in the field in different ways at different moments, and the army's feelings and preparation differed as well in the different campaigns of World War II. Unlike in other conflicts, in this war they had to make the most of weapons that were rarely greatly improved or increased in number in the course of the war, unlike in other countries. All this needs to be studied more closely, including concepts such as primary groups and learning curves.

In terms of content as well, the gradual expansion of horizons and timelines led to a considerable change in judging the Fascist regime. Fascist contribution to disintegrating the international system of Versailles and the League of Nations should by now be a given for historians, apart from the few who still believe in Fascist pacifism. In an international perspective, however, the actions of a comparatively minor player, next to Germany and Japan, seemed more and more decisive to Italian historiography as it moved from one phase to the next. Hitler's Germany did not trust – and indeed scorned[53] – Italy's military contribution, starting its world war without it. But it is doubtful that Hitler would have started his war if he could not have counted with certainty on some support from a wide range of fascist governments, among which the Italian one was the most important.[54]

Once the war had begun, no Blitzkrieg or Weltpolitik could have lasted without the support of occupation troops,[55] the kind of troops Italy always provided in places as far away as Russia, France and the Balkans. Military historians have too often focused on the face of the battle, but occupation, consolidating conquests and counterinsurgency were also decisive. Recent studies on Italy as a force of occupation are extremely important in this regard and have decidedly moved beyond all attempts to minimize the past.

At the same time, we should not overstate the case. Paradoxically, sometimes we find a sole focus in the most critical, often German-speaking, scholars as well. They have sought to assign the blame upon (or share it with) Italian troops that had usually been credited to the German armed forces before and especially after the Hamburg exhibition of 1995. These scholars hold that it was Fascist Italy that invented[56] and implemented for the first time the war of extermination, from Ethiopia onwards. But growing awareness of the Fascist regime's great historic responsibility should not lead us to exaggerate it beyond what it deserves.

Also in terms of content, expanded perspectives are re-evaluating the responsibility of Italians as a people (not only, as above, as a regime) in this long
cycle of wars. Of course, we should not neglect complex analysis here: it has
been much debated by scholars whether speaking of unity or identity among
Italians makes historical sense. Moreover, we should avoid repeating the vague
discussions about the 'morte della patria' after the events of 8 September 1943.

Yet, even recently, we have seen similar generalities come out again from different historiographical perspectives. Three different images emerged from three
recent publications on the Italians at war, depending on the sources they considered. First, those who studied Fascist sources[57] have been quick to maintain
that all Italians in 1940–1943 were fascists, with few exceptions, changing their
mind only at the very end of that period. Second, those who studied the trials of
war deserters[58] have seemed likely to regard all Italians as already 'out of' (if not
against) the war, as Fascism's military judges considered them at the time. Third,
those who looked only at oral interviews to former soldiers disbanded on 8 September 1943 conducted during the 1990s[59] have maintained that the Italians saw
the war only as horror and took every opportunity to escape it.

Happily, in the face of these generalizations, the best historians of the Resistance
continue to maintain that in 1943–1945 combatants in the mountains were
a minority – noticeable, sometimes more so than in other countries, but still a
minority[60] – and not once again a 'popolo alla macchia' (underground people).
Fascist totalitarianism[61] did not succeed in erasing the enormous variety of social,
political and cultural geography included under the single umbrella of 'Italians'. The
concept of war anti-fascism,[62] first restricted to just one of these wars, should perhaps
be reconsidered and better applied to the whole 1935–1945 period.

On the other hand, expanding and lengthening the perspective beyond the
regular war to the total war and to the longer 'cycle of wars' 1935–1945
clearly allows, and requires, historians to give more attention to reconsidering
Italian responsibilities in all of these wars and their changes over time, space
and in the society. From a social point of view, within the ruling classes,
breaking off from the regime's myths had a different pace than in the middle
classes and especially in the working classes, within which anti-fascism had
never been eliminated despite the totalitarian regime. From a geographical point
of view, cities and countryside, north, central, south and inland areas responded
to Fascism's wars very differently, depending on how much these wars affected
and involved them. Compared to the British or US 'people's war',[63] or even
more so, to nazified society within Nazi Germany, which Hitler managed to protect to an extent from the war's suffering and hardships,[64] 'le mille pieghe' (the
thousand crinkles) of Italian society, which had suffered since 1940–1943 the
hardships of war as well as regime's unpreparedness and inequalities, should
advise historians to get a quite varied image.

One rather recent area of research has concentrated on Italian popular opinion
and the Fascist regime.[65] Unfortunately, the bulk of these studies focused on
peacetime. If the same efforts could be applied to the study of the home front
during the Fascist wars (colonial, in Ethiopia[66] and Libya, and then world and

global wars), what we already know[67] about the Fascist totalitarian radicalization in war would certainly be improved by better differentiating the picture rather than exaggerating it.

In conclusion, the continuing expansion of the historiographic perspective in Italian studies is, as a whole, quite positive. Italian scholars have garnered lessons from the best international historiography, which is to say that there has been a quite significant and increasing integration between Italian and international studies. But this should be said without any assumption about the superiority of international ideas or Italian national subordination. In fact, international studies on World War II are going through a rather particular, challenging moment seventy years after the end of the war. They have yet to fully incorporate new information that has come in the last twenty years from Eastern European archives, and from the global moment in analysis perspectives. As is true of Cold War studies, it is no easy task to reconcile the needed global expansion of viewpoints with the fact the war was fought mainly over the control of Europe. A quick look through recent years of major journals in the field immediately shows the difficulties and the historiographical uncertainties.

This should be said because it is still far from a given that scholarly studies will manage to reach a better understanding of what happened in Italy during the 1930s to 1940s. Thanks to the changing historiographical perspectives along the three phases, much more is now known about the history of a (not so) secondary player in the international system, its political and military decision-makers and its society, all so much more diverse and complex than often suggested by facile stereotypes.

Paradoxically, however, seventy years after the fact, many of these themes still need to be (re)studied. In all likelihood, doing it could only be the goal of a new generation of scholars. Scholars trained in a truly transnational (and transcontinental) context, able to write a local history of Italy in the 1935–1945 cycle of wars from a global perspective, is what we need. Yet, even this new generation's efforts could vanish[68] if the knowledge produced by the historiography of the previous generations is superficially ignored. Only this effort will let these younger historians avoid both the nationalism and narrow sectorial approach that we see in many studies nowadays, looking and pretending to be so new, but too often lacking a proper and necessary historiographical depth.

Notes

1 C. Baldoli, *A History of Italy* (Basingstoke: Palgrave Macmillan, 2009); L. Riall, *Risorgimento: The History of Italy from Napoleon to Nation State* (Basingstoke: Palgrave Macmillan, 2009); N. Carter, *Modern Italy in Historical Perspective* (London: Bloomsbury Academic, 2009); C. Duggan, *The Force of Destiny: A History of Italy since 1796* (London: Allen Lane, 2007); J. Foot, *Modern Italy* (Basingstoke: Palgrave Macmillan, 2003); A. Lyttelton (ed.), *Liberal and Fascist Italy, 1900–1945* (Oxford: Oxford University Press, 2002); M.F. Gilbert and K.R. Nilsson, *Historical*

Dictionary of Modern Italy (Lanham, MD and London: Scarecrow Press, 1999);
D. Sassoon, *Contemporary Italy: Economy, Society, and Politics since 1945*
(New York and London: Longman, 1997); M.J. Bull, *Contemporary Italy:
A Research Guide* (Westport, CT and London: Greenwood, 1996); G. Holmes (ed.),
The Oxford Illustrated History of Italy (Oxford: Oxford University Press, 1997);
M. Clark, *Modern Italy, 1871–1995* (London: Longman, 1996); P. Ginsborg,
A History of Contemporary Italy: Society and Politics, 1943–1988 (Harmondsworth:
Penguin, 1990).

2   G. Rochat, *Le guerre italiane 1935–1943. Dall'impero d'Etiopia alla disfatta* (Turin:
Einaudi, 2005) (about the title, see G. Rochat, *Guerre italiane in Libia e in Etiopia.
Studi militari 1921–1939* (Pagus: Paese 1991)).

3   A. Del Boca, *Italiani, brava gente?* (Vicenza: Neri Pozza, 2005).

4   E. Mawdsley, 'General Introduction', in E. Mawdsley (ed.), *The Cambridge History
of the Second World War*, vol. I, J. Ferris and E. Mawdsley (eds.), *Fighting the War*
(Cambridge: Cambridge University Press, 2015).

5   M. Howard, *La guerra e le armi nella storia d'Europa* (Rome and Bari: Laterza,
1978).

6   J. Keegan, *Uomini e battaglie della seconda guerra mondiale* (Milan: Rizzoli,
1989); J. Keegan, *La seconda guerra mondiale* (Milan: Rizzoli, 2000).

7   G.L. Weinberg, *Il mondo in armi. Storia globale della Seconda guerra mondiale*
(Turin: Utet, 2007).

8   E. Mawdsley, *World War II: A New History* (Cambridge: Cambridge University
Press, 2009).

9   N. Labanca, 'The Italian Wars', in R. Overy (ed.), *The Oxford Illustrated History of
World War II* (Oxford: Oxford University Press, 2015), pp. 74–109.

10 D. Mack Smith, *Le guerre del duce* (Rome and Bari: Laterza, 1976).

11 J. Gooch, *Mussolini and his Generals: The Armed Forces and Fascist Foreign
Policy,1922–1940* (Cambridge: Cambridge University Press, 2007).

12 M. Knox, *La guerra di Mussolini* (Rome: Editori riuniti, 1984); M. Knox, *To the
Threshold of Power, 1922/33: Origins and Dynamics of the Fascist and National
Socialist Dictatorships*, vol. I (Cambridge: Cambridge University Press, 2007).

13 A.J. Bacevich, 'The Revisionist Imperative: Rethinking Twentieth Century Wars',
The Journal of Military History, 76 (2012), pp. 333–42.

14 J. Winter (ed.), *The Cambridge History of the First World War*, vol. I, *Global War*
(Cambridge: Cambridge University Press, 2014).

15 Ferris and Mawdsley, *Introduction*, in *Fighting the War*.

16 E. Collotti, 'Seconda guerra mondiale', in *Il mondo contemporaneo, Politica internazionale* (Florence: La nuova Italia, 1979); G. Rochat, 'Seconda guerra mondiale', in *Il
mondo contemporaneo, Storia d'Italia*, vol. II (Florence: La nuova Italia, 1978).

17 F. Focardi, *Il cattivo tedesco e il bravo italiano. La rimozione delle colpe della seconda guerra mondiale* (Rome and Bari: Laterza, 2013).

18 P. Cooke, *The Legacy of the Italian Resistance* (New York: Palgrave Macmillan,
2011) [transl. *L'eredità della Resistenza. Storia, cultura, politiche dal dopoguerra
a oggi* (Rome: Viella, 2015)].

19 G. Rochat, *Seconda guerra mondiale*, in *La storiografia militare italiana negli ultimi
venti anni* (Milan: Angeli, 1985); F. Ferratini Tosi, G. Grassi and M. Legnani (eds.),
L'Italia nella seconda guerra mondiale e nella resistenza (Milan: Angeli, 1988);
C. Pavone, 'La resistenza oggi: problema storiografico e problema civile', *Rivista di
storia contemporanea*, 2–3 (1992), pp. 456–80 (also in E. Collotti, R. Sandri and
F. Sessi (eds.), *Dizionario della Resistenza*, vol. II (Turin: Einaudi, 2000), pp.
701–10); G. Santomassimo, S. Rogari, G. Perona, F. Malgeri and M. Legnani (eds.),
In/formazione, 25–26 (1994); A. Ballone, *Bibliografia della Resistenza*, in *Dizionario
della Resistenza*, vol. II, pp. 719–34; N. Labanca, 'Resistenza/resistenze. Un bilancio

tra discorso pubblico e studi storici', in M. Fioravanzo and C. Fumian (eds.), *1943 Strategie militari, collaborazionismi, Resistenze* (Rome: Viella, 2015), pp. 27–76.

20 M. Legnani, *L'Italia dal fascismo alla Repubblica. Sistema di potere e alleanze sociali*, L. Baldissara, S. Battilossi and P. Ferrari (eds.), foreword by E. Collotti, (Rome: Carocci, 2000); N. Gallerano (ed.), *L'altro dopoguerra. Roma e il Sud 1943–1945. Atti del convegno*, foreword by G. Quazza, introduction by E. Forcella, (Milan: Angeli, 1985); G. Rochat, E. Santarelli and P. Sorcinelli (eds.), *Linea gotica 1944: eserciti, popolazioni, partigiani* (Milan: F. Angeli, 1986).

21 C. Pavone, *Una guerra civile. Saggio storico sulla moralità nella Resistenza* (Turin: Bollati Boringhieri, 1991).

22 A.J.P. Taylor, *The Origins of the Second World War* (London: Hamish Hamilton, 1961).

23 R. De Felice, *Mussolini il rivoluzionario 1883–1920*, foreword by D. Cantimori (Turin: Einaudi, 1965); R. De Felice, *Mussolini il fascista*, vol. 1, *La conquista del potere 1921–1925*, 1966, and vol. 2, *L'organizzazione dello Stato fascista 1925–1929*, 1968; *Mussolini il duce*, vol. 1, *Gli anni del consenso, 1929–1936*, 1974, and vol. 2, *Lo Stato totalitario, 1936–1940*, 1981; *Mussolini l'alleato*, vol. I, *L'Italia in guerra, 1940–1943*, t. I, *Dalla guerra breve alla guerra lunga*, 1990, and t. II, *Crisi e agonia del regime*, 1990; also see the last and unfinished volume II, *La guerra civile 1943–1945*, 1997.

24 *Una storia di tutti. Prigionieri, internati, deportati italiani nella seconda guerra mondiale* (Milan: F. Angeli, 1989).

25 A. Marwick, *War and Social Change in the Twentieth Century: A Comparative Study of Britain, France, Germany, Russia and the United States* (Basingstoke: Macmillan, 1974).

26 *Alltagsgeschichte der NS-Zeit neue perspektive oder trivialisierung?* (Munchen: Oldenbourg, 1984); A. Ludtke (ed.), *Alltagsgeschichte. Zur Rekonstruktion historischer Erfahrungen und Lebensweisen* (Frankfurt/Main and New York: Campus Verlag, 1989) (*The History of Everyday Life: Reconstructing Historical Experiences and Ways of Life* (Princeton, NJ: Princeton University Press, 1995)).

27 See Pavone, *Una guerra civile*.

28 See Rochat, *Le guerre italiane 1935–1943*.

29 E. Galli della Loggia, *La morte della patria. La crisi dell'idea di nazione tra Resistenza, antifascismo e Repubblica* (Rome and Bari: Laterza, 1996).

30 G. Pansa, *Il sangue dei vinti (quello che accadde in Italia dopo il 25 aprile)* (Milan: Sperling & Kupfer, 2003); G. Pansa, *La grande bugia (le sinistre italiane e il sangue dei vinti)* (Milan: Sperling paperback, 2010).

31 G. Oliva, *La resa dei conti. Aprile-maggio 1945. Foibe, piazzale Loreto e giustizia partigiana* (Milan: Mondadori, 1999); R. Pupo and R. Spazzali, *Foibe* (Milan: B. Mondadori, 2003); G. Oliva, *Profughi. Dalle foibe all'esodo: la tragedia degli italiani d'Istria, Fiume e Dalmazia* (Milan: Mondadori, 2005); R. Pupo, *Il lungo esodo. Istria: le persecuzioni, le foibe, l'esilio* (Milan: Rizzoli, 2005).

32 Rochat, *Le guerre italiane 1935–1943*.

33 P. Corner, *The Fascist Party and Popular Opinion in Mussolini's Italy* (Oxford: Oxford University Press, 2012).

34 A. Prost and J. Winter, *Penser la Grande Guerre. Un essai d'historiographie* (Paris: Editions du Seuil, 2004).

35 M. Geyer and A. Tooze, 'Introduction', in E. Mawdsley (ed.), *The Cambridge History of the Second World War*, vol. III, Michael Geyer and Adam Tooze (eds.), *Total War: Economy, Society and Culture*.

36 Basil Henry Liddell Hart, *History of the Second World War* (London: Cassel, 1970) [transl. *Storia militare della seconda guerra mondiale* (Milan: Mondadori, 1970)].

37 Howard, *La guerra e le armi nella storia d'Europa*.

38 P. Fussell, *La Grande Guerra e la memoria moderna (1975)* (Bologna: il Mulino, 1984); P. Fussell, *Tempo di guerra. Psicologia, emozioni e cultura nella seconda guerra mondiale (1989)* (Milan: Mondadori, 1991).

39 J. Keegan, *The Face of Battle* (London: Cape, 1976) [transl. *Il volto della battaglia*, Milan: Mondadori, 1978]; J. Keegan, *A History of Warfare* (London: Pimlico, 1994) [transl. *La grande storia della guerra. Dalla preistoria ai giorni nostri*, Milan: A. Mondadori, 1994]; J. Keegan, *The First World War* (London: Hutchinson, 1998) (transl. *La prima guerra mondiale. Una storia politico-militare*, Rome: Carocci, 2000).

40 N. Labanca, 'Combat style. Studi recenti sulle istituzioni militari alla prova del fuoco', in N. Labanca and G. Rochat (eds.), *Il soldato, la guerra e il rischio di morire* (Milan: Unicopli, 2006), pp. 339–78.

41 A.R. Millett, W. Murray and K.H. Watman, 'The Effectiveness of Military Organization', in A.R. Millett and W. Murray (eds.), *Military Effectiveness*, vol. I, *The First World War*, and vol. III, *The Second World War* (Boston, MA: Allen & Unwin, 1988).

42 M. van Creveld, *Supplying War: Logistic from Wallenstein to Patton* (Cambridge: Cambridge University Press, 1977); M. van Creveld, *Technology and War. From 2000 B.C. to the Present* (London: Collier Macmillan, 1989); M. van Creveld, *The Transformation of War* (New York: Free Press, 1991).

43 V. Davis Hanson, *The Western Way of War: Infantry Battle in Classical Greece*, introduction by J. Keegan (New York: Knopf, 1989) (transl. *L'arte occidentale della guerra. Descrizione di una battaglia nella Grecia classica*, Milan: Mondadori, 1990); Id., *Carnage and culture: Landmark Battles in the rise of Western Power* (New York: Doubleday, 2001) (British edition title *Why the West has Won: Carnage and Culture from Salamis to Vietnam*, London: Faber, 2001) (transl. *Massacri e cultura. Le battaglie che hanno portato la civiltà occidentale a dominare il mondo*, Milan: Garzanti, 2002).

44 J. Lynn, *Battle. A History of Combat and Culture* (New York: Westview, 2003).

45 A. Gat, *A History of Military Thought: From the Enlightenment to the Cold War* (Oxford: Oxford University Press, 2001); A. Gat, *War in Human Civilization* (Oxford: Oxford University Press, 2006).

46 S. Audoin-Rouzeau, *14–18. Les combattants des tranchées. A travers leurs journaux* (Paris: Colin, 1986); S. Audoin-Rouzeau, *La guerre des enfants, 1914–1918. Essai d'histoire culturelle* (Paris: Colin, 1993); S. Audoin-Rouzeau, *L'enfant de l'ennemi, 1914–1918. Viol, avortement, infanticide pendant la grande guerre* (Paris: Aubier, 1995); S. Audoin-Rouzeau and A. Becker, *14–18, retrouver la guerre* (Paris: Gallimard, 2000); S. Audouin-Rouzeau, *Combattre. Une anthropologie historique de la guerre moderne (19.-21. siècle)* (Paris: Seuil, 2008); S. Audoin-Rouzeau, *1914–1918. La violence de guerre* (Paris: Gallimard-Ministère de la Défense-DMPA, 2014).

47 A. Becker, *Les monuments aux morts. Patrimoine et mémoire de la grande guerre* (Paris: Errance, 1988); Ead., *Guerre et la foi. De la mort á la mémoire, 1914–1930* (Paris: A. Colin, 1994); Ead., *Oubliés de la Grande Guerre. Humanitaire et culture de guerre, 1914–1918. Populations occupées, déportés civils, prisonniers de guerre* (Paris, Noesis, 1998); Ead., *Les cicatrices rouges '14–15. France et Belgique occupées* (Paris: Fayard, 2010); and her contribution to D. El Kenz and F.-X. Nérard (eds.), *Commémorer les victimes en Europe 16-21. Siècles* (Seyssel: Champ Vallon, 2011); A. Becker, *Voir la Grande Guerre. Un autre récit, 1914–2014*, postface by Pierre Bergounioux (Paris: Armand Colin, 2014).

48 G.L. Weinberg, *Il mondo in armi. Storia globale della Seconda guerra mondiale* (Turin: Utet, 2007).

49 C.R. Browning, *Uomini comuni. Polizia tedesca e 'soluzione finale' in Polonia* (Turin: Einaudi, 1995).

50 R.J. Overy, *The Air War, 1939–1945* (London: Europa, 1980); R. J. Overy, *Why the Allies Won* (New York: W.W. Norton, 1995); R. J. Overy, *War and Economy in the Third Reich* (Oxford: Clarendon Press, 1994); R.J. Overy, *Russia's War: Blood upon the Snow* (New York: TV Books, 1997); R.J. Overy (ed.), *The Oxford Illustrated History of World War II* (Oxford: Oxford University Press, 2015).

51 *Das Deutsche Reich und der Zweite Weltkrieg*, herausgegeben vom Militärgeschichtlichen Forschungsamt, Stuttgart, Deutsche Verlags-Anstalt, 1979–2008, 10 vol. (also available as *Germany and the Second World War*, edited by the Militärgeschichtliches Forschungsamt (Oxford and New York: Clarendon Press and Oxford University Press, 1990–2014).

52 Recently see M.M. Aterrano, *Mediterranean-First? La pianificazione strategica anglo-americana e le origini dell'occupazione alleata in Italia (1939–1943)* (Napoli: FedOA Press, 2017).

53 G. Schreiber, *I militari italiani nei campi di concentramento del Terzo Reich 1943–1945. Traditi disprezzati dimenticati* (Rome: USSME, 1992).

54 L. Klinkhammer, A. Osti Guerrazzi and T. Schlemmer (eds.), *Die 'Achse' im Krieg. Politik, Ideologie und Kriegführung 1939–1945* (Paderborn: Ferdinand Schöningh, 2010), pp. 194–210.

55 T. Sala, *Le potenze dell'Asse e la Jugoslavia. Saggi e documenti 1941/1943* (Milan: Feltrinelli, 1974); G. Scotti and L. Viazzi, *Le aquile delle montagne nere. Storia dell'occupazione e della guerra italiana in Montenegro (1941–1943)* (Milan: Mursia, 1987); M. Cuzzi, *L'occupazione italiana della Slovenia (1941–1943)* (Rome: USSME, 1998); E. Collotti, 'L'occupazione italiana in Grecia: problemi generali', in G. Rigo (ed.), *Studi e strumenti di storia contemporanea*, Annali 5, Istituto milanese per la storia dell'età contemporanea, della resistenza e del movimento operaio (Milan: Angeli, 2000), pp. 365–79; L. Santarelli., 'Il sistema dell'occupazione italiana in Grecia. Aspetti e problemi di ricerca', in Rigo (ed.), *Studi e strumenti di storia contemporanea*, pp. 381–407; B. Mantelli (ed.), 'L'Italia fascista potenza occupante: lo scacchiere balcanico', *QualeStoria*, XXX:1 (2002); B. Mantelli, 'Gli Italiani in Jugoslavia 1941–1943: occupazione militare, politiche persecutorie, crimini di guerra', *Storia e memoria*, 1 (2004), pp. 23–37; S. Neri Serneri (ed.), 'Il fascismo come potenza occupante. Storia e memoria', *Contemporanea*, VIII:2 (2005), pp. 311–35; D. Schipsi, *L'occupazione italiana dei territori metropolitani francesi (1940–1943)* (Rome: USSME, 2007); P. Iuso, *Esercito, guerra e nazione. I soldati italiani tra Balcani e Mediterraneo orientale 1940–1945* (Rome: Ediesse, 2008); F. Caccamo and L. Monzali (eds.), *L'occupazione della Iugoslavia (1941–1943)* (Florence: Le Lettere, 2008); Istituto romano per la storia d'Italia dal fascismo alla Resistenza, *Politiche di occupazione dell'Italia fascista*, A. Irsifar (ed.) (Milan: Franco Angeli, 2008); D. Conti, *L'occupazione italiana dei Balcani. Crimini di guerra e mito della 'brava gente' (1940–1943)* (Rome: Odradek, 2008); T. Schlemmer, *Invasori, non vittime. La campagna italiana di Russia 1941–1943* (Bari and Rome: Laterza, 2009); A. Osti Guerrazzi, *L'Esercito italiano in Slovenia 1941–1943. Strategie di repressione antipartigiana* (Rome: Viella, 2011); G. Scotti, *'Bono taliano'. Militari italiani in Jugoslavia dal 1941 al 1943: da occupatori a 'disertori'* (Rome: Odradek, 2012); M. Clementi, *Camicie nere sull'Acropoli. L'occupazione italiana in Grecia (1941–1943)* (Rome: DeriveApprodi, 2013); E. Gobetti, *Alleati del nemico. L'occupazione italiana in Jugoslavia (1941–1943)* (Rome and Bari: Laterza, 2013); F. Goddi, *Fronte Montenegro. Occupazione italiana e giustizia militare (1941–1943)* (Gorizia: Leg, 2015); D. Grillere, *L'occupation italienne face à l'occupation allemande. Analyse et enjeux de l'autre occupation en France métropolitaine 1938–1943*, Ph.D. dissertation, Université Paris-Sorbonne,

2012; E. Sica, *Mussolini's Army in the French Riviera: Italy's Occupation of France* (Urbana, IL: University of Illinois Press, 2016); A. Becherelli and P. Formiconi, *La quinta sponda. Una storia dell'occupazione italiana della Croazia 1941–1943* (Rome: Stato Maggiore della Difesa, 2015).

56 A. Mattioli, *Experimentierfeld der Gewalt. Der Abessinienkrieg und seine internationale Bedeutung 1935–1941*, foreword by A. Del Boca (Zürich: Orell Füssli, 2005); also see G. Schneider, *Mussolini in Afrika: die faschistische Rassenpolitik in den italienischen Kolonien, 1936–1941* (Köln: SH-Verlag, 2000), and G. Brogini Künzi, *Italien und der Abessinienkrieg 1935/36. Kolonialkrieg oder Totaler Krieg?* (Paderborn: Schöningh, 2006). For a critique see N. Labanca, 'Kolonialkrieg in Ostafrika 1935/35: der erste faschistische Vernichtungskrieg?', in Klinkhammer, Osti Guerrazzi, Schlemmer (eds.), *Die 'Achse' im Krieg*, pp. 194–210.

57 M. Avagliano and M. Palmieri, *Vincere e vinceremo! Gli italiani al fronte, 1940–1943* (Bologna: Il Mulino, 2014).

58 M. Franzinelli, *Disertori. Una storia mai raccontata della seconda guerra mondiale* (Milan: Mondadori, 2016).

59 G. Gribaudi, *Combattenti, sbandati, prigionieri. Esperienze e memorie di reduci della seconda guerra mondiale* (Rome: Donzelli, 2016).

60 S. Peli, *La Resistenza in Italia. Storia e critica* (Turin: Einaudi, 2004) [second edition as *Storia della Resistenza in Italia* (Turin: Einaudi, 2006)].

61 E. Gentile, *La via italiana al totalitarismo. Il partito e lo Stato nel regime fascista* (Rome: NIS, 1995) (n.e. 2008).

62 R. Battaglia, *Storia della Resistenza italiana* (Turin: Einaudi, 1953).

63 A. Calder, *The People's War: Britain 1939–1945* (London: Jonathan Cape, 1969); D. Todman, *Britain's War: Into Battle 1937–1941* (London: Allan Lane, 2016).

64 R. J. Evans, *The Third Reich at War 1939–1945* (London: Penguin, 2008); N. Stargardt, *The German War: A Nation under Arms, 1939–1945* (London: Penguin, 2015).

65 P. Corner and V. Galimi (eds.), *Il fascismo in provincia. Articolazioni e gestione del potere tra centro e periferia* (Rome: Viella, 2014); 'Fascismo: itinerari storiografici da un secolo all'altro', *Studi storici*, 1 (2014); G. Albanese and R. Pergher (eds.), *In the Society of Fascists: Acclamation, Acquiescence, and Agency in Mussolini's Italy* (New York: Palgrave Macmillan, 2012); 'Fascismi periferici. Nuove ricerche', *L'Annale Irsifar* (Milan: Angeli, 2010); A.M. Vinci (ed.), *Regime fascista, nazione e periferie. Atti del Convegno: Regime fascista, nazione e periferie, Udine, dicembre 2007* (Udine: Istituto friulano per la storia del movimento di liberazione, 2010).

66 P. Corner, *L'opinione popolare italiana di fronte alla guerra di Etiopia*, in *L'Impero fascista. Italia ed Etiopia, 1935–1941* (Bologna: Il Mulino, 2008).

67 S. Colarizi, *L'opinione degli italiani sotto il regime 1929–1943* (Rome and Bari: Laterza, 1991); A. Ventura (ed.), *Sulla crisi del regime fascista 1938–1943: la società italiana dal consenso alla Resistenza. Atti del Convegno nazionale di studi, Padova, 4–6 novembre 1993* (Venezia: Marsilio, 1996).

68 Very recently see E. Sica and R. Carrier (eds.), *Italy and the Second World War: Alternative Perspectives* (Leiden: Brill, 2018).

Index